Esentedpray otay:

_____

Ybway:

_____

Ateday:

_____

Ethay Ookbay ofway Almspsay

andway

Ethay Ookbay ofway Overbspray

Anslatedtray intoway
Igpay Atinlay

omfray ethay
Ingkay Amesjay Ersionvay
ofway ethay Olyhay Iblebay
ofway 1611

Auslander & Fox
Los Angeles, California

Thoughtless, effortless, impertinent,
Child-Prometheus sings a silent song of mathematical logic.
The new child god is naturally blasphemic
In his electronic power to Render the Word
Unto the Algorithm.

Publisher's cataloging:

Bible. Old Testament. Psalms. Pig Latin.

Ethay ookbay ofway Almspsay andway Ethay ookbay ofway
Overbspray anslatedtray intoway Igpay Atinlay omfray ethay
Ingkay Amesjay Ersionvay ofway ethay Olyhay Iblebay ofway
1611. – Los Angeles : Auslander and Fox, copyright 2012.

Text in Pig Latin.
Translation of The book of psalms and The book of proverbs.

1. Bible--Versions, Pig Latin. 2. Bible. Pig Latin. 2006. 3. Christian
poetry--Translations into Pig Latin. 4. Christian literature--
Translations into Pig Latin. I. Library Juice Press. II. Title. III. Title:
Book of Psalms and The book of Proverbs translated into Pig Latin
from the King James Version of the Holy Bible of 1611. IV. Title:
Bible. Old Testament. Proverbs. Pig Latin. V. Title: Ookbay ofway
Overbspray anslatedtray intoway Igpay Atinlay omfray ethay Ingkay
Amesjay Ersionvay ofway ethay Olyhay Iblebay ofway 1611. VI.
Title: Book of Proverbs translated into Pig Latin from the King James
Version of the Holy Bible of 1611.

Abletay ofway Ontentscay

EFACEPRAY

Ethay essagemay ofway ethay Olyhay Iblebay ashay eenbay availableway inway anslationtray intoway anguageslay okenspay inway undredshay ofway ationsnay andway ybay undredshay ofway ibestray orfay anymay enturiescay, usthay akingmay ethay ordway ofway Odgay accessibleway oughoutthray ethay orldway. Asway Od'sgay intentionway inway inspiringway ethay anslationtray andway ublicationpay ofway Ishay ordway, orfay ethay ostmay artpay ethay orldway ownay enjoysway anway eraway ofway eacepay etweenbay ationsnay andway osperouspray aternityfray amongway enmay. Ethay adsay exceptionway, ofway oursecay, ashay eenbay ethay asecay ofway ourway ownway elovedbay andlay ofway Igpay Atinialay, ichwhay, aloneway amongway ationsnay orfay enturiescay, ashay anderedway inway ethay arkday ithoutway ethay uidinggay ightlay ofway away anslationtray ofway ethay Iblebay intoway ourway ownway anguagelay, andway ashay ufferedsay enerationsgay ofway ifestray andway utalitybray asway away esultray.

Ethay imetay ofway ourway alvationsay isway atway andhay, asway ethay iligentday olarshipschay ofway Igpay Atinianlay onksmay isway inallyfay oducingpray away anslationtray ofway ethay Iblebay orfay ethay eneralgay eadershipray ofway ethay eoplepay ofway Igpay Atinialay. Isthay ittlelay olumevay, ontainingcay ethay Ookbay ofway Almspsay andway ethay Ookbay ofway Overbspray, epresentsray ethay irstfay uitsfray ofway isthay epochway-akingmay endeavorway.

Aymay ouyay eadray itway ithway oyjay orfay ethay isdomway itway impartsway!

Oryray Itwinlay
Aprilway, 2006

ETHAY OOKBAY OFWAY ALMSPSAY

ALMPSAY 1

1 Essedblay [isway] ethay anmay atthay alkethway otnay inway ethay ounselcay ofway ethay ungodlyway, ornay andethstay inway ethay ayway ofway innerssay, ornay ittethsay inway ethay eatsay ofway ethay ornfulscay.

2 Utbay ishay elightday [isway] inway ethay awlay ofway ethay ORDLAY; andway inway ishay awlay othday ehay editatemay ayday andway ightnay.

3 Andway ehay allshay ebay ikelay away eetray antedplay byay ethay iversray ofway aterway, atthay ingethbray orthfay ishay uitfray inway ishay easonsay; ishay eaflay alsoway allshay otnay itherway; andway atsoeverwhay ehay oethday allshay osperpray.

4 Ethay ungodlyway [areway] otnay osay: utbay [areway] ikelay ethay affchay ichwhay ethay indway ivethdray awayway.

5 Ereforethay ethay ungodlyway allshay otnay andstay inway ethay udgmentjay, ornay innerssay inway ethay ongregationcay ofway ethay ighteousray.

6 Orfay ethay ORDLAY owethknay ethay ayway ofway ethay ighteousray: utbay ethay ayway ofway ethay ungodlyway allshay erishpay.

ALMPSAY 2

1 Whyay oday ethay eathenhay ageray, andway ethay eoplepay imagineway away ainvay ingthay?

2 Ethay ingskay ofway ethay earthway etsay emselvesthay, andway ethay ulersray aketay ounselcay ogethertay, againstway ethay ORDLAY, andway againstway ishay anointedway, [ayingsay],

3 Etlay usway eakbray eirthay andsbay asunderway, andway astcay awayway eirthay ordscay omfray usway.

4 Ehay atthay ittethsay inway ethay eavenshay allshay aughlay: ethay Ordlay allshay avehay emthay inway erisionday.

5 Enthay allshay ehay eakspay untoway emthay inway ishay athwray, andway exvay emthay inway ishay oresay ispleasureday.

6 Etyay avehay IWAY etsay myay ingkay uponway myay olyhay illhay ofway Ionzay.

7 IWAY illway eclareday ethay ecreeday: ethay ORDLAY athhay aidsay untoway emay, Outhay [artway] myay Onsay; isthay ayday avehay IWAY egottenbay eethay.
8 Askway ofway emay, andway IWAY allshay ivegay [eethay] ethay eathenhay [orfay] inethay inheritanceway, andway ethay uttermostway artspay ofway ethay earthway [orfay] thyay ossessionpay.
9 Outhay altshay eakbray emthay ithway away odray ofway ironway; outhay altshay ashday emthay inway iecespay ikelay away otterpay'say esselvay.
10 Ebay iseway ownay ereforethay, OWAY eyay ingskay: ebay instructedway, eyay udgesjay ofway ethay earthway.
11 Ervesay ethay ORDLAY ithway earfay, andway ejoiceray ithway emblingtray.
12 Isskay ethay Onsay, estlay ehay ebay angryway, andway eyay erishpay [omfray] ethay ayway, enwhay ishay athwray isway indledkay utbay away ittlelay. Essedblay [areway] allway eythay atthay utpay eirthay usttray inway imhay.

ALMPSAY 3
AWAY Almpsay ofway Avidday, enwhay ehay edflay omfray Absalomway ishay onsay.
1 ORDLAY, owhay areway eythay increasedway atthay oubletray emay! anymay [areway] eythay atthay iseray upway againstway emay.
2 Anymay [erethay ebay] ichwhay aysay ofway myay oulsay, [Erethay isway] onay elphay orfay imhay inway Odgay. Elahsay.
3 Utbay outhay, OWAY ORDLAY, [artway] away ieldshay orfay emay; myay oryglay, andway ethay ifterlay upway ofway inemay eadhay.
4 IWAY iedcray untoway ethay ORDLAY ithway myay oicevay, andway ehay eardhay emay outway ofway ishay olyhay illhay. Elahsay.
5 IWAY aidlay emay ownday andway eptslay; IWAY awakedway; orfay ethay ORDLAY ustainedsay emay.
6 IWAY illway otnay ebay afraidway ofway entay ousandsthay ofway eoplepay, atthay avehay etsay [emselvesthay] againstway emay oundray aboutway.
7 Ariseway, OWAY ORDLAY; avesay emay, OWAY myay Odgay: orfay outhay asthay ittensmay allway inemay enemiesway [uponway] ethay eekchay onebay; outhay asthay okenbray ethay eethtay ofway ethay ungodlyway.
8 Alvationsay [elongethbay] untoway ethay ORDLAY: thyay essingblay [isway] uponway thyay eoplepay. Elahsay.

ALMPSAY 4
Otay ethay iefchay Usicianmay onway Eginothnay, AWAY Almpsay
ofway Avidday.
1 Earhay emay enwhay IWAY allcay, OWAY Odgay ofway myay
ighteousnessray: outhay asthay enlargedway emay [enwhay IWAY asway]
inway istressday; avehay ercymay uponway emay, andway earhay myay
ayerpray.
2 OWAY eyay onssay ofway enmay, owhay onglay [illway eyay urntay]
myay oryglay intoway ameshay? [owhay onglay] illway eyay ovelay
anityvay, [andway] eeksay afterway easinglay? Elahsay.
3 Utbay owknay atthay ethay ORDLAY athhay etsay apartway imhay
atthay isway odlygay orfay imselfhay: ethay ORDLAY illway earhay
enwhay IWAY allcay untoway imhay.
4 Andstay inway aweway, andway insay otnay: ommunecay ithway ouryay
ownway earthay uponway ouryay edbay, andway ebay illstay. Elahsay.
5 Offerway ethay acrificessay ofway ighteousnessray, andway utpay
ouryay usttray inway ethay ORDLAY.
6 [Erethay ebay] anymay atthay aysay, Owhay illway ewshay usway
[anyway] oodgay? ORDLAY, iftlay outhay upway ethay ightlay ofway
thyay ountenancecay uponway usway.
7 Outhay asthay utpay adnessglay inway myay earthay, oremay anthay
inway ethay imetay [atthay] eirthay orncay andway eirthay ineway
increasedway.
8 IWAY illway othbay aylay emay ownday inway eacepay, andway
eepslay: orfay outhay, ORDLAY, onlyway akestmay emay elldway inway
afetysay.

ALMPSAY 5
Otay ethay iefchay Usicianmay uponway Ehilothnay, AWAY Almpsay
ofway Avidday.
1 Ivegay earway otay myay ordsway, OWAY ORDLAY, onsidercay myay
editationmay.
2 Earkenhay untoway ethay oicevay ofway myay cryay, myay Ingkay,
andway myay Odgay: orfay untoway eethay illway IWAY aypray.
3 Myay oicevay altshay outhay earhay inway ethay orningmay, OWAY
ORDLAY; inway ethay orningmay illway IWAY irectday [myay
ayerpray] untoway eethay, andway illway ooklay upway.
4 Orfay outhay [artway] otnay away Odgay atthay athhay easureplay
inway ickednessway: eithernay allshay evilway elldway ithway eethay.

5 Ethay oolishfay allshay otnay andstay inway thyay ightsay: outhay atesthay allway orkersway ofway iniquityway.

6 Outhay altshay estroyday emthay atthay eakspay easinglay: ethay ORDLAY illway abhorway ethay oodyblay andway eceitfulday anmay.

7 Utbay asway orfay emay, IWAY illway omecay [intoway] thyay ousehay inway ethay ultitudemay ofway thyay ercymay: [andway] inway thyay earfay illway IWAY orshipway owardtay thyay olyhay empletay.

8 Eadlay emay, OWAY ORDLAY, inway thyay ighteousnessray ecausebay ofway inemay enemiesway; akemay thyay ayway aightstray eforebay myay acefay.

9 Orfay [erethay isway] onay aithfulnessfay inway eirthay outhmay; eirthay inwardway artpay [isway] eryvay ickednessway; eirthay oatthray [isway] anway openway epulchresay; eythay atterflay ithway eirthay onguetay.

10 Estroyday outhay emthay, OWAY Odgay; etlay emthay allfay byay eirthay ownway ounselscay; astcay emthay outway inway ethay ultitudemay ofway eirthay ansgressionstray; orfay eythay avehay ebelledray againstway eethay.

11 Utbay etlay allway osethay atthay utpay eirthay usttray inway eethay ejoiceray: etlay emthay everway outshay orfay oyjay, ecausebay outhay efendestday emthay: etlay emthay alsoway atthay ovelay thyay amenay ebay oyfuljay inway eethay.

12 Orfay outhay, ORDLAY, iltway essblay ethay ighteousray; ithway avourfay iltway outhay ompasscay imhay asway [ithway] away ieldshay.

ALMPSAY 6
Otay ethay iefchay Usicianmay onway Eginothnay uponway Eminithshay, AWAY Almpsay ofway Avidday.

1 OWAY ORDLAY, ebukeray emay otnay inway inethay angerway, eithernay astenchay emay inway thyay othay ispleasureday.

2 Avehay ercymay uponway emay, OWAY ORDLAY; orfay IWAY [amway] eakway: OWAY ORDLAY, ealhay emay; orfay myay onesbay areway exedvay.

3 Myay oulsay isway alsoway oresay exedvay: utbay outhay, OWAY ORDLAY, owhay onglay?

4 Eturnray, OWAY ORDLAY, eliverday myay oulsay: ohway avesay emay orfay thyay erciesmay' akesay.

5 Orfay inway eathday [erethay isway] onay emembranceray ofway eethay: inway ethay avegray owhay allshay ivegay eethay anksthay?

6 IWAY amway earyway ithway myay oaninggray; allway ethay ightnay akemay IWAY myay edbay otay imsway; IWAY aterway myay ouchcay ithway myay earstay.

7 Inemay eyeway isway onsumedcay ecausebay ofway iefgray; itway axethway oldway ecausebay ofway allway inemay enemiesway.

8 Epartday omfray emay, allway eyay orkersway ofway iniquityway; orfay ethay ORDLAY athhay eardhay ethay oicevay ofway myay eepingway.

9 Ethay ORDLAY athhay eardhay myay upplicationsay; ethay ORDLAY illway eceiveray myay ayerpray.

10 Etlay allway inemay enemiesway ebay ashamedway andway oresay exedvay: etlay emthay eturnray [andway] ebay ashamedway uddenlysay.

ALMPSAY 7
Iggaionshay ofway Avidday, ichwhay ehay angsay untoway ethay ORDLAY, oncerningcay ethay ordsway ofway Ushcay ethay Enjamitebay.

1 OWAY ORDLAY myay Odgay, inway eethay oday IWAY utpay myay usttray: avesay emay omfray allway emthay atthay ersecutepay emay, andway eliverday emay:

2 Estlay ehay eartay myay oulsay ikelay away ionlay, endingray [itway] inway iecespay, ilewhay [erethay isway] onenay otay eliverday.

3 OWAY ORDLAY myay Odgay, ifway IWAY avehay oneday isthay; ifway erethay ebay iniquityway inway myay andshay;

4 Ifway IWAY avehay ewardedray evilway untoway imhay atthay asway atway eacepay ithway emay; (eayay, IWAY avehay eliveredday imhay atthay ithoutway ausecay isway inemay enemyway:)

5 Etlay ethay enemyway ersecutepay myay oulsay, andway aketay [itway]; eayay, etlay imhay eadtray ownday myay ifelay uponway ethay earthway, andway aylay inemay onourhay inway ethay ustday. Elahsay.

6 Ariseway, OWAY ORDLAY, inway inethay angerway, iftlay upway elfthysay ecausebay ofway ethay ageray ofway inemay enemiesway: andway awakeway orfay emay [otay] ethay udgmentjay [atthay] outhay asthay ommandedcay.

7 Osay allshay ethay ongregationcay ofway ethay eoplepay ompasscay eethay aboutway: orfay eirthay akessay ereforethay eturnray outhay onway ighhay.

8 Ethay ORDLAY allshay udgejay ethay eoplepay: udgejay emay, OWAY ORDLAY, accordingway otay myay ighteousnessray, andway accordingway otay inemay integrityway [atthay isway] inway emay.

9 Ohway etlay ethay ickednessway ofway ethay ickedway omecay otay anway endway; utbay establishway ethay ustjay: orfay ethay ighteousray Odgay iethtray ethay eartshay andway einsray.

10 Myay efenceday [isway] ofway Odgay, ichwhay avethsay ethay uprightway inway earthay.

11 Odgay udgethjay ethay ighteousray, andway Odgay isway angryway [ithway ethay ickedway] everyway ayday.

12 Ifway ehay urntay otnay, ehay illway etwhay ishay ordsway; ehay athhay entbay ishay owbay, andway ademay itway eadyray.

13 Ehay athhay alsoway eparedpray orfay imhay ethay instrumentsway ofway eathday; ehay ordainethway ishay arrowsway againstway ethay ersecutorspay.

14 Eholdbay, ehay availethtray ithway iniquityway, andway athhay onceivedcay ischiefmay, andway oughtbray orthfay alsehoodfay.

15 Ehay ademay away itpay, andway iggedday itway, andway isway allenfay intoway ethay itchday [ichwhay] ehay ademay.

16 Ishay ischiefmay allshay eturnray uponway ishay ownway eadhay, andway ishay iolentvay ealingday allshay omecay ownday uponway ishay ownway atepay.

17 IWAY illway aisepray ethay ORDLAY accordingway otay ishay ighteousnessray: andway illway ingsay aisepray otay ethay amenay ofway ethay ORDLAY ostmay ighhay.

ALMPSAY 8

Otay ethay iefchay Usicianmay uponway Ittithgay, AWAY Almpsay ofway Avidday.

1 OWAY ORDLAY ourway Ordlay, owhay excellentway [isway] thyay amenay inway allway ethay earthway! owhay asthay etsay thyay oryglay aboveway ethay eavenshay.

2 Outway ofway ethay outhmay ofway abesbay andway ucklingssay asthay outhay ordainedway engthstray ecausebay ofway inethay enemiesway, atthay outhay ightestmay illstay ethay enemyway andway ethay avengerway.

3 Enwhay IWAY onsidercay thyay eavenshay, ethay orkway ofway thyay ingersfay, ethay oonmay andway ethay arsstay, ichwhay outhay asthay ordainedway;

4 Atwhay isway anmay, atthay outhay artway indfulmay ofway imhay? andway ethay onsay ofway anmay, atthay outhay isitestvay imhay?

5 Orfay outhay asthay ademay imhay away ittlelay owerlay anthay ethay angelsway, andway asthay ownedcray imhay ithway oryglay andway onourhay.
6 Outhay adestmay imhay otay avehay ominionday overway ethay orksway ofway thyay andshay; outhay asthay utpay allway [ingsthay] underway ishay eetfay:
7 Allway eepshay andway oxenway, eayay, andway ethay eastsbay ofway ethay ieldfay;
8 Ethay owlfay ofway ethay airway, andway ethay ishfay ofway ethay easay, [andway atsoeverwhay] assethpay oughthray ethay athspay ofway ethay eassay.
9 OWAY ORDLAY ourway Ordlay, owhay excellentway [isway] thyay amenay inway allway ethay earthway!

ALMPSAY 9
Otay ethay iefchay Usicianmay uponway Uthmay-abbenlay, AWAY Almpsay ofway Avidday.
1 IWAY illway aisepray [eethay], OWAY ORDLAY, ithway myay olewhay earthay; IWAY illway ewshay orthfay allway thyay arvellousmay orksway.
2 IWAY illway ebay adglay andway ejoiceray inway eethay: IWAY illway ingsay aisepray otay thyay amenay, OWAY outhay ostmay Ighhay.
3 Enwhay inemay enemiesway areway urnedtay ackbay, eythay allshay allfay andway erishpay atway thyay esencepray.
4 Orfay outhay asthay aintainedmay myay ightray andway myay ausecay; outhay atestsay inway ethay onethray udgingjay ightray.
5 Outhay asthay ebukedray ethay eathenhay, outhay asthay estroyedday ethay ickedway, outhay asthay utpay outway eirthay amenay orfay everway andway everway.
6 OWAY outhay enemyway, estructionsday areway omecay otay away erpetualpay endway: andway outhay asthay estroyedday itiescay; eirthay emorialmay isway erishedpay ithway emthay.
7 Utbay ethay ORDLAY allshay endureway orfay everway: ehay athhay eparedpray ishay onethray orfay udgmentjay.
8 Andway ehay allshay udgejay ethay orldway inway ighteousnessray, ehay allshay inistermay udgmentjay otay ethay eoplepay inway uprightnessway.
9 Ethay ORDLAY alsoway illway ebay away efugeray orfay ethay oppressedway, away efugeray inway imestay ofway oubletray.

10 Andway eythay atthay owknay thyay amenay illway utpay eirthay usttray inway eethay: orfay outhay, ORDLAY, asthay otnay orsakenfay emthay atthay eeksay eethay.

11 Ingsay aisesþray otay ethay ORDLAY, ichwhay ellethdway inway Ionzay: eclareday amongway ethay eoplepay ishay oingsday.

12 Enwhay ehay akethmay inquisitionway orfay oodblay, ehay ememberethray emthay: ehay orgettethfay otnay ethay cryay ofway ethay umblehay.

13 Avehay ercymay uponway emay, OWAY ORDLAY; onsidercay myay oubletray [ichwhay IWAY uffersay] ofway emthay atthay atehay emay, outhay atthay iftestlay emay upway omfray ethay atesgay ofway eathday:

14 Atthay IWAY aymay ewshay orthfay allway thyay aisepray inway ethay atesgay ofway ethay aughterday ofway Ionzay: IWAY illway ejoiceray inway thyay alvationsay.

15 Ethay eathenhay areway unksay ownday inway ethay itpay [atthay] eythay ademay: inway ethay etnay ichwhay eythay idhay isway eirthay ownway ootfay akentay.

16 Ethay ORDLAY isway ownknay [byay] ethay udgmentjay [ichwhay] ehay executethway: ethay ickedway isway aredsnay inway ethay orkway ofway ishay ownway andshay. Iggaionhay. Elahsay.

17 Ethay ickedway allshay ebay urnedtay intoway ellhay, [andway] allway ethay ationsnay atthay orgetfay Odgay.

18 Orfay ethay eedynay allshay otnay alwayway ebay orgottenfay: ethay expectationway ofway ethay oorpay allshay [otnay] erishpay orfay everway.

19 Ariseway, OWAY ORDLAY; etlay otnay anmay evailpray: etlay ethay eathenhay ebay udgedjay inway thyay ightsay.

20 Utpay emthay inway earfay, OWAY ORDLAY: [atthay] ethay ationsnay aymay owknay emselvesthay [otay ebay utbay] enmay. Elahsay.

ALMPSAY 10

1 Whyay andeststay outhay afarway offway, OWAY ORDLAY? [whyay] idesthay outhay [elfthysay] inway imestay ofway oubletray?

2 Ethay ickedway inway [ishay] idepray othday ersecutepay ethay oorpay: etlay emthay ebay akentay inway ethay evicesday atthay eythay avehay imaginedway.

3 Orfay ethay ickedway oastethbay ofway ishay earthay'say esireday, andway essethblay ethay ovetouscay, [omwhay] ethay ORDLAY abhorrethway.

4 Ethay ickedway, oughthray ethay idepray ofway ishay ountenancecay, illway otnay eeksay [afterway Odgay]: Odgay [isway] otnay inway allway ishay oughtsthay.

5 Ishay aysway areway alwaysway ievousgray; thyay udgmentsjay [areway] arfay aboveway outway ofway ishay ightsay: [asway orfay] allway ishay enemiesway, ehay uffethpay atway emthay.

6 Ehay athhay aidsay inway ishay earthay, IWAY allshay otnay ebay ovedmay: orfay [IWAY allshay] evernay [ebay] inway adversityway.

7 Ishay outhmay isway ullfay ofway ursingcay andway eceitday andway audfray: underway ishay onguetay [isway] ischiefmay andway anityvay.

8 Ehay ittethsay inway ethay urkinglay acesplay ofway ethay illagesvay: inway ethay ecretsay acesplay othday ehay urdermay ethay innocentway: ishay eyesway areway ivilypray etsay againstway ethay oorpay.

9 Ehay iethlay inway aitway ecretlysay asway away ionlay inway ishay enday: ehay iethlay inway aitway otay atchcay ethay oorpay: ehay othday atchcay ethay oorpay, enwhay ehay awethdray imhay intoway ishay etnay.

10 Ehay ouchethcray, [andway] umblethhay imselfhay, atthay ethay oorpay aymay allfay byay ishay ongstray onesway.

11 Ehay athhay aidsay inway ishay earthay, Odgay athhay orgottenfay: ehay idethhay ishay acefay; ehay illway evernay eesay [itway].

12 Ariseway, OWAY ORDLAY; OWAY Odgay, iftlay upway inethay andhay: orgetfay otnay ethay umblehay.

13 Ereforewhay othday ethay ickedway ontemncay Odgay? ehay athhay aidsay inway ishay earthay, Outhay iltway otnay equireray [itway].

14 Outhay asthay eensay [itway]; orfay outhay eholdestbay ischiefmay andway itespay, otay equiteray [itway] ithway thyay andhay: ethay oorpay ommittethcay imselfhay untoway eethay; outhay artway ethay elperhay ofway ethay atherlessfay.

15 Eakbray outhay ethay armway ofway ethay ickedway andway ethay evilway [anmay]: eeksay outway ishay ickednessway [illtay] outhay indfay onenay.

16 Ethay ORDLAY [isway] Ingkay orfay everway andway everway: ethay eathenhay areway erishedpay outway ofway ishay andlay.

17 ORDLAY, outhay asthay eardhay ethay esireday ofway ethay umblehay: outhay iltway eparepray eirthay earthay, outhay iltway ausecay inethay earway otay earhay:

18 Otay udgejay ethay atherlessfay andway ethay oppressedway, atthay ethay anmay ofway ethay earthway aymay onay oremay oppressway.

ALMPSAY 11

Otay ethay iefchay Usicianmay, [AWAY Almpsay] ofway Avidday.

1 Inway ethay ORDLAY utpay IWAY myay usttray: owhay aysay eyay otay myay oulsay, Eeflay [asway] away irdbay otay ouryay ountainmay?

2 Orfay, olay, ethay ickedway endbay [eirthay] owbay, eythay akemay eadyray eirthay arrowway uponway ethay ingstray, atthay eythay aymay ivilypray ootshay atway ethay uprightway inway earthay.

3 Ifway ethay oundationsfay ebay estroyedday, atwhay ancay ethay ighteousray oday?

4 Ethay ORDLAY [isway] inway ishay olyhay empletay, ethay ORDLAY'SAY onethray [isway] inway eavenhay: ishay eyesway eholdbay, ishay eyelidsway tryay, ethay ildrenchay ofway enmay.

5 Ethay ORDLAY iethtray ethay ighteousray: utbay ethay ickedway andway imhay atthay ovethlay iolencevay ishay oulsay atethhay.

6 Uponway ethay ickedway ehay allshay ainray aressnay, irefay andway imstonebray, andway anway orriblehay empesttay: [isthay allshay ebay] ethay ortionpay ofway eirthay upcay.

7 Orfay ethay ighteousray ORDLAY ovethlay ighteousnessray; ishay ountenancecay othday eholdbay ethay uprightway.

ALMPSAY 12

Otay ethay iefchay Usicianmay uponway Eminithshay, AWAY Almpsay ofway Avidday.

1 Elphay, ORDLAY; orfay ethay odlygay anmay easethcay; orfay ethay aithfulfay ailfay omfray amongway ethay ildrenchay ofway enmay.

2 Eythay eakspay anityvay everyway oneway ithway ishay eighbournay: [ithway] atteringflay ipslay [andway] ithway away oubleday earthay oday eythay eakspay.

3 Ethay ORDLAY allshay utcay offway allway atteringflay ipslay, [andway] ethay onguetay atthay eakethspay oudpray ingsthay:

4 Owhay avehay aidsay, Ithway ourway onguetay illway eway evailpray; ourway ipslay [areway] ourway ownway: owhay [isway] ordlay overway usway?

5 Orfay ethay oppressionway ofway ethay oorpay, orfay ethay ighingsay ofway ethay eedynay, ownay illway IWAY ariseway, aithsay ethay ORDLAY; IWAY illway etsay [imhay] inway afetysay [omfray imhay atthay] uffethpay atway imhay.

6 Ethay ordsway ofway ethay ORDLAY [areway] urepay ordsway: [asway] ilversay iedtray inway away urnacefay ofway earthway, urifiedpay evensay imestay.

7 Outhay altshay eepkay emthay, OWAY ORDLAY, outhay altshay eservepray emthay omfray isthay enerationgay orfay everway.
8 Ethay ickedway alkway onway everyway idesay, enwhay ethay ilestvay enmay areway exaltedway.

ALMPSAY 13
Otay ethay iefchay Usicianmay, AWAY Almpsay ofway Avidday.
1 Owhay onglay iltway outhay orgetfay emay, OWAY ORDLAY? orfay everway? owhay onglay iltway outhay idehay thyay acefay omfray emay?
2 Owhay onglay allshay IWAY aketay ounselcay inway myay oulsay, [avinghay] orrowsay inway myay earthay ailyday? owhay onglay allshay inemay enemyway ebay exaltedway overway emay?
3 Onsidercay [andway] earhay emay, OWAY ORDLAY myay Odgay: ightenlay inemay eyesway, estlay IWAY eepslay ethay [eepslay ofway] eathday;
4 Estlay inemay enemyway aysay, IWAY avehay evailedpray againstway imhay; [andway] osethay atthay oubletray emay ejoiceray enwhay IWAY amway ovedmay.
5 Utbay IWAY avehay ustedtray inway thyay ercymay; myay earthay allshay ejoiceray inway thyay alvationsay.
6 IWAY illway ingsay untoway ethay ORDLAY, ecausebay ehay athhay ealtday ountifullybay ithway emay.

ALMPSAY 14
Otay ethay iefchay Usicianmay, [AWAY Almpsay] ofway Avidday.
1 Ethay oolfay athhay aidsay inway ishay earthay, [Erethay isway] onay Odgay. Eythay areway orruptcay, eythay avehay oneday abominableway orksway, [erethay isway] onenay atthay oethday oodgay.
2 Ethay ORDLAY ookedlay ownday omfray eavenhay uponway ethay ildrenchay ofway enmay, otay eesay ifway erethay ereway anyway atthay idday understandway, [andway] eeksay Odgay.
3 Eythay areway allway onegay asideway, eythay areway [allway] ogethertay ecomebay ilthyfay: [erethay isway] onenay atthay oethday oodgay, onay, otnay oneway.
4 Avehay allway ethay orkersway ofway iniquityway onay owledgeknay? owhay eatway upway myay eoplepay [asway] eythay eatway eadbray, andway allcay otnay uponway ethay ORDLAY.
5 Erethay ereway eythay inway eatgray earfay: orfay Odgay [isway] inway ethay enerationgay ofway ethay ighteousray.

6 Eyay avehay amedshay ethay ounselcay ofway ethay oorpay, ecausebay ethay ORDLAY [isway] ishay efugeray.

7 Ohway atthay ethay alvationsay ofway Israelway [ereway omecay] outway ofway Ionzay! enwhay ethay ORDLAY ingethbray ackbay ethay aptivitycay ofway ishay eoplepay, Acobjay allshay ejoiceray, [andway] Israelway allshay ebay adglay.

ALMPSAY 15
AWAY Almpsay ofway Avidday.

1 ORDLAY, owhay allshay abideway inway thyay abernacletay? owhay allshay elldway inway thyay olyhay illhay?

2 Ehay atthay alkethway uprightlyway, andway orkethway ighteousnessray, andway eakethspay ethay uthtray inway ishay earthay.

3 [Ehay atthay] ackbitethbay otnay ithway ishay onguetay, ornay oethday evilway otay ishay eighbournay, ornay akethtay upway away eproachray againstway ishay eighbournay.

4 Inway osewhay eyesway away ilevay ersonpay isway ontemnedcay; utbay ehay onourethhay emthay atthay earfay ethay ORDLAY. [Ehay atthay] earethsway otay [ishay ownway] urthay, andway angethchay otnay.

5 [Ehay atthay] uttethpay otnay outway ishay oneymay otay usuryway, ornay akethtay ewardray againstway ethay innocentway. Ehay atthay oethday esethay [ingsthay] allshay evernay ebay ovedmay.

ALMPSAY 16
Ichtammay ofway Avidday.

1 Eservepray emay, OWAY Odgay: orfay inway eethay oday IWAY utpay myay usttray.

2 [OWAY myay oulsay], outhay asthay aidsay untoway ethay ORDLAY, Outhay [artway] myay Ordlay: myay oodnessgay [extendethway] otnay otay eethay;

3 [Utbay] otay ethay aintssay atthay [areway] inway ethay earthway, andway [otay] ethay excellentway, inway omwhay [isway] allway myay elightday.

4 Eirthay orrowssay allshay ebay ultipliedmay [atthay] astenhay [afterway] anotherway [odgay]: eirthay inkdray offeringsway ofway oodblay illway IWAY otnay offerway, ornay aketay upway eirthay amesnay intoway myay ipslay.

5 Ethay ORDLAY [isway] ethay ortionpay ofway inemay inheritanceway andway ofway myay upcay: outhay aintainestmay myay otlay.

6 Ethay ineslay areway allenfay untoway emay inway easantplay [acesplay]; eayay, IWAY avehay away oodlygay eritagehay.

7 IWAY illway essblay ethay ORDLAY, owhay athhay ivengay emay ounselcay: myay einsray alsoway instructway emay inway ethay ightnay easonssay.

8 IWAY avehay etsay ethay ORDLAY alwaysway eforebay emay: ecausebay [ehay isway] atway myay ightray andhay, IWAY allshay otnay ebay ovedmay.

9 Ereforethay myay earthay isway adglay, andway myay oryglay ejoicethray: myay eshflay alsoway allshay estray inway opehay.

10 Orfay outhay iltway otnay eavelay myay oulsay inway ellhay; eithernay iltway outhay uffersay inethay Olyhay Oneway otay eesay orruptioncay.

11 Outhay iltway ewshay emay ethay athpay ofway ifelay: inway thyay esencepray [isway] ulnessfay ofway oyjay; atway thyay ightray andhay [erethay areway] easuresplay orfay evermoreway.

ALMPSAY 17
AWAY Ayerpray ofway Avidday.
1 Earhay ethay ightray, OWAY ORDLAY, attendway untoway myay cryay, ivegay earway untoway myay ayerpray, [atthay oethgay] otnay outway ofway eignedfay ipslay.

2 Etlay myay entencesay omecay orthfay omfray thyay esencepray; etlay inethay eyesway eholdbay ethay ingsthay atthay areway equalway.

3 Outhay asthay ovedpray inemay earthay; outhay asthay isitedvay [emay] inway ethay ightnay; outhay asthay iedtray emay, [andway] altshay indfay othingnay; IWAY amway urposedpay [atthay] myay outhmay allshay otnay ansgresstray.

4 Oncerningcay ethay orksway ofway enmay, byay ethay ordway ofway thyay ipslay IWAY avehay eptkay [emay omfray] ethay athspay ofway ethay estroyerday.

5 Oldhay upway myay oingsgay inway thyay athspay, [atthay] myay ootstepsfay ipslay otnay.

6 IWAY avehay alledcay uponway eethay, orfay outhay iltway earhay emay, OWAY Odgay: inclineway inethay earway untoway emay, [andway earhay] myay eechspay.

7 Ewshay thyay arvellousmay ovingkindnesslay, OWAY outhay atthay avestsay byay thyay ightray andhay emthay ichwhay utpay eirthay usttray [inway eethay] omfray osethay atthay iseray upway [againstway emthay].

8 Eepkay emay asway ethay appleway ofway ethay eyeway, idehay emay underway ethay adowshay ofway thyay ingsway,

9 Omfray ethay ickedway atthay oppressway emay, [omfray] myay eadlyday enemiesway, [owhay] ompasscay emay aboutway.

10 Eythay areway inclosedway inway eirthay ownway atfay: ithway eirthay outhmay eythay eakspay oudlypray.

11 Eythay avehay ownay ompassedcay usway inway ourway epsstay: eythay avehay etsay eirthay eyesway owingbay ownday otay ethay earthway;

12 Ikelay asway away ionlay [atthay] isway eedygray ofway ishay eypray, andway asway itway ereway away oungyay ionlay urkinglay inway ecretsay acesplay.

13 Ariseway, OWAY ORDLAY, isappointday imhay, astcay imhay ownday: eliverday myay oulsay omfray ethay ickedway, [ichwhay isway] thyay ordsway:

14 Omfray enmay [ichwhay areway] thyay andhay, OWAY ORDLAY, omfray enmay ofway ethay orldway, [ichwhay avehay] eirthay ortionpay inway [isthay] ifelay, andway osewhay ellybay outhay illestfay ithway thyay idhay [easuretray]: eythay areway ullfay ofway ildrenchay, andway eavelay ethay estray ofway eirthay [ubstancesay] otay eirthay abesbay.

15 Asway orfay emay, IWAY illway eholdbay thyay acefay inway ighteousnessray: IWAY allshay ebay atisfiedsay, enwhay IWAY awakeway, ithway thyay ikenesslay.

ALMPSAY 18
Otay ethay iefchay Usicianmay, [AWAY Almpsay] ofway Avidday, ethay ervantsay ofway ethay ORDLAY, owhay akespay untoway ethay ORDLAY ethay ordsway ofway isthay ongsay inway ethay ayday [atthay] ethay ORDLAY eliveredday imhay omfray ethay andhay ofway allway ishay enemiesway, andway omfray ethay andhay ofway Aulsay: Andway ehay aidsay,

1 IWAY illway ovelay eethay, OWAY ORDLAY, myay engthstray.

2 Ethay ORDLAY [isway] myay ockray, andway myay ortressfay, andway myay elivererday; myay Odgay, myay engthstray, inway omwhay IWAY illway usttray; myay ucklerbay, andway ethay ornhay ofway myay alvationsay, [andway] myay ighhay owertay.

3 IWAY illway allcay uponway ethay ORDLAY, [owhay isway orthyway] otay ebay aisedpray: osay allshay IWAY ebay avedsay omfray inemay enemiesway.

4 Ethay orrowssay ofway eathday ompassedcay emay, andway ethay oodsflay ofway ungodlyway enmay ademay emay afraidway.

5 Ethay orrowssay ofway ellhay ompassedcay emay aboutway: ethay aressnay ofway eathday eventedpray emay.

6 Inway myay istressday IWAY alledcay uponway ethay ORDLAY, andway iedcray untoway myay Odgay: ehay eardhay myay oicevay outway ofway ishay empletay, andway myay cryay amecay eforebay imhay, [evenway] intoway ishay earsway.

7 Enthay ethay earthway ookshay andway embledtray; ethay oundationsfay alsoway ofway ethay illshay ovedmay andway ereway akenshay, ecausebay ehay asway othwray.

8 Erethay entway upway away okesmay outway ofway ishay ostrilsnay, andway irefay outway ofway ishay outhmay evouredday: oalscay ereway indledkay byay itway.

9 Ehay owedbay ethay eavenshay alsoway, andway amecay ownday: andway arknessday [asway] underway ishay eetfay.

10 Andway ehay oderay uponway away erubchay, andway idday flyay: eayay, ehay idday flyay uponway ethay ingsway ofway ethay indway.

11 Ehay ademay arknessday ishay ecretsay aceplay; ishay avilionpay oundray aboutway imhay [ereway] arkday atersway [andway] ickthay oudsclay ofway ethay iesskay.

12 Atway ethay ightnessbray [atthay asway] eforebay imhay ishay ickthay oudsclay assedpay, ailhay [onesstay] andway oalscay ofway irefay.

13 Ethay ORDLAY alsoway underedthay inway ethay eavenshay, andway ethay Ighesthay avegay ishay oicevay; ailhay [onesstay] andway oalscay ofway irefay.

14 Eayay, ehay entsay outway ishay arrowsway, andway atteredscay emthay; andway ehay otshay outway ightningslay, andway iscomfitedday emthay.

15 Enthay ethay annelschay ofway atersway ereway eensay, andway ethay oundationsfay ofway ethay orldway ereway iscoveredday atway thyay ebukeray, OWAY ORDLAY, atway ethay astblay ofway ethay eathbray ofway thyay ostrilsnay.

16 Ehay entsay omfray aboveway, ehay ooktay emay, ehay ewdray emay outway ofway anymay atersway.

17 Ehay eliveredday emay omfray myay ongstray enemyway, andway omfray emthay ichwhay atedhay emay: orfay eythay ereway ootay ongstray orfay emay.

18 Eythay eventedpray emay inway ethay ayday ofway myay alamitycay: utbay ethay ORDLAY asway myay aystay.

19 Ehay oughtbray emay orthfay alsoway intoway away argelay aceplay; ehay eliveredday emay, ecausebay ehay elightedday inway emay.

20 Ethay ORDLAY ewardedray emay accordingway otay myay ighteousnessray; accordingway otay ethay eannessclay ofway myay andshay athhay ehay ecompensedray emay.

21 Orfay IWAY avehay eptkay ethay aysway ofway ethay ORDLAY, andway avehay otnay ickedlyway epartedday omfray myay Odgay.

22 Orfay allway ishay udgmentsjay [ereway] eforebay emay, andway IWAY idday otnay utpay awayway ishay atutesstay omfray emay.

23 IWAY asway alsoway uprightway eforebay imhay, andway IWAY eptkay elfmysay omfray inemay iniquityway.

24 Ereforethay athhay ethay ORDLAY ecompensedray emay accordingway otay myay ighteousnessray, accordingway otay ethay eannessclay ofway myay andshay inway ishay eyesightway.

25 Ithway ethay ercifulmay outhay iltway ewshay elfthysay ercifulmay; ithway anway uprightway anmay outhay iltway ewshay elfthysay uprightway;

26 Ithway ethay urepay outhay iltway ewshay elfthysay urepay; andway ithway ethay owardfray outhay iltway ewshay elfthysay owardfray.

27 Orfay outhay iltway avesay ethay afflictedway eoplepay; utbay iltway ingbray ownday ighhay ookslay.

28 Orfay outhay iltway ightlay myay andlecay: ethay ORDLAY myay Odgay illway enlightenway myay arknessday.

29 Orfay byay eethay IWAY avehay unray oughthray away ooptray; andway byay myay Odgay avehay IWAY eapedlay overway away allway.

30 [Asway orfay] Odgay, ishay ayway [isway] erfectpay: ethay ordway ofway ethay ORDLAY isway iedtray: ehay [isway] away ucklerbay otay allway osethay atthay usttray inway imhay.

31 Orfay owhay [isway] Odgay avesay ethay ORDLAY? orway owhay [isway] away ockray avesay ourway Odgay?

32 [Itway isway] Odgay atthay irdethgay emay ithway engthstray, andway akethmay myay ayway erfectpay.

33 Ehay akethmay myay eetfay ikelay indshay' [eetfay], andway ettethsay emay uponway myay ighhay acesplay.

34 Ehay eachethtay myay andshay otay arway, osay atthay away owbay ofway eelstay isway okenbray byay inemay armsway.

35 Outhay asthay alsoway ivengay emay ethay ieldshay ofway thyay alvationsay: andway thyay ightray andhay athhay oldenhay emay upway, andway thyay entlenessgay athhay ademay emay eatgray.

36 Outhay asthay enlargedway myay epsstay underway emay, atthay myay eetfay idday otnay ipslay.

37 IWAY avehay ursuedpay inemay enemiesway, andway overtakenway emthay: eithernay idday IWAY urntay againway illtay eythay ereway onsumedcay.

38 IWAY avehay oundedway emthay atthay eythay ereway otnay ableway otay iseray: eythay areway allenfay underway myay eetfay.

39 Orfay outhay asthay irdedgay emay ithway engthstray untoway ethay attlebay: outhay asthay ubduedsay underway emay osethay atthay oseray upway againstway emay.

40 Outhay asthay alsoway ivengay emay ethay ecksnay ofway inemay enemiesway; atthay IWAY ightmay estroyday emthay atthay atehay emay.

41 Eythay iedcray, utbay [erethay asway] onenay otay avesay [emthay: evenway] untoway ethay ORDLAY, utbay ehay answeredway emthay otnay.

42 Enthay idday IWAY eatbay emthay allsmay asway ethay ustday eforebay ethay indway: IWAY idday astcay emthay outway asway ethay irtday inway ethay eetsstray.

43 Outhay asthay eliveredday emay omfray ethay ivingsstray ofway ethay eoplepay; [andway] outhay asthay ademay emay ethay eadhay ofway ethay eathenhay: away eoplepay [omwhay] IWAY avehay otnay ownknay allshay ervesay emay.

44 Asway oonsay asway eythay earhay ofway emay, eythay allshay obeyway emay: ethay angersstray allshay ubmitsay emselvesthay untoway emay.

45 Ethay angersstray allshay adefay awayway, andway ebay afraidway outway ofway eirthay oseclay acesplay.

46 Ethay ORDLAY ivethlay; andway essedblay [ebay] myay ockray; andway etlay ethay Odgay ofway myay alvationsay ebay exaltedway.

47 [Itway isway] Odgay atthay avengethway emay, andway ubduethsay ethay eoplepay underway emay.

48 Ehay eliverethday emay omfray inemay enemiesway: eayay, outhay iftestlay emay upway aboveway osethay atthay iseray upway againstway emay: outhay asthay eliveredday emay omfray ethay iolentvay anmay.

49 Ereforethay illway IWAY ivegay ansksthay untoway eethay, OWAY ORDLAY, amongway ethay eathenhay, andway ingsay aisespray untoway thyay amenay.

50 Eatgray eliveranceday ivethgay ehay otay ishay ingkay; andway ewethshay ercymay otay ishay anointedway, otay Avidday, andway otay ishay eedsay orfay evermoreway.

ALMPSAY 19
Otay ethay iefchay Usicianmay, AWAY Almpsay ofway Avidday.
1 Ethay eavenshay eclareday ethay oryglay ofway Odgay; andway ethay
irmamentfay ewethshay ishay andyworkhay.
2 Ayday untoway ayday utterethway eechspay, andway ightnay untoway
ightnay ewethshay owledgeknay.
3 [Erethay isway] onay eechspay ornay anguagelay, [erewhay] eirthay
oicevay isway otnay eardhay.
4 Eirthay inelay isway onegay outway oughthray allway ethay earthway,
andway eirthay ordsway otay ethay endway ofway ethay orldway. Inway
emthay athhay ehay etsay away abernacletay orfay ethay unsay,
5 Ichwhay [isway] asway away idegroombray omingcay outway ofway
ishay amberchay, [andway] ejoicethray asway away ongstray anmay otay
unray away aceray.
6 Ishay oinggay orthfay [isway] omfray ethay endway ofway ethay
eavenhay, andway ishay ircuitcay untoway ethay endsway ofway itway:
andway erethay isway othingnay idhay omfray ethay eathay ereofthay.
7 Ethay awlay ofway ethay ORDLAY [isway] erfectpay, onvertingcay
ethay oulsay: ethay estimonytay ofway ethay ORDLAY [isway] uresay,
akingmay iseway ethay implesay.
8 Ethay atutesstay ofway ethay ORDLAY [areway] ightray, ejoicingray
ethay earthay: ethay ommandmentcay ofway ethay ORDLAY [isway]
urepay, enlighteningway ethay eyesway.
9 Ethay earfay ofway ethay ORDLAY [isway] eanclay, enduringway orfay
everway: ethay udgmentsjay ofway ethay ORDLAY [areway] uetray
[andway] ighteousray altogetherway.
10 Oremay otay ebay esiredday [areway eythay] anthay oldgay, eayay,
anthay uchmay inefay oldgay: eetersway alsoway anthay oneyhay andway
ethay oneycombhay.
11 Oreovermay byay emthay isway thyay ervantsay arnedway: [andway]
inway eepingkay ofway emthay [erethay isway] eatgray ewardray.
12 Owhay ancay understandway [ishay] errorsway? eanseclay outhay
emay omfray ecretsay [aultsfay].
13 Eepkay ackbay thyay ervantsay alsoway omfray esumptuouspray
[inssay]; etlay emthay otnay avehay ominionday overway emay: enthay
allshay IWAY ebay uprightway, andway IWAY allshay ebay innocentway
omfray ethay eatgray ansgressiontray.
14 Etlay ethay ordsway ofway myay outhmay, andway ethay editationmay
ofway myay earthay, ebay acceptableway inway thyay ightsay, OWAY
ORDLAY, myay engthstray, andway myay edeemerray.

ALMPSAY 20
Otay ethay iefchay Usicianmay, AWAY Almpsay ofway Avidday.
1 Ethay ORDLAY earhay eethay inway ethay ayday ofway oubletray;
ethay amenay ofway ethay Odgay ofway Acobjay efendday eethay;
2 Endsay eethay elphay omfray ethay anctuarysay, andway engthenstray
eethay outway ofway Ionzay;
3 Ememberray allway thyay offeringsway, andway acceptway thyay
urntbay acrificesay; Elahsay.
4 Antgray eethay accordingway otay inethay ownway earthay, andway
ulfilfay allway thyay ounselcay.
5 Eway illway ejoiceray inway thyay alvationsay, andway inway ethay
amenay ofway ourway Odgay eway illway etsay upway [ourway]
annersbay: ethay ORDLAY ulfilfay allway thyay etitionspay.
6 Ownay owknay IWAY atthay ethay ORDLAY avethsay ishay
anointedway; ehay illway earhay imhay omfray ishay olyhay eavenhay
ithway ethay avingsay engthstray ofway ishay ightray andhay.
7 Omesay [usttray] inway ariotschay, andway omesay inway orseshay:
utbay eway illway ememberray ethay amenay ofway ethay ORDLAY
ourway Odgay.
8 Eythay areway oughtbray ownday andway allenfay: utbay eway areway
isenray, andway andstay uprightway.
9 Avesay, ORDLAY: etlay ethay ingkay earhay usway enwhay eway
allcay.

ALMPSAY 21
Otay ethay iefchay Usicianmay, AWAY Almpsay ofway Avidday.
1 Ethay ingkay allshay oyjay inway thyay engthstray, OWAY ORDLAY;
andway inway thyay alvationsay owhay eatlygray allshay ehay ejoiceray!
2 Outhay asthay ivengay imhay ishay earthay'say esireday, andway asthay
otnay ithholdenway ethay equestray ofway ishay ipslay. Elahsay.
3 Orfay outhay eventestpray imhay ithway ethay essingsblay ofway
oodnessgay: outhay ettestsay away owncray ofway urepay oldgay onway
ishay eadhay.
4 Ehay askedway ifelay ofway eethay, [andway] outhay avestgay [itway]
imhay, [evenway] engthlay ofway aysday orfay everway andway everway.
5 Ishay oryglay [isway] eatgray inway thyay alvationsay: onourhay
andway ajestymay asthay outhay aidlay uponway imhay.

6 Orfay outhay asthay ademay imhay ostmay essedblay orfay everway: outhay asthay ademay imhay exceedingway adglay ithway thyay ountenancecay.

7 Orfay ethay ingkay ustethtray inway ethay ORDLAY, andway oughthray ethay ercymay ofway ethay ostmay Ighhay ehay allshay otnay ebay ovedmay.

8 Inethay andhay allshay indfay outway allway inethay enemiesway: thyay ightray andhay allshay indfay outway osethay atthay atehay eethay.

9 Outhay altshay akemay emthay asway away ieryfay ovenway inway ethay imetay ofway inethay angerway: ethay ORDLAY allshay allowsway emthay upway inway ishay athwray, andway ethay irefay allshay evourday emthay.

10 Eirthay uitfray altshay outhay estroyday omfray ethay earthway, andway eirthay eedsay omfray amongway ethay ildrenchay ofway enmay.

11 Orfay eythay intendedway evilway againstway eethay: eythay imaginedway away ischievousmay eviceday, [ichwhay] eythay areway otnay ableway [otay erformpay].

12 Ereforethay altshay outhay akemay emthay urntay eirthay ackbay, [enwhay] outhay altshay akemay eadyray [inethay arrowsway] uponway thyay ingsstray againstway ethay acefay ofway emthay.

13 Ebay outhay exaltedway, ORDLAY, inway inethay ownway engthstray: [osay] illway eway ingsay andway aisepray thyay owerpay.

ALMPSAY 22

Otay ethay iefchay Usicianmay uponway Aijelethway Aharshay, AWAY Almpsay ofway Avidday.

1 Myay Odgay, myay Odgay, whyay asthay outhay orsakenfay emay? [whyay artway outhay osay] arfay omfray elpinghay emay, [andway omfray] ethay ordsway ofway myay oaringray?

2 OWAY myay Odgay, IWAY cryay inway ethay aytimeday, utbay outhay earesthay otnay; andway inway ethay ightnay easonsay, andway amway otnay ilentsay.

3 Utbay outhay [artway] olyhay, [OWAY outhay] atthay inhabitestway ethay aisespray ofway Israelway.

4 Ourway athersfay ustedtray inway eethay: eythay ustedtray, andway outhay idstday eliverday emthay.

5 Eythay iedcray untoway eethay, andway ereway eliveredday: eythay ustedtray inway eethay, andway ereway otnay onfoundedcay.

6 Utbay IWAY [amway] away ormway, andway onay anmay; away eproachray ofway enmay, andway espisedday ofway ethay eoplepay.

7 Allway eythay atthay eesay emay aughlay emay otay ornscay: eythay
ootshay outway ethay iplay, eythay akeshay ethay eadhay, [ayingsay],
8 Ehay ustedtray onway ethay ORDLAY [atthay] ehay ouldway eliverday
imhay: etlay imhay eliverday imhay, eeingsay ehay elightedday inway
imhay.
9 Utbay outhay [artway] ehay atthay ooktay emay outway ofway ethay
ombway: outhay idstday akemay emay opehay [enwhay IWAY asway]
uponway myay othermay'say eastsbray.
10 IWAY asway astcay uponway eethay omfray ethay ombway: outhay
[artway] myay Odgay omfray myay othermay'say ellybay.
11 Ebay otnay arfay omfray emay; orfay oubletray [isway] earnay; orfay
[erethay isway] onenay otay elphay.
12 Anymay ullsbay avehay ompassedcay emay: ongstray [ullsbay] ofway
Ashanbay avehay esetbay emay oundray.
13 Eythay apedgay uponway emay [ithway] eirthay outhsmay, [asway]
away aveningray andway away oaringray ionlay.
14 IWAY amway ouredpay outway ikelay aterway, andway allway myay
onesbay areway outway ofway ointjay: myay earthay isway ikelay axway;
itway isway eltedmay inway ethay idstmay ofway myay owelsbay.
15 Myay engthstray isway ieddray upway ikelay away otsherdpay; andway
myay onguetay eavethclay otay myay awsjay; andway outhay asthay
oughtbray emay intoway ethay ustday ofway eathday.
16 Orfay ogsday avehay ompassedcay emay: ethay assemblyway ofway
ethay ickedway avehay inclosedway emay: eythay iercedpay myay
andshay andway myay eetfay.
17 IWAY aymay elltay allway myay onesbay: eythay ooklay [andway]
arestay uponway emay.
18 Eythay artpay myay armentsgay amongway emthay, andway astcay
otslay uponway myay esturevay.
19 Utbay ebay otnay outhay arfay omfray emay, OWAY ORDLAY:
OWAY myay engthstray, astehay eethay otay elphay emay.
20 Eliverday myay oulsay omfray ethay ordsway; myay arlingday omfray
ethay owerpay ofway ethay ogday.
21 Avesay emay omfray ethay ionlay'say outhmay: orfay outhay asthay
eardhay emay omfray ethay ornshay ofway ethay unicornsway.
22 IWAY illway eclareday thyay amenay untoway myay ethrenbray:
inway ethay idstmay ofway ethay ongregationcay illway IWAY aisepray
eethay.

23 Eyay atthay earfay ethay ORDLAY, aisepray imhay; allway eyay ethay eedsay ofway Acobjay, orifyglay imhay; andway earfay imhay, allway eyay ethay eedsay ofway Israelway.

24 Orfay ehay athhay otnay espisedday ornay abhorredway ethay afflictionway ofway ethay afflictedway; eithernay athhay ehay idhay ishay acefay omfray imhay; utbay enwhay ehay iedcray untoway imhay, ehay eardhay.

25 Myay aisepray [allshay ebay] ofway eethay inway ethay eatgray ongregationcay: IWAY illway aypay myay owsvay eforebay emthay atthay earfay imhay.

26 Ethay eekmay allshay eatway andway ebay atisfiedsay: eythay allshay aisepray ethay ORDLAY atthay eeksay imhay: ouryay earthay allshay ivelay orfay everway.

27 Allway ethay endsway ofway ethay orldway allshay ememberray andway urntay untoway ethay ORDLAY: andway allway ethay indredskay ofway ethay ationsnay allshay orshipway eforebay eethay.

28 Orfay ethay ingdomkay [isway] ethay ORDLAY'SAY: andway ehay [isway] ethay overnorgay amongway ethay ationsnay.

29 Allway [eythay atthay ebay] atfay uponway earthway allshay eatway andway orshipway: allway eythay atthay ogay ownday otay ethay ustday allshay owbay eforebay imhay: andway onenay ancay eepkay aliveway ishay ownway oulsay.

30 AWAY eedsay allshay ervesay imhay; itway allshay ebay accountedway otay ethay Ordlay orfay away enerationgay.

31 Eythay allshay omecay, andway allshay eclareday ishay ighteousnessray untoway away eoplepay atthay allshay ebay ornbay, atthay ehay athhay oneday [isthay].

ALMPSAY 23
AWAY Almpsay ofway Avidday.

1 Ethay ORDLAY [isway] myay epherdshay; IWAY allshay otnay antway.

2 Ehay akethmay emay otay ielay ownday inway eengray asturespay: ehay eadethlay emay esidebay ethay illstay atersway.

3 Ehay estorethray myay oulsay: ehay eadethlay emay inway ethay athspay ofway ighteousnessray orfay ishay amenay'say akesay.

4 Eayay, oughthay IWAY alkway oughthray ethay alleyvay ofway ethay adowshay ofway eathday, IWAY illway earfay onay evilway: orfay outhay [artway] ithway emay; thyay odray andway thyay affstay eythay omfortcay emay.

5 Outhay eparestpray away abletay eforebay emay inway ethay esencepray ofway inemay enemiesway: outhay anointestway myay eadhay ithway oilway; myay upcay unnethray overway.

6 Urelysay oodnessgay andway ercymay allshay ollowfay emay allway ethay aysday ofway myay ifelay: andway IWAY illway elldway inway ethay ousehay ofway ethay ORDLAY orfay everway.

ALMPSAY 24
AWAY Almpsay ofway Avidday.

1 Ethay earthway [isway] ethay ORDLAY'SAY, andway ethay ulnessfay ereofthay; ethay orldway, andway eythay atthay elldway ereinthay.

2 Orfay ehay athhay oundedfay itway uponway ethay eassay, andway establishedway itway uponway ethay oodsflay.

3 Owhay allshay ascendway intoway ethay illhay ofway ethay ORDLAY? orway owhay allshay andstay inway ishay olyhay aceplay?

4 Ehay atthay athhay eanclay andshay, andway away urepay earthay; owhay athhay otnay iftedlay upway ishay oulsay untoway anityvay, ornay ornsway eceitfullyday.

5 Ehay allshay eceiveray ethay essingblay omfray ethay ORDLAY, andway ighteousnessray omfray ethay Odgay ofway ishay alvationsay.

6 Isthay [isway] ethay enerationgay ofway emthay atthay eeksay imhay, atthay eeksay thyay acefay, OWAY Acobjay. Elahsay.

7 Iftlay upway ouryay eadshay, OWAY eyay atesgay; andway ebay eyay iftlay upway, eyay everlastingway oorsday; andway ethay Ingkay ofway oryglay allshay omecay inway.

8 Owhay [isway] isthay Ingkay ofway oryglay? Ethay ORDLAY ongstray andway ightymay, ethay ORDLAY ightymay inway attlebay.

9 Iftlay upway ouryay eadshay, OWAY eyay atesgay; evenway iftlay [emthay] upway, eyay everlastingway oorsday; andway ethay Ingkay ofway oryglay allshay omecay inway.

10 Owhay isway isthay Ingkay ofway oryglay? Ethay ORDLAY ofway ostshay, ehay [isway] ethay Ingkay ofway oryglay. Elahsay.

ALMPSAY 25
[AWAY Almpsay] ofway Avidday.

1 Untoway eethay, OWAY ORDLAY, oday IWAY iftlay upway myay oulsay.

2 OWAY myay Odgay, IWAY usttray inway eethay: etlay emay otnay ebay ashamedway, etlay otnay inemay enemiesway iumphtray overway emay.

3 Eayay, etlay onenay atthay aitway onway eethay ebay ashamedway: etlay emthay ebay ashamedway ichwhay ansgresstray ithoutway ausecay.

4 Ewshay emay thyay aysway, OWAY ORDLAY; eachtay emay thyay athspay.

5 Eadlay emay inway thyay uthtray, andway eachtay emay: orfay outhay [artway] ethay Odgay ofway myay alvationsay; onway eethay oday IWAY aitway allway ethay ayday.

6 Ememberray, OWAY ORDLAY, thyay endertay erciesmay andway thyay ovingkindnesseslay; orfay eythay [avehay eenbay] everway ofway oldway.

7 Ememberray otnay ethay inssay ofway myay outhyay, ornay myay ansgressionstray: accordingway otay thyay ercymay ememberray outhay emay orfay thyay oodnessgay' akesay, OWAY ORDLAY.

8 Oodgay andway uprightway [isway] ethay ORDLAY: ereforethay illway ehay eachtay innerssay inway ethay ayway.

9 Ethay eekmay illway ehay uidegay inway udgmentjay: andway ethay eekmay illway ehay eachtay ishay ayway.

10 Allway ethay athspay ofway ethay ORDLAY [areway] ercymay andway uthtray untoway uchsay asway eepkay ishay ovenantcay andway ishay estimoniestay.

11 Orfay thyay amenay'say akesay, OWAY ORDLAY, ardonpay inemay iniquityway; orfay itway [isway] eatgray.

12 Atwhay anmay [isway] ehay atthay earethfay ethay ORDLAY? imhay allshay ehay eachtay inway ethay ayway [atthay] ehay allshay oosechay.

13 Ishay oulsay allshay elldway atway easeway; andway ishay eedsay allshay inheritway ethay earthway.

14 Ethay ecretsay ofway ethay ORDLAY [isway] ithway emthay atthay earfay imhay; andway ehay illway ewshay emthay ishay ovenantcay.

15 Inemay eyesway [areway] everway owardtay ethay ORDLAY; orfay ehay allshay uckplay myay eetfay outway ofway ethay etnay.

16 Urntay eethay untoway emay, andway avehay ercymay uponway emay; orfay IWAY [amway] esolateday andway afflictedway.

17 Ethay oublestray ofway myay earthay areway enlargedway: [OWAY] ingbray outhay emay outway ofway myay istressesday.

18 Ooklay uponway inemay afflictionway andway myay ainpay; andway orgivefay allway myay inssay.

19 Onsidercay inemay enemiesway; orfay eythay areway anymay; andway eythay atehay emay ithway uelcray atredhay.

20 OWAY eepkay myay oulsay, andway eliverday emay: etlay emay otnay ebay ashamedway; orfay IWAY utpay myay usttray inway eethay.

21 Etlay integrityway andway uprightnessway eservepray emay; orfay IWAY aitway onway eethay.
22 Edeemray Israelway, OWAY Odgay, outway ofway allway ishay oublestray.

ALMPSAY 26
[AWAY Almpsay] ofway Avidday.

1 Udgejay emay, OWAY ORDLAY; orfay IWAY avehay alkedway inway inemay integrityway: IWAY avehay ustedtray alsoway inway ethay ORDLAY; [ereforethay] IWAY allshay otnay ideslay.
2 Examineway emay, OWAY ORDLAY, andway ovepray emay; tryay myay einsray andway myay earthay.
3 Orfay thyay ovingkindnesslay [isway] eforebay inemay eyesway: andway IWAY avehay alkedway inway thyay uthtray.
4 IWAY avehay otnay atsay ithway ainvay ersonspay, eithernay illway IWAY ogay inway ithway issemblersday.
5 IWAY avehay atedhay ethay ongregationcay ofway evilway oersday; andway illway otnay itsay ithway ethay ickedway.
6 IWAY illway ashway inemay andshay inway innocencyway: osay illway IWAY ompasscay inethay altarway, OWAY ORDLAY:
7 Atthay IWAY aymay ublishpay ithway ethay oicevay ofway anksgivingthay, andway elltay ofway allway thyay ondrousway orksway.
8 ORDLAY, IWAY avehay ovedlay ethay abitationhay ofway thyay ousehay, andway ethay aceplay erewhay inethay onourhay ellethdway.
9 Athergay otnay myay oulsay ithway innerssay, ornay myay ifelay ithway oodyblay enmay:
10 Inway osewhay andshay [isway] ischiefmay, andway eirthay ightray andhay isway ullfay ofway ibesbray.
11 Utbay asway orfay emay, IWAY illway alkway inway inemay integrityway: edeemray emay, andway ebay ercifulmay untoway emay.
12 Myay ootfay andethstay inway anway evenway aceplay: inway ethay ongregationscay illway IWAY essblay ethay ORDLAY.

ALMPSAY 27
[AWAY Almpsay] ofway Avidday.
1 Ethay ORDLAY [isway] myay ightlay andway myay alvationsay; omwhay allshay IWAY earfay? ethay ORDLAY [isway] ethay engthstray ofway myay ifelay; ofway omwhay allshay IWAY ebay afraidway?

2 Enwhay ethay ickedway, [evenway] inemay enemiesway andway myay oesfay, amecay uponway emay otay eatway upway myay eshflay, eythay umbledstay andway ellfay.

3 Oughthay anway osthay ouldshay encampway againstway emay, myay earthay allshay otnay earfay: oughthay arway ouldshay iseray againstway emay, inway isthay [illway] IWAY [ebay] onfidentcay.

4 Oneway [ingthay] avehay IWAY esiredday ofway ethay ORDLAY, atthay illway IWAY eeksay afterway; atthay IWAY aymay elldway inway ethay ousehay ofway ethay ORDLAY allway ethay aysday ofway myay ifelay, otay eholdbay ethay eautybay ofway ethay ORDLAY, andway otay enquireway inway ishay empletay.

5 Orfay inway ethay imetay ofway oubletray ehay allshay idehay emay inway ishay avilionpay: inway ethay ecretsay ofway ishay abernacletay allshay ehay idehay emay; ehay allshay etsay emay upway uponway away ockray.

6 Andway ownay allshay inemay eadhay ebay iftedlay upway aboveway inemay enemiesway oundray aboutway emay: ereforethay illway IWAY offerway inway ishay abernacletay acrificessay ofway oyjay; IWAY illway ingsay, eayay, IWAY illway ingsay aisespray untoway ethay ORDLAY.

7 Earhay, OWAY ORDLAY, [enwhay] IWAY cryay ithway myay oicevay: avehay ercymay alsoway uponway emay, andway answerway emay.

8 [Enwhay outhay aidstsay], Eeksay eyay myay acefay; myay earthay aidsay untoway eethay, Thyay acefay, ORDLAY, illway IWAY eeksay.

9 Idehay otnay thyay acefay [arfay] omfray emay; utpay otnay thyay ervantsay awayway inway angerway: outhay asthay eenbay myay elphay; eavelay emay otnay, eithernay orsakefay emay, OWAY Odgay ofway myay alvationsay.

10 Enwhay myay atherfay andway myay othermay orsakefay emay, enthay ethay ORDLAY illway aketay emay upway.

11 Eachtay emay thyay ayway, OWAY ORDLAY, andway eadlay emay inway away ainplay athpay, ecausebay ofway inemay enemiesway.

12 Eliverday emay otnay overway untoway ethay illway ofway inemay enemiesway: orfay alsefay itnessesway areway isenray upway againstway emay, andway uchsay asway eathebray outway ueltycray.

13 [IWAY adhay aintedfay], unlessway IWAY adhay elievedbay otay eesay ethay oodnessgay ofway ethay ORDLAY inway ethay andlay ofway ethay ivinglay.

14 Aitway onway ethay ORDLAY: ebay ofway oodgay ouragecay, andway ehay allshay engthenstray inethay earthay: aitway, IWAY aysay, onway ethay ORDLAY.

ALMPSAY 28
[AWAY Almpsay] ofway Avidday.

1 Untoway eethay illway IWAY cryay, OWAY ORDLAY myay ockray; ebay otnay ilentsay otay emay: estlay, [ifway] outhay ebay ilentsay otay emay, IWAY ecomebay ikelay emthay atthay ogay ownday intoway ethay itpay.

2 Earhay ethay oicevay ofway myay upplicationssay, enwhay IWAY cryay untoway eethay, enwhay IWAY iftlay upway myay andshay owardtay thyay olyhay oracleway.

3 Awdray emay otnay awayway ithway ethay ickedway, andway ithway ethay orkersway ofway iniquityway, ichwhay eakspay eacepay otay eirthay eighboursnay, utbay ischiefmay [isway] inway eirthay eartshay.

4 Ivegay emthay accordingway otay eirthay eedsday, andway accordingway otay ethay ickednessway ofway eirthay endeavoursway: ivegay emthay afterway ethay orkway ofway eirthay andshay; enderray otay emthay eirthay esertday.

5 Ecausebay eythay egardray otnay ethay orksway ofway ethay ORDLAY, ornay ethay operationway ofway ishay andshay, ehay allshay estroyday emthay, andway otnay uildbay emthay upway.

6 Essedblay [ebay] ethay ORDLAY, ecausebay ehay athhay eardhay ethay oicevay ofway myay upplicationssay.

7 Ethay ORDLAY [isway] myay engthstray andway myay ieldshay; myay earthay ustedtray inway imhay, andway IWAY amway elpedhay: ereforethay myay earthay eatlygray ejoicethray; andway ithway myay ongsay illway IWAY aisepray imhay.

8 Ethay ORDLAY [isway] eirthay engthstray, andway ehay [isway] ethay avingsay engthstray ofway ishay anointedway.

9 Avesay thyay eoplepay, andway essblay inethay inheritanceway: eedfay emthay alsoway, andway iftlay emthay upway orfay everway.

ALMPSAY 29
AWAY Almpsay ofway Avidday.
1 Ivegay untoway ethay ORDLAY, OWAY eyay ightymay, ivegay untoway ethay ORDLAY oryglay andway engthstray.

2 Ivegay untoway ethay ORDLAY ethay oryglay ueday untoway ishay amenay; orshipway ethay ORDLAY inway ethay eautybay ofway olinesshay.

3 Ethay oicevay ofway ethay ORDLAY [isway] uponway ethay atersway: ethay Odgay ofway oryglay undereththay: ethay ORDLAY [isway] uponway anymay atersway.

4 Ethay oicevay ofway ethay ORDLAY [isway] owerfulpay; ethay oicevay ofway ethay ORDLAY [isway] ullfay ofway ajestymay.

5 Ethay oicevay ofway ethay ORDLAY eakethbray ethay edarscay; eayay, ethay ORDLAY eakethbray ethay edarscay ofway Ebanonlay.

6 Ehay akethmay emthay alsoway otay ipskay ikelay away alfcay; Ebanonlay andway Irionsay ikelay away oungyay unicornway.

7 Ethay oicevay ofway ethay ORDLAY ividethday ethay amesflay ofway irefay.

8 Ethay oicevay ofway ethay ORDLAY akethshay ethay ildernessway; ethay ORDLAY akethshay ethay ildernessway ofway Adeshkay.

9 Ethay oicevay ofway ethay ORDLAY akethmay ethay indshay otay alvecay, andway iscoverethday ethay orestsfay: andway inway ishay empletay othday everyway oneway eakspay ofway [ishay] oryglay.

10 Ethay ORDLAY ittethsay uponway ethay oodflay; eayay, ethay ORDLAY ittethsay Ingkay orfay everway.

11 Ethay ORDLAY illway ivegay engthstray untoway ishay eoplepay; ethay ORDLAY illway essblay ishay eoplepay ithway eacepay.

ALMPSAY 30
AWAY Almpsay [andway] Ongsay [atway] ethay edicationday ofway ethay ousehay ofway Avidday.

1 IWAY illway extolway eethay, OWAY ORDLAY; orfay outhay asthay iftedlay emay upway, andway asthay otnay ademay myay oesfay otay ejoiceray overway emay.

2 OWAY ORDLAY myay Odgay, IWAY iedcray untoway eethay, andway outhay asthay ealedhay emay.

3 OWAY ORDLAY, outhay asthay oughtbray upway myay oulsay omfray ethay avegray: outhay asthay eptkay emay aliveway, atthay IWAY ouldshay otnay ogay ownday otay ethay itpay.

4 Ingsay untoway ethay ORDLAY, OWAY eyay aintssay ofway ishay, andway ivegay anksthay atway ethay emembranceray ofway ishay olinesshay.

5 Orfay ishay angerway [endurethway utbay] away omentmay; inway
ishay avourfay [isway] ifelay: eepingway aymay endureway orfay away
ightnay, utbay oyjay [omethcay] inway ethay orningmay.
6 Andway inway myay osperitypray IWAY aidsay, IWAY allshay evernay
ebay ovedmay.
7 ORDLAY, byay thyay avourfay outhay asthay ademay myay
ountainmay otay andstay ongstray: outhay idstday idehay thyay acefay,
[andway] IWAY asway oubledtray.
8 IWAY iedcray otay eethay, OWAY ORDLAY; andway untoway ethay
ORDLAY IWAY ademay upplicationsay.
9 Atwhay ofitpray [isway erethay] inway myay oodblay, enwhay IWAY
ogay ownday otay ethay itpay? Allshay ethay ustday aisepray eethay?
allshay itway eclareday thyay uthtray?
10 Earhay, OWAY ORDLAY, andway avehay ercymay uponway emay:
ORDLAY, ebay outhay myay elperhay.
11 Outhay asthay urnedtay orfay emay myay ourningmay intoway
ancingday: outhay asthay utpay offway myay ackclothsay, andway
irdedgay emay ithway adnessglay;
12 Otay ethay endway atthay [myay] oryglay aymay ingsay aisepray otay
eethay, andway otnay ebay ilentsay. OWAY ORDLAY myay Odgay,
IWAY illway ivegay anksthay untoway eethay orfay everway.

ALMPSAY 31
Otay ethay iefchay Usicianmay, AWAY Almpsay ofway Avidday.
1 Inway eethay, OWAY ORDLAY, oday IWAY utpay myay usttray;
etlay emay evernay ebay ashamedway: eliverday emay inway thyay
ighteousnessray.
2 Owbay ownday inethay earway otay emay; eliverday emay eedilyspay:
ebay outhay myay ongstray ockray, orfay anway ousehay ofway efenceday
otay avesay emay.
3 Orfay outhay [artway] myay ockray andway myay ortressfay;
ereforethay orfay thyay amenay'say akesay eadlay emay, andway uidegay
emay.
4 Ullpay emay outway ofway ethay etnay atthay eythay avehay aidlay
ivilypray orfay emay: orfay outhay [artway] myay engthstray.
5 Intoway inethay andhay IWAY ommitcay myay iritspay: outhay asthay
edeemedray emay, OWAY ORDLAY Odgay ofway uthtray.
6 IWAY avehay atedhay emthay atthay egardray inglyay anitiesvay: utbay
IWAY usttray inway ethay ORDLAY.

7 IWAY illway ebay adglay andway ejoiceray inway thyay ercymay: orfay outhay asthay onsideredcay myay oubletray; outhay asthay ownknay myay oulsay inway adversitiesway;

8 Andway asthay otnay utshay emay upway intoway ethay andhay ofway ethay enemyway: outhay asthay etsay myay eetfay inway away argelay oomray.

9 Avehay ercymay uponway emay, OWAY ORDLAY, orfay IWAY amway inway oubletray: inemay eyeway isway onsumedcay ithway iefgray, [eayay], myay oulsay andway myay ellybay.

10 Orfay myay ifelay isway entspay ithway iefgray, andway myay earsyay ithway ighingsay: myay engthstray ailethfay ecausebay ofway inemay iniquityway, andway myay onesbay areway onsumedcay.

11 IWAY asway away eproachray amongway allway inemay enemiesway, utbay especiallyway amongway myay eighboursnay, andway away earfay otay inemay acquaintanceway: eythay atthay idday eesay emay ithoutway edflay omfray emay.

12 IWAY amway orgottenfay asway away eadday anmay outway ofway indmay: IWAY amway ikelay away okenbray esselvay.

13 Orfay IWAY avehay eardhay ethay anderslay ofway anymay: earfay [asway] onway everyway idesay: ilewhay eythay ooktay ounselcay ogethertay againstway emay, eythay evisedday otay aketay awayway myay ifelay.

14 Utbay IWAY ustedtray inway eethay, OWAY ORDLAY: IWAY aidsay, Outhay [artway] myay Odgay.

15 Myay imestay [areway] inway thyay andhay: eliverday emay omfray ethay andhay ofway inemay enemiesway, andway omfray emthay atthay ersecutepay emay.

16 Akemay thyay acefay otay ineshay uponway thyay ervantsay: avesay emay orfay thyay erciesmay' akesay.

17 Etlay emay otnay ebay ashamedway, OWAY ORDLAY; orfay IWAY avehay alledcay uponway eethay: etlay ethay ickedway ebay ashamedway, [andway] etlay emthay ebay ilentsay inway ethay avegray.

18 Etlay ethay inglyay ipslay ebay utpay otay ilencesay; ichwhay eakspay ievousgray ingsthay oudlypray andway ontemptuouslycay againstway ethay ighteousray.

19 [Ohway] owhay eatgray [isway] thyay oodnessgay, ichwhay outhay asthay aidlay upway orfay emthay atthay earfay eethay; [ichwhay] outhay asthay oughtwray orfay emthay atthay usttray inway eethay eforebay ethay onssay ofway enmay!

20 Outhay altshay idehay emthay inway ethay ecretsay ofway thyay esencepray omfray ethay idepray ofway anmay: outhay altshay eepkay emthay ecretlysay inway away avilionpay omfray ethay ifestray ofway onguestay.

21 Essedblay [ebay] ethay ORDLAY: orfay ehay athhay ewedshay emay ishay arvellousmay indnesskay inway away ongstray itycay.

22 Orfay IWAY aidsay inway myay astehay, IWAY amway utcay offway omfray eforebay inethay eyesway: everthelessnay outhay eardesthay ethay oicevay ofway myay upplicationssay enwhay IWAY iedcray untoway eethay.

23 OWAY ovelay ethay ORDLAY, allway eyay ishay aintssay: [orfay] ethay ORDLAY eservethpray ethay aithfulfay, andway entifullyplay ewardethray ethay oudpray oerday.

24 Ebay ofway oodgay ouragecay, andway ehay allshay engthenstray ouryay earthay, allway eyay atthay opehay inway ethay ORDLAY.

ALMPSAY 32
[AWAY Almpsay] ofway Avidday, Aschilmay.

1 Essedblay [isway ehay osewhay] ansgressiontray [isway] orgivenfay, [osewhay] insay [isway] overedcay.

2 Essedblay [isway] ethay anmay untoway omwhay ethay ORDLAY imputethway otnay iniquityway, andway inway osewhay iritspay [erethay isway] onay uilegay.

3 Enwhay IWAY eptkay ilencesay, myay onesbay axedway oldway oughthray myay oaringray allway ethay ayday onglay.

4 Orfay ayday andway ightnay thyay andhay asway eavyhay uponway emay: myay oisturemay isway urnedtay intoway ethay oughtdray ofway ummersay. Elahsay.

5 IWAY acknowledgedway myay insay untoway eethay, andway inemay iniquityway avehay IWAY otnay idhay. IWAY aidsay, IWAY illway onfesscay myay ansgressionstray untoway ethay ORDLAY; andway outhay orgavestfay ethay iniquityway ofway myay insay. Elahsay.

6 Orfay isthay allshay everyway oneway atthay isway odlygay aypray untoway eethay inway away imetay enwhay outhay ayestmay ebay oundfay: urelysay inway ethay oodsflay ofway eatgray atersway eythay allshay otnay omecay ighnay untoway imhay.

7 Outhay [artway] myay idinghay aceplay; outhay altshay eservepray emay omfray oubletray; outhay altshay ompasscay emay aboutway ithway ongssay ofway eliveranceday. Elahsay.

8 IWAY illway instructway eethay andway eachtay eethay inway ethay
ayway ichwhay outhay altshay ogay: IWAY illway uidegay eethay ithway
inemay eyeway.

9 Ebay eyay otnay asway ethay orsehay, [orway] asway ethay ulemay,
[ichwhay] avehay onay understandingway: osewhay outhmay ustmay
ebay eldhay inway ithway itbay andway idlebray, estlay eythay omecay
earnay untoway eethay.

10 Anymay orrowssay [allshay ebay] otay ethay ickedway: utbay ehay
atthay ustethtray inway ethay ORDLAY, ercymay allshay ompasscay
imhay aboutway.

11 Ebay adglay inway ethay ORDLAY, andway ejoiceray, eyay
ighteousray: andway outshay orfay oyjay, allway [eyay atthay areway]
uprightway inway earthay.

ALMPSAY 33

1 Ejoiceray inway ethay ORDLAY, OWAY eyay ighteousray: [orfay]
aisepray isway omelycay orfay ethay uprightway.

2 Aisepray ethay ORDLAY ithway arphay: ingsay untoway imhay ithway
ethay alterypsay [andway] anway instrumentway ofway entay ingsstray.

3 Ingsay untoway imhay away ewnay ongsay; ayplay ilfullyskay ithway
away oudlay oisenay.

4 Orfay ethay ordway ofway ethay ORDLAY [isway] ightray; andway
allway ishay orksway [areway oneday] inway uthtray.

5 Ehay ovethlay ighteousnessray andway udgmentjay: ethay earthway
isway ullfay ofway ethay oodnessgay ofway ethay ORDLAY.

6 Byay ethay ordway ofway ethay ORDLAY ereway ethay eavenshay
ademay; andway allway ethay osthay ofway emthay byay ethay eathbray
ofway ishay outhmay.

7 Ehay atherethgay ethay atersway ofway ethay easay ogethertay asway
anway eaphay: ehay ayethlay upway ethay epthday inway orehousesstay.

8 Etlay allway ethay earthway earfay ethay ORDLAY: etlay allway ethay
inhabitantsway ofway ethay orldway andstay inway aweway ofway imhay.

9 Orfay ehay akespay, andway itway asway [oneday]; ehay
ommandedcay, andway itway oodstay astfay.

10 Ethay ORDLAY ingethbray ethay ounselcay ofway ethay eathenhay
otay oughtnay: ehay akethmay ethay evicesday ofway ethay eoplepay
ofway onenay effectway.

11 Ethay ounselcay ofway ethay ORDLAY andethstay orfay everway,
ethay oughtsthay ofway ishay earthay otay allway enerationsgay.

12 Essedblay [isway] ethay ationnay osewhay Odgay [isway] ethay ORDLAY; [andway] ethay eoplepay [omwhay] ehay athhay osenchay orfay ishay ownway inheritanceway.

13 Ethay ORDLAY ookethlay omfray eavenhay; ehay eholdethbay allway ethay onssay ofway enmay.

14 Omfray ethay aceplay ofway ishay abitationhay ehay ookethlay uponway allway ethay inhabitantsway ofway ethay earthway.

15 Ehay ashionethfay eirthay eartshay alikeway; ehay onsiderethcay allway eirthay orksway.

16 Erethay isway onay ingkay avedsay byay ethay ultitudemay ofway anway osthay: away ightymay anmay isway otnay eliveredday byay uchmay engthstray.

17 Anway orsehay [isway] away ainvay ingthay orfay afetysay: eithernay allshay ehay eliverday [anyway] byay ishay eatgray engthstray.

18 Eholdbay, ethay eyeway ofway ethay ORDLAY [isway] uponway emthay atthay earfay imhay, uponway emthay atthay opehay inway ishay ercymay;

19 Otay eliverday eirthay oulsay omfray eathday, andway otay eepkay emthay aliveway inway aminefay.

20 Ourway oulsay aitethway orfay ethay ORDLAY: ehay [isway] ourway elphay andway ourway ieldshay.

21 Orfay ourway earthay allshay ejoiceray inway imhay, ecausebay eway avehay ustedtray inway ishay olyhay amenay.

22 Etlay thyay ercymay, OWAY ORDLAY, ebay uponway usway, accordingway asway eway opehay inway eethay.

ALMPSAY 34

[AWAY Almpsay] ofway Avidday, enwhay ehay angedchay ishay ehaviourbay eforebay Abimelechway; owhay ovedray imhay awayway, andway ehay epartedday.

1 IWAY illway essblay ethay ORDLAY atway allway imestay: ishay aisepray [allshay] ontinuallycay [ebay] inway myay outhmay.

2 Myay oulsay allshay akemay erhay oastbay inway ethay ORDLAY: ethay umblehay allshay earhay [ereofthay], andway ebay adglay.

3 OWAY agnifymay ethay ORDLAY ithway emay, andway etlay usway exaltway ishay amenay ogethertay.

4 IWAY oughtsay ethay ORDLAY, andway ehay eardhay emay, andway eliveredday emay omfray allway myay earsfay.

5 Eythay ookedlay untoway imhay, andway ereway ightenedlay: andway eirthay acesfay ereway otnay ashamedway.

6 Isthay oorpay anmay iedcray, andway ethay ORDLAY eardhay [imhay], andway avedsay imhay outway ofway allway ishay oublestray.

7 Ethay angelway ofway ethay ORDLAY encampethway oundray aboutway emthay atthay earfay imhay, andway eliverethday emthay.

8 OWAY astetay andway eesay atthay ethay ORDLAY [isway] oodgay: essedblay [isway] ethay anmay [atthay] ustethtray inway imhay.

9 OWAY earfay ethay ORDLAY, eyay ishay aintssay: orfay [erethay isway] onay antway otay emthay atthay earfay imhay.

10 Ethay oungyay ionslay oday acklay, andway uffersay ungerhay: utbay eythay atthay eeksay ethay ORDLAY allshay otnay antway anyway oodgay [ingthay].

11 Omecay, eyay ildrenchay, earkenhay untoway emay: IWAY illway eachtay ouyay ethay earfay ofway ethay ORDLAY.

12 Atwhay anmay [isway ehay atthay] esirethday ifelay, [andway] ovethlay [anymay] aysday, atthay ehay aymay eesay oodgay?

13 Eepkay thyay onguetay omfray evilway, andway thyay ipslay omfray eakingspay uilegay.

14 Epartday omfray evilway, andway oday oodgay; eeksay eacepay, andway ursuepay itway.

15 Ethay eyesway ofway ethay ORDLAY [areway] uponway ethay ighteousray, andway ishay earsway [areway openway] untoway eirthay cryay.

16 Ethay acefay ofway ethay ORDLAY [isway] againstway emthay atthay oday evilway, otay utcay offway ethay emembranceray ofway emthay omfray ethay earthway.

17 [Ethay ighteousray] cryay, andway ethay ORDLAY earethhay, andway eliverethday emthay outway ofway allway eirthay oublestray.

18 Ethay ORDLAY [isway] ighnay untoway emthay atthay areway ofway away okenbray earthay; andway avethsay uchsay asway ebay ofway away ontritecay iritspay.

19 Anymay [areway] ethay afflictionsway ofway ethay ighteousray: utbay ethay ORDLAY eliverethday imhay outway ofway emthay allway.

20 Ehay eepethkay allway ishay onesbay: otnay oneway ofway emthay isway okenbray.

21 Evilway allshay ayslay ethay ickedway: andway eythay atthay atehay ethay ighteousray allshay ebay esolateday.

22 Ethay ORDLAY edeemethray ethay oulsay ofway ishay ervantssay: andway onenay ofway emthay atthay usttray inway imhay allshay ebay esolateday.

ALMPSAY 35
[AWAY Almpsay] ofway Avidday.
1 Eadplay [myay ausecay], OWAY ORDLAY, ithway emthay atthay ivestray ithway emay: ightfay againstway emthay atthay ightfay againstway emay.
2 Aketay oldhay ofway ieldshay andway ucklerbay, andway andstay upway orfay inemay elphay.
3 Awdray outway alsoway ethay earspay, andway opstay [ethay ayway] againstway emthay atthay ersecutepay emay: aysay untoway myay oulsay, IWAY [amway] thyay alvationsay.
4 Etlay emthay ebay onfoundedcay andway utpay otay ameshay atthay eeksay afterway myay oulsay: etlay emthay ebay urnedtay ackbay andway oughtbray otay onfusioncay atthay eviseday myay urthay.
5 Etlay emthay ebay asway affchay eforebay ethay indway: andway etlay ethay angelway ofway ethay ORDLAY asechay [emthay].
6 Etlay eirthay ayway ebay arkday andway ipperyslay: andway etlay ethay angelway ofway ethay ORDLAY ersecutepay emthay.
7 Orfay ithoutway ausecay avehay eythay idhay orfay emay eirthay etnay [inway] away itpay, [ichwhay] ithoutway ausecay eythay avehay iggedday orfay myay oulsay.
8 Etlay estructionday omecay uponway imhay atway unawaresway; andway etlay ishay etnay atthay ehay athhay idhay atchcay imselfhay: intoway atthay eryvay estructionday etlay imhay allfay.
9 Andway myay oulsay allshay ebay oyfuljay inway ethay ORDLAY: itway allshay ejoiceray inway ishay alvationsay.
10 Allway myay onesbay allshay aysay, ORDLAY, owhay [isway] ikelay untoway eethay, ichwhay eliverestday ethay oorpay omfray imhay atthay isway ootay ongstray orfay imhay, eayay, ethay oorpay andway ethay eedynay omfray imhay atthay oilethspay imhay?
11 Alsefay itnessesway idday iseray upway; eythay aidlay otay myay argechay [ingsthay] atthay IWAY ewknay otnay.
12 Eythay ewardedray emay evilway orfay oodgay [otay] ethay oilingspay ofway myay oulsay.
13 Utbay asway orfay emay, enwhay eythay ereway icksay, myay othingclay [asway] ackclothsay: IWAY umbledhay myay oulsay ithway astingfay; andway myay ayerpray eturnedray intoway inemay ownway osombay.
14 IWAY ehavedbay elfmysay asway oughthay [ehay adhay eenbay] myay iendfray [orway] otherbray: IWAY owedbay ownday eavilyhay, asway oneway atthay ournethmay [orfay ishay] othermay.

15 Utbay inway inemay adversityway eythay ejoicedray, andway atheredgay emselvesthay ogethertay: [eayay], ethay abjectsway atheredgay emselvesthay ogethertay againstway emay, andway IWAY ewknay [itway] otnay; eythay idday eartay [emay], andway easedcay otnay:

16 Ithway ocriticalhypay ockersmay inway eastsfay, eythay ashedgnay uponway emay ithway eirthay eethtay.

17 Ordlay, owhay onglay iltway outhay ooklay onway? escueray myay oulsay omfray eirthay estructionsday, myay arlingday omfray ethay ionslay.

18 IWAY illway ivegay eethay anksthay inway ethay eatgray ongregationcay: IWAY illway aisepray eethay amongway uchmay eoplepay.

19 Etlay otnay emthay atthay areway inemay enemiesway ongfullywray ejoiceray overway emay: [eithernay] etlay emthay inkway ithway ethay eyeway atthay atehay emay ithoutway away ausecay.

20 Orfay eythay eakspay otnay eacepay: utbay eythay eviseday eceitfulday attersmay againstway [emthay atthay areway] uietqay inway ethay andlay.

21 Eaay, eythay openedway eirthay outhmay ideway againstway emay, [andway] aidsay, Ahaway, ahaway, ourway eyeway athhay eensay [itway].

22 [Isthay] outhay asthay eensay, OWAY ORDLAY: eepkay otnay ilencesay: OWAY Ordlay, ebay otnay arfay omfray emay.

23 Irstay upway elfthysay, andway awakeway otay myay udgmentjay, [evenway] untoway myay ausecay, myay Odgay andway myay Ordlay.

24 Udgejay emay, OWAY ORDLAY myay Odgay, accordingway otay thyay ighteousnessray; andway etlay emthay otnay ejoiceray overway emay.

25 Etlay emthay otnay aysay inway eirthay eartshay, Ahway, osay ouldway eway avehay itway: etlay emthay otnay aysay, Eway avehay allowedsway imhay upway.

26 Etlay emthay ebay ashamedway andway oughtbray otay onfusioncay ogethertay atthay ejoiceray atway inemay urthay: etlay emthay ebay othedclay ithway ameshay andway ishonourday atthay agnifymay [emselvesthay] againstway emay.

27 Etlay emthay outshay orfay oyjay, andway ebay adglay, atthay avourfay myay ighteousray ausecay: eaay, etlay emthay aysay ontinuallycay, Etlay ethay ORDLAY ebay agnifiedmay, ichwhay athhay easureplay inway ethay osperitypray ofway ishay ervantsay.

28 Andway myay onguetay allshay eakspay ofway thyay ighteousnessray [andway] ofway thyay aisepray allway ethay ayday onglay.

ALMPSAY 36
Otay ethay iefchay Usicianmay, [AWAY Almpsay] ofway Avidday ethay
ervantsay ofway ethay ORDLAY.

1 Ethay ansgressiontray ofway ethay ickedway aithsay ithinway myay
earthay, [atthay erethay isway] onay earfay ofway Odgay eforebay ishay
eyesway.

2 Orfay ehay atterethflay imselfhay inway ishay ownway eyesway,
untilway ishay iniquityway ebay oundfay otay ebay atefulhay.

3 Ethay ordsway ofway ishay outhmay [areway] iniquityway andway
eceitday: ehay athhay eftlay offway otay ebay iseway, [andway] otay oday
oodgay.

4 Ehay evisethday ischiefmay uponway ishay edbay; ehay ettethsay
imselfhay inway away ayway [atthay isway] otnay oodgay; ehay
abhorrethway otnay evilway.

5 Thyay ercymay, OWAY ORDLAY, [isway] inway ethay eavenshay;
[andway] thyay aithfulnessfay [eachethray] untoway ethay oudsclay.

6 Thyay ighteousnessray [isway] ikelay ethay eatgray ountainsmay; thyay
udgmentsjay [areway] away eatgray eepday: OWAY ORDLAY, outhay
eservestpray anmay andway eastbay.

7 Owhay excellentway [isway] thyay ovingkindnesslay, OWAY Odgay!
ereforethay ethay ildrenchay ofway enmay utpay eirthay usttray underway
ethay adowshay ofway thyay ingsway.

8 Eythay allshay ebay abundantlyway atisfiedsay ithway ethay atnessfay
ofway thyay ousehay; andway outhay altshay akemay emthay inkdray
ofway ethay iverray ofway thyay easuresplay.

9 Orfay ithway eethay [isway] ethay ountainfay ofway ifelay: inway thyay
ightlay allshay eway eesay ightlay.

10 OWAY ontinuecay thyay ovingkindnesslay untoway emthay atthay
owknay eethay; andway thyay ighteousnessray otay ethay uprightway
inway earthay.

11 Etlay otnay ethay ootfay ofway idepray omecay againstway emay,
andway etlay otnay ethay andhay ofway ethay ickedway emoveray emay.

12 Erethay areway ethay orkersway ofway iniquityway allenfay: eythay
areway astcay ownday, andway allshay otnay ebay ableway otay iseray.

ALMPSAY 37
[AWAY Almpsay] ofway Avidday.
1 Etfray otnay elfthysay ecausebay ofway evildoersway, eithernay ebay
outhay enviousway againstway ethay orkersway ofway iniquityway.

2 Orfay eythay allshay oonsay ebay utcay ownday ikelay ethay assgray, andway itherway asway ethay eengray erbhay.

3 Usttray inway ethay ORDLAY, andway oday oodgay; [osay] altshay outhay elldway inway ethay andlay, andway erilyvay outhay altshay ebay edfay.

4 Elightday elfthysay alsoway inway ethay ORDLAY; andway ehay allshay ivegay eethay ethay esiresday ofway inethay earthay.

5 Ommitcay thyay ayway untoway ethay ORDLAY; usttray alsoway inway imhay; andway ehay allshay ingbray [itway] otay asspay.

6 Andway ehay allshay ingbray orthfay thyay ighteousnessray asway ethay ightlay, andway thyay udgmentjay asway ethay oondaynay.

7 Estray inway ethay ORDLAY, andway aitway atientlypay orfay imhay: etfray otnay elfthysay ecausebay ofway imhay owhay osperethpray inway ishay ayway, ecausebay ofway ethay anmay owhay ingethbray ickedway evicesday otay asspay.

8 Easecay omfray angerway, andway orsakefay athwray: etfray otnay elfthysay inway anyway iseway otay oday evilway.

9 Orfay evildoersway allshay ebay utcay offway: utbay osethay atthay aitway uponway ethay ORDLAY, eythay allshay inheritway ethay earthway.

10 Orfay etyay away ittlelay ilewhay, andway ethay ickedway [allshay] otnay [ebay]: eayay, outhay altshay iligentlyday onsidercay ishay aceplay, andway itway [allshay] otnay [ebay].

11 Utbay ethay eekmay allshay inheritway ethay earthway; andway allshay elightday emselvesthay inway ethay abundanceway ofway eacepay.

12 Ethay ickedway ottethplay againstway ethay ustjay, andway ashethgnay uponway imhay ithway ishay eethtay.

13 Ethay Ordlay allshay aughlay atway imhay: orfay ehay eethsay atthay ishay ayday isway omingcay.

14 Ethay ickedway avehay awndray outway ethay ordsway, andway avehay entbay eirthay owbay, otay astcay ownday ethay oorpay andway eedynay, [andway] otay ayslay uchsay asway ebay ofway uprightway onversationcay.

15 Eirthay ordsway allshay enterway intoway eirthay ownway earthay, andway eirthay owsbay allshay ebay okenbray.

16 AWAY ittlelay atthay away ighteousray anmay athhay [isway] etterbay anthay ethay ichesray ofway anymay ickedway.

17 Orfay ethay armsway ofway ethay ickedway allshay ebay okenbray: utbay ethay ORDLAY upholdethway ethay ighteousray.

18 Ethay ORDLAY owethknay ethay aysday ofway ethay uprightway: andway eirthay inheritanceway allshay ebay orfay everway.

19 Eythay allshay otnay ebay ashamedway inway ethay evilway imetay: andway inway ethay aysday ofway aminefay eythay allshay ebay atisfiedsay.

20 Utbay ethay ickedway allshay erishpay, andway ethay enemiesway ofway ethay ORDLAY [allshay ebay] asway ethay atfay ofway ambslay: eythay allshay onsumecay; intoway okesmay allshay eythay onsumecay awayway.

21 Ethay ickedway orrowethbay, andway ayethpay otnay againway: utbay ethay ighteousray ewethshay ercymay, andway ivethgay.

22 Orfay [uchsay asway ebay] essedblay ofway imhay allshay inheritway ethay earthway; andway [eythay atthay ebay] ursedcay ofway imhay allshay ebay utcay offway.

23 Ethay epsstay ofway away [oodgay] anmay areway orderedway byay ethay ORDLAY: andway ehay elightethday inway ishay ayway.

24 Oughthay ehay allfay, ehay allshay otnay ebay utterlyway astcay ownday: orfay ethay ORDLAY upholdethway [imhay ithway] ishay andhay.

25 IWAY avehay eenbay oungyay, andway [ownay] amway oldway; etyay avehay IWAY otnay eensay ethay ighteousray orsakenfay, ornay ishay eedsay eggingbay eadbray.

26 [Ehay isway] everway ercifulmay, andway endethlay; andway ishay eedsay [isway] essedblay.

27 Epartday omfray evilway, andway oday oodgay; andway elldway orfay evermoreway.

28 Orfay ethay ORDLAY ovethlay udgmentjay, andway orsakethfay otnay ishay aintssay; eythay areway eservedpray orfay everway: utbay ethay eedsay ofway ethay ickedway allshay ebay utcay offway.

29 Ethay ighteousray allshay inheritway ethay andlay, andway elldway ereinthay orfay everway.

30 Ethay outhmay ofway ethay ighteousray eakethspay isdomway, andway ishay onguetay alkethtay ofway udgmentjay.

31 Ethay awlay ofway ishay Odgay [isway] inway ishay earthay; onenay ofway ishay epsstay allshay ideslay.

32 Ethay ickedway atchethway ethay ighteousray, andway eekethsay otay ayslay imhay.

33 Ethay ORDLAY illway otnay eavelay imhay inway ishay andhay, ornay ondemncay imhay enwhay ehay isway udgedjay.

34 Aitway onway ethay ORDLAY, andway eepkay ishay ayway, andway ehay allshay exaltway eethay otay inheritway ethay andlay: enwhay ethay ickedway areway utcay offway, outhay altshay eesay [itway].
35 IWAY avehay eensay ethay ickedway inway eatgray owerpay, andway eadingspray imselfhay ikelay away eengray aybay eetray.
36 Etyay ehay assedpay awayway, andway, olay, ehay [asway] otnay: eayay, IWAY oughtsay imhay, utbay ehay ouldcay otnay ebay oundfay.
37 Arkmay ethay erfectpay [anmay], andway eholdbay ethay uprightway: orfay ethay endway ofway [atthay] anmay [isway] eacepay.
38 Utbay ethay ansgressorstray allshay ebay estroyedday ogethertay: ethay endway ofway ethay ickedway allshay ebay utcay offway.
39 Utbay ethay alvationsay ofway ethay ighteousray [isway] ofway ethay ORDLAY: [ehay isway] eirthay engthstray inway ethay imetay ofway oubletray.
40 Andway ethay ORDLAY allshay elphay emthay, andway eliverday emthay: ehay allshay eliverday emthay omfray ethay ickedway, andway avesay emthay, ecausebay eythay usttray inway imhay.

ALMPSAY 38
AWAY Almpsay ofway Avidday, otay ingbray otay emembranceray.
1 OWAY ORDLAY, ebukeray emay otnay inway thyay athwray: eithernay astenchay emay inway thyay othay ispleasureday.
2 Orfay inethay arrowsway ickstay astfay inway emay, andway thyay andhay essethpray emay oresay.
3 [Erethay isway] onay oundnesssay inway myay eshflay ecausebay ofway inethay angerway; eithernay [isway erethay anyway] estray inway myay onesbay ecausebay ofway myay insay.
4 Orfay inemay iniquitiesway areway onegay overway inemay eadhay: asway anway eavyhay urdenbay eythay areway ootay eavyhay orfay emay.
5 Myay oundsway inkstay [andway] areway orruptcay ecausebay ofway myay oolishnessfay.
6 IWAY amway oubledtray; IWAY amway owedbay ownday eatlygray; IWAY ogay ourningmay allway ethay ayday onglay.
7 Orfay myay oinslay areway illedfay ithway away oathsomelay [iseaseday]: andway [erethay isway] onay oundnesssay inway myay eshflay.
8 IWAY amway eeblefay andway oresay okenbray: IWAY avehay oaredray byay easonray ofway ethay isquietnessday ofway myay earthay.
9 Ordlay, allway myay esireday [isway] eforebay eethay; andway myay oaninggray isway otnay idhay omfray eethay.

10 Myay earthay antethpay, myay engthstray ailethfay emay: asway orfay ethay ightlay ofway inemay eyesway, itway alsoway isway onegay omfray emay.

11 Myay overslay andway myay iendsfray andstay aloofway omfray myay oresay; andway myay insmenkay andstay afarway offway.

12 Eythay alsoway atthay eeksay afterway myay ifelay aylay aressnay [orfay emay]: andway eythay atthay eeksay myay urthay eakspay ischievousmay ingsthay, andway imagineway eceitsday allway ethay ayday onglay.

13 Utbay IWAY, asway away eafday [anmay], eardhay otnay; andway [IWAY asway] asway away umbday anmay [atthay] openethway otnay ishay outhmay.

14 Usthay IWAY asway asway away anmay atthay earethhay otnay, andway inway osewhay outhmay [areway] onay eproofsray.

15 Orfay inway eethay, OWAY ORDLAY, oday IWAY opehay: outhay iltway earhay, OWAY Ordlay myay Odgay.

16 Orfay IWAY aidsay, [Earhay emay], estlay [otherwiseway] eythay ouldshay ejoiceray overway emay: enwhay myay ootfay ippethslay, eythay agnifymay [emselvesthay] againstway emay.

17 Orfay IWAY [amway] eadyray otay althay, andway myay orrowsay [isway] ontinuallycay eforebay emay.

18 Orfay IWAY illway eclareday inemay iniquityway; IWAY illway ebay orrysay orfay myay insay.

19 Utbay inemay enemiesway [areway] ivelylay, [andway] eythay areway ongstray: andway eythay atthay atehay emay ongfullywray areway ultipliedmay.

20 Eythay alsoway atthay enderray evilway orfay oodgay areway inemay adversariesway; ecausebay IWAY ollowfay [ethay ingthay atthay] oodgay [isway].

21 Orsakefay emay otnay, OWAY ORDLAY: OWAY myay Odgay, ebay otnay arfay omfray emay.

22 Akemay astehay otay elphay emay, OWAY Ordlay myay alvationsay.

ALMPSAY 39
Otay ethay iefchay Usicianmay, [evenway] otay Eduthunjay, AWAY Almpsay ofway Avidday.

1 IWAY aidsay, IWAY illway aketay eedhay otay myay aysway, atthay IWAY insay otnay ithway myay onguetay: IWAY illway eepkay myay outhmay ithway away idlebray, ilewhay ethay ickedway isway eforebay emay.

2 IWAY asway umbday ithway ilencesay, IWAY eldhay myay eacepay, [evenway] omfray oodgay; andway myay orrowsay asway irredstay.
3 Myay earthay asway othay ithinway emay, ilewhay IWAY asway usingmay ethay irefay urnedbay: [enthay] akespay IWAY ithway myay onguetay,
4 ORDLAY, akemay emay otay owknay inemay endway, andway ethay easuremay ofway myay aysday, atwhay itway [isway; atthay] IWAY aymay owknay owhay ailfray IWAY [amway].
5 Eholdbay, outhay asthay ademay myay aysday [asway] anway andbreadthhay; andway inemay ageway [isway] asway othingnay eforebay eethay: erilyvay everyway anmay atway ishay estbay atestay [isway] altogetherway anityvay. Elahsay.
6 Urelysay everyway anmay alkethway inway away ainvay ewshay: urelysay eythay areway isquietedday inway ainvay: ehay eapethhay upway [ichesray], andway owethknay otnay owhay allshay athergay emthay.
7 Andway ownay, Ordlay, atwhay aitway IWAY orfay? myay opehay [isway] inway eethay.
8 Eliverday emay omfray allway myay ansgressionstray: akemay emay otnay ethay eproachray ofway ethay oolishfay.
9 IWAY asway umbday, IWAY openedway otnay myay outhmay; ecausebay outhay idstday [itway].
10 Emoveray thyay okestray awayway omfray emay: IWAY amway onsumedcay byay ethay owblay ofway inethay andhay.
11 Enwhay outhay ithway ebukesray ostday orrectcay anmay orfay iniquityway, outhay akestmay ishay eautybay otay onsumecay awayway ikelay away othmay: urelysay everyway anmay [isway] anityvay. Elahsay.
12 Earhay myay ayerpray, OWAY ORDLAY, andway ivegay earway untoway myay cryay; oldhay otnay thyay eacepay atway myay earstay: orfay IWAY [amway] away angerstray ithway eethay, [andway] away ojournersay, asway allway myay athersfay [ereway].
13 OWAY arespay emay, atthay IWAY aymay ecoverray engthstray, eforebay IWAY ogay encehay, andway ebay onay oremay.

ALMPSAY 40
Otay ethay iefchay Usicianmay, AWAY Almpsay ofway Avidday.
1 IWAY aitedway atientlypay orfay ethay ORDLAY; andway ehay inclinedway untoway emay, andway eardhay myay cryay.
2 Ehay oughtbray emay upway alsoway outway ofway anway orriblehay itpay, outway ofway ethay irymay ayclay, andway etsay myay eetfay uponway away ockray, [andway] establishedway myay oingsgay.

3 Andway ehay athhay utpay away ewnay ongsay inway myay outhmay, [evenway] aisepray untoway ourway Odgay: anymay allshay eesay [itway], andway earfay, andway allshay usttray inway ethay ORDLAY.

4 Essedblay [isway] atthay anmay atthay akethmay ethay ORDLAY ishay usttray, andway espectethray otnay ethay oudpray, ornay uchsay asway urntay asideway otay ieslay.

5 Anymay, OWAY ORDLAY myay Odgay, [areway] thyay onderfulway orksway [ichwhay] outhay asthay oneday, andway thyay oughtsthay [ichwhay areway] otay usway-ardway: eythay annotcay ebay eckonedray upway inway orderway untoway eethay: [ifway] IWAY ouldway eclareday andway eakspay [ofway emthay], eythay areway oremay anthay ancay ebay umberednay.

6 Acrificesay andway offeringway outhay idstday otnay esireday; inemay earsway asthay outhay openedway: urntbay offeringway andway insay offeringway asthay outhay otnay equiredray.

7 Enthay aidsay IWAY, Olay, IWAY omecay: inway ethay olumevay ofway ethay ookbay [itway isway] ittenwray ofway emay,

8 IWAY elightday otay oday thyay illway, OWAY myay Odgay: eayay, thyay awlay [isway] ithinway myay earthay.

9 IWAY avehay eachedpray ighteousnessray inway ethay eatgray ongregationcay: olay, IWAY avehay otnay efrainedray myay ipslay, OWAY ORDLAY, outhay owestknay.

10 IWAY avehay otnay idhay thyay ighteousnessray ithinway myay earthay; IWAY avehay eclaredday thyay aithfulnessfay andway thyay alvationsay: IWAY avehay otnay oncealedcay thyay ovingkindnesslay andway thyay uthtray omfray ethay eatgray ongregationcay.

11 Ithholdway otnay outhay thyay endertay erciesmay omfray emay, OWAY ORDLAY: etlay thyay ovingkindnesslay andway thyay uthtray ontinuallycay eservepray emay.

12 Orfay innumerableway evilsway avehay ompassedcay emay aboutway: inemay iniquitiesway avehay akentay oldhay uponway emay, osay atthay IWAY amway otnay ableway otay ooklay upway; eythay areway oremay anthay ethay airshay ofway inemay eadhay: ereforethay myay earthay ailethfay emay.

13 Ebay easedplay, OWAY ORDLAY, otay eliverday emay: OWAY ORDLAY, akemay astehay otay elphay emay.

14 Etlay emthay ebay ashamedway andway onfoundedcay ogethertay atthay eeksay afterway myay oulsay otay estroyday itway; etlay emthay ebay ivendray ackwardbay andway utpay otay ameshay atthay ishway emay evilway.

15 Etlay emthay ebay esolateday orfay away ewardray ofway eirthay ameshay atthay aysay untoway emay, Ahaway, ahaway.

16 Etlay allway osethay atthay eeksay eethay ejoiceray andway ebay adglay inway eethay: etlay uchsay asway ovelay thyay alvationsay aysay ontinuallycay, Ethay ORDLAY ebay agnifiedmay.

17 Utbay IWAY [amway] oorpay andway eedynay; [etyay] ethay Ordlay inkeththay uponway emay: outhay [artway] myay elphay andway myay elivererday; akemay onay arryingtay, OWAY myay Odgay.

ALMPSAY 41

Otay ethay iefchay Usicianmay, AWAY Almpsay ofway Avidday.

1 Essedblay [isway] ehay atthay onsiderethcay ethay oorpay: ethay ORDLAY illway eliverday imhay inway imetay ofway oubletray.

2 Ethay ORDLAY illway eservepray imhay, andway eepkay imhay aliveway; [andway] ehay allshay ebay essedblay uponway ethay earthway: andway outhay iltway otnay eliverday imhay untoway ethay illway ofway ishay enemiesway.

3 Ethay ORDLAY illway engthenstray imhay uponway ethay edbay ofway anguishinglay: outhay iltway akemay allway ishay edbay inway ishay icknesssay.

4 IWAY aidsay, ORDLAY, ebay ercifulmay untoway emay: ealhay myay oulsay; orfay IWAY avehay innedsay againstway eethay.

5 Inemay enemiesway eakspay evilway ofway emay, Enwhay allshay ehay ieday, andway ishay amenay erishpay?

6 Andway ifway ehay omecay otay eesay [emay], ehay eakethspay anityvay: ishay earthay atherethgay iniquityway otay itselfway; [enwhay] ehay oethgay abroadway, ehay ellethtay [itway].

7 Allway atthay atehay emay isperwhay ogethertay againstway emay: againstway emay oday eythay eviseday myay urthay.

8 Anway evilway iseaseday, [aysay eythay], eavethclay astfay untoway imhay: andway [ownay] atthay ehay iethlay ehay allshay iseray upway onay oremay.

9 Eaay, inemay ownway amiliarfay iendfray, inway omwhay IWAY ustedtray, ichwhay idday eatway ofway myay eadbray, athhay iftedlay upway [ishay] eelhay againstway emay.

10 Utbay outhay, OWAY ORDLAY, ebay ercifulmay untoway emay, andway aiseray emay upway, atthay IWAY aymay equiteray emthay.

11 Byay isthay IWAY owknay atthay outhay avourestfay emay, ecausebay inemay enemyway othday otnay iumphtray overway emay.

12 Andway asway orfay emay, outhay upholdestway emay inway inemay integrityway, andway ettestsay emay eforebay thyay acefay orfay everway.
13 Essedblay [ebay] ethay ORDLAY Odgay ofway Israelway omfray everlastingway, andway otay everlastingway. Amenway, andway Amenway.

ALMPSAY 42

Otay ethay iefchay Usicianmay, Aschilmay, orfay ethay onssay ofway Orahkay.

1 Asway ethay arthay antethpay afterway ethay aterway ooksbray, osay antethpay myay oulsay afterway eethay, OWAY Odgay.
2 Myay oulsay irsteththay orfay Odgay, orfay ethay ivinglay Odgay: enwhay allshay IWAY omecay andway appearway eforebay Odgay?
3. Myay earstay avehay eenbay myay eatmay ayday andway ightnay, ilewhay eythay ontinuallycay aysay untoway emay, Erewhay [isway] thyay Odgay?
4 Enwhay IWAY ememberray esethay [ingsthay], IWAY ourpay outway myay oulsay inway emay: orfay IWAY adhay onegay ithway ethay ultitudemay, IWAY entway ithway emthay otay ethay ousehay ofway Odgay, ithway ethay oicevay ofway oyjay andway aisepray, ithway away ultitudemay atthay eptkay olydayhay.
5 Whyay artway outhay astcay ownday, OWAY myay oulsay? andway [whyay] artway outhay isquietedday inway emay? opehay outhay inway Odgay: orfay IWAY allshay etyay aisepray imhay [orfay] ethay elphay ofway ishay ountenancecay.
6 OWAY myay Odgay, myay oulsay isway astcay ownday ithinway emay: ereforethay illway IWAY ememberray eethay omfray ethay andlay ofway Ordanjay, andway ofway ethay Ermoniteshay, omfray ethay illhay Izarmay.
7 Eepday allethcay untoway eepday atway ethay oisenay ofway thyay aterspoutsway: allway thyay avesway andway thyay illowsbay areway onegay overway emay.
8 [Etyay] ethay ORDLAY illway ommandcay ishay ovingkindnesslay inway ethay aytimeday, andway inway ethay ightnay ishay ongsay [allshay ebay] ithway emay, [andway] myay ayerpray untoway ethay Odgay ofway myay ifelay.
9 IWAY illway aysay untoway Odgay myay ockray, Whyay asthay outhay orgottenfay emay? whyay ogay IWAY ourningmay ecausebay ofway ethay oppressionway ofway ethay enemyway?

10 [Asway] ithway away ordsway inway myay onesbay, inemay enemiesway eproachray emay; ilewhay eythay aysay ailyday untoway emay, Erewhay [isway] thyay Odgay?
11 Whyay artway outhay astcay ownday, OWAY myay oulsay? andway whyay artway outhay isquietedday ithinway emay? opehay outhay inway Odgay: orfay IWAY allshay etyay aisepray imhay, [owhay isway] ethay ealthhay ofway myay ountenancecay, andway myay Odgay.

ALMPSAY 43

1 Udgejay emay, OWAY Odgay, andway eadplay myay ausecay againstway anway ungodlyway ationnay: OWAY eliverday emay omfray ethay eceitfulday andway unjustway anmay.
2 Orfay outhay [artway] ethay Odgay ofway myay engthstray: whyay ostday outhay astcay emay offway? whyay ogay IWAY ourningmay ecausebay ofway ethay oppressionway ofway ethay enemyway?
3 OWAY endsay outway thyay ightlay andway thyay uthtray: etlay emthay eadlay emay; etlay emthay ingbray emay untoway thyay olyhay illhay, andway otay thyay abernaclestay.
4 Enthay illway IWAY ogay untoway ethay altarway ofway Odgay, untoway Odgay myay exceedingway oyjay: eayay, uponway ethay arphay illway IWAY aisepray eethay, OWAY Odgay myay Odgay.
5 Whyay artway outhay astcay ownday, OWAY myay oulsay? andway whyay artway outhay isquietedday ithinway emay? opehay inway Odgay: orfay IWAY allshay etyay aisepray imhay, [owhay isway] ethay ealthhay ofway myay ountenancecay, andway myay Odgay.

ALMPSAY 44

Otay ethay iefchay Usicianmay orfay ethay onssay ofway Orahkay, Aschilmay.
1 Eway avehay eardhay ithway ourway earsway, OWAY Odgay, ourway athersfay avehay oldtay usway, [atwhay] orkway outhay idstday inway eirthay aysday, inway ethay imestay ofway oldway.
2 [Owhay] outhay idstday ivedray outway ethay eathenhay ithway thyay andhay, andway antedstplay emthay; [owhay] outhay idstday afflictway ethay eoplepay, andway astcay emthay outway.
3 Orfay eythay otgay otnay ethay andlay inway ossessionpay byay eirthay ownway ordsway, eithernay idday eirthay ownway armway avesay emthay: utbay thyay ightray andhay, andway inethay armway, andway ethay ightlay ofway thyay ountenancecay, ecausebay outhay adsthay away avourfay untoway emthay.

4 Outhay artway myay Ingkay, OWAY Odgay: ommandcay eliverancesday orfay Acobjay.

5 Oughthray eethay illway eway ushpay ownday ourway enemiesway: oughthray thyay amenay illway eway eadtray emthay underway atthay iseray upway againstway usway.

6 Orfay IWAY illway otnay usttray inway myay owbay, eithernay allshay myay ordsway avesay emay.

7 Utbay outhay asthay avedsay usway omfray ourway enemiesway, andway asthay utpay emthay otay ameshay atthay atedhay usway.

8 Inway Odgay eway oastbay allway ethay ayday onglay, andway aisepray thyay amenay orfay everway. Elahsay.

9 Utbay outhay asthay astcay offway, andway utpay usway otay ameshay; andway oestgay otnay orthfay ithway ourway armiesway.

10 Outhay akestmay usway otay urntay ackbay omfray ethay enemyway: andway eythay ichwhay atehay usway oilspay orfay emselvesthay.

11 Outhay asthay ivengay usway ikelay eepshay [appointedway] orfay eatmay; andway asthay atteredscay usway amongway ethay eathenhay.

12 Outhay ellestsay thyay eoplepay orfay oughtnay, andway ostday otnay increaseway [thyay ealthway] byay eirthay icepray.

13 Outhay akestmay usway away eproachray otay ourway eighboursnay, away ornscay andway away erisionday otay emthay atthay areway oundray aboutway usway.

14 Outhay akestmay usway away ordbyway amongway ethay eathenhay, away akingshay ofway ethay eadhay amongway ethay eoplepay.

15 Myay onfusioncay [isway] ontinuallycay eforebay emay, andway ethay ameshay ofway myay acefay athhay overedcay emay,

16 Orfay ethay oicevay ofway imhay atthay eproachethray andway asphemethblay; byay easonray ofway ethay enemyway andway avengerway.

17 Allway isthay isway omecay uponway usway; etyay avehay eway otnay orgottenfay eethay, eithernay avehay eway ealtday alselyfay inway thyay ovenantcay.

18 Ourway earthay isway otnay urnedtay ackbay, eithernay avehay ourway epsstay eclinedday omfray thyay ayway;

19 Oughthay outhay asthay oresay okenbray usway inway ethay aceplay ofway agonsdray, andway overedcay usway ithway ethay adowshay ofway eathday.

20 Ifway eway avehay orgottenfay ethay amenay ofway ourway Odgay, orway etchedstray outway ourway andshay otay away angestray odgay;

21 Allshay otnay Odgay earchsay isthay outway? orfay ehay owethknay ethay ecretssay ofway ethay earthay.

22 Eayay, orfay thyay akesay areway eway illedkay allway ethay ayday onglay; eway areway ountedcay asway eepshay orfay ethay aughterslay.

23 Awakeway, whyay eepestslay outhay, OWAY Ordlay? ariseway, astcay [usway] otnay offway orfay everway.

24 Ereforewhay idesthay outhay thyay acefay, [andway] orgettestfay ourway afflictionway andway ourway oppressionway?

25 Orfay ourway oulsay isway owedbay ownday otay ethay ustday: ourway ellybay eavethclay untoway ethay earthway.

26 Ariseway orfay ourway elphay, andway edeemray usway orfay thyay erciesmay' akesay.

ALMPSAY 45

Otay ethay iefchay Usicianmay uponway Oshannimshay, orfay ethay onssay ofway Orahkay, Aschilmay, AWAY Ongsay ofway oveslay.

1 Myay earthay isway inditingway away oodgay attermay: IWAY eakspay ofway ethay ingsthay ichwhay IWAY avehay ademay ouchingtay ethay ingkay: myay onguetay [isway] ethay enpay ofway away eadyray iterwray.

2 Outhay artway airerfay anthay ethay ildrenchay ofway enmay: acegray isway ouredpay intoway thyay ipslay: ereforethay Odgay athhay essedblay eethay orfay everway.

3 Irdgay thyay ordsway uponway [thyay] ighthay, OWAY [ostmay] ightymay, ithway thyay oryglay andway thyay ajestymay.

4 Andway inway thyay ajestymay ideray osperouslypray ecausebay ofway uthtray andway eeknessmay [andway] ighteousnessray; andway thyay ightray andhay allshay eachtay eethay erribletay ingsthay.

5 Inethay arrowssway [areway] arpshay inway ethay earthay ofway ethay ingkay'say enemiesway; [erebywhay] ethay eoplepay allfay underway eethay.

6 Thyay onethray, OWAY Odgay, [isway] orfay everway andway everway: ethay eptrescay ofway thyay ingdomkay [isway] away ightray eptrescay.

7 Outhay ovestlay ighteousnessray, andway atesthay ickednessway: ereforethay Odgay, thyay Odgay, athhay anointedway eethay ithway ethay oilway ofway adnessglay aboveway thyay ellowsfay.

8 Allway thyay armentsgay [ellsmay] ofway myrrhay, andway aloesway, [andway] assiacay, outway ofway ethay ivoryway alacespay, erebywhay eythay avehay ademay eethay adglay.

9 Ingskay' aughtersday [ereway] amongway thyay onourablehay omenway: uponway thyay ightray andhay idday andstay ethay ueenqay inway oldgay ofway Ophirway.

10 Earkenhay, OWAY aughterday, andway onsidercay, andway inclineway inethay earway; orgetfay alsoway inethay ownway eoplepay, andway thyay atherfay'say ousehay;

11 Osay allshay ethay ingkay eatlygray esireday thyay eautybay: orfay ehay [isway] thyay Ordlay; andway orshipway outhay imhay.

12 Andway ethay aughterday ofway Etyray [allshay ebay erethay] ithway away iftgay; [evenway] ethay ichray amongway ethay eoplepay allshay intreatway thyay avourfay.

13 Ethay ingkay'say aughterday [isway] allway oriousglay ithinway: erhay othingclay [isway] ofway oughtwray oldgay.

14 Eshay allshay ebay oughtbray untoway ethay ingkay inway aimentray ofway eedleworknay: ethay irginsvay erhay ompanionscay atthay ollowfay erhay allshay ebay oughtbray untoway eethay.

15 Ithway adnessglay andway ejoicingray allshay eythay ebay oughtbray: eythay allshay enterway intoway ethay ingkay'say alacepay.

16 Insteadway ofway thyay athersfay allshay ebay thyay ildrenchay, omwhay outhay ayestmay akemay incespray inway allway ethay earthway.

17 IWAY illway akemay thyay amenay otay ebay ememberedray inway allway enerationsgay: ereforethay allshay ethay eoplepay aisepray eethay orfay everway andway everway.

ALMPSAY 46
Otay ethay iefchay Usicianmay orfay ethay onssay ofway Orahkay, AWAY Ongsay uponway Alamothway.

1 Odgay [isway] ourway efugeray andway engthstray, away eryvay esentpray elphay inway oubletray.

2 Ereforethay illway otnay eway earfay, oughthay ethay earthway ebay emovedray, andway oughthay ethay ountainsmay ebay arriedcay intoway ethay idstmay ofway ethay easay;

3 [Oughthay] ethay atersway ereofthay oarray [andway] ebay oubledtray, [oughthay] ethay ountainsmay akeshay ithway ethay ellingsway ereofthay. Elahsay.

4 [Erethay isway] away iverray, ethay eamsstray ereofwhay allshay akemay adglay ethay itycay ofway Odgay, ethay olyhay [aceplay] ofway ethay abernaclestay ofway ethay ostmay Ighhay.

5 Odgay [isway] inway ethay idstmay ofway erhay; eshay allshay otnay ebay ovedmay: Odgay allshay elphay erhay, [andway atthay] ightray earlyway.

6 Ethay eathenhay agedray, ethay ingdomskay ereway ovedmay: ehay utteredway ishay oicevay, ethay earthway eltedmay.

7 Ethay ORDLAY ofway ostshay [isway] ithway usway; ethay Odgay ofway Acobjay [isway] ourway efugeray. Elahsay.

8 Omecay, eholdbay ethay orksway ofway ethay ORDLAY, atwhay esolationsday ehay athhay ademay inway ethay earthway.

9 Ehay akethmay arsway otay easecay untoway ethay endway ofway ethay earthway; ehay eakethbray ethay owbay, andway uttethcay ethay earspay inway undersay; ehay urnethbay ethay ariotchay inway ethay irefay.

10 Ebay illstay, andway owknay atthay IWAY [amway] Odgay: IWAY illway ebay exaltedway amongway ethay eathenhay, IWAY illway ebay exaltedway inway ethay earthway.

11 Ethay ORDLAY ofway ostshay [isway] ithway usway; ethay Odgay ofway Acobjay [isway] ourway efugeray. Elahsay.

ALMPSAY 47
Otay ethay iefchay Usicianmay, AWAY Almpsay orfay ethay onssay ofway Orahkay.

1 OWAY apclay ouryay andshay, allway eyay eoplepay; outshay untoway Odgay ithway ethay oicevay ofway iumphtray.

2 Orfay ethay ORDLAY ostmay ighhay [isway] erribletay; [ehay isway] away eatgray Ingkay overway allway ethay earthway.

3 Ehay allshay ubduesay ethay eoplepay underway usway, andway ethay ationsnay underway ourway eetfay.

4 Ehay allshay oosechay ourway inheritanceway orfay usway, ethay excellencyway ofway Acobjay omwhay ehay ovedlay. Elahsay.

5 Odgay isway onegay upway ithway away outshay, ethay ORDLAY ithway ethay oundsay ofway away umpettray.

6 Ingsay aisespray otay Odgay, ingsay aisespray: ingsay aisespray untoway ourway Ingkay, ingsay aisespray.

7 Orfay Odgay [isway] ethay Ingkay ofway allway ethay earthway: ingsay eyay aisespray ithway understandingway.

8 Odgay eignethray overway ethay eathenhay: Odgay ittethsay uponway ethay onethray ofway ishay olinesshay.

9 Ethay incespray ofway ethay eoplepay areway atheredgay ogethertay, [evenway] ethay eoplepay ofway ethay Odgay ofway Abrahamway: orfay

ethay ieldsshay ofway ethay earthway [elongbay] untoway Odgay: ehay isway eatlygray exaltedway.

ALMPSAY 48
AWAY Ongsay [andway] Almpsay orfay ethay onssay ofway Orahkay.

1 Eatgray [isway] ethay ORDLAY, andway eatlygray otay ebay aisedpray inway ethay itycay ofway ourway Odgay, [inway] ethay ountainmay ofway ishay olinesshay.

2 Eautifulbay orfay ituationsay, ethay oyjay ofway ethay olewhay earthway, [isway] ountmay Ionzay, [onway] ethay idessay ofway ethay orthnay, ethay itycay ofway ethay eatgray Ingkay.

3 Odgay isway ownknay inway erhay alacespay orfay away efugeray.

4 Orfay, olay, ethay ingskay ereway assembledway, eythay assedpay byay ogethertay.

5 Eythay awsay [itway, andway] osay eythay arvelledmay; eythay ereway oubledtray, [andway] astedhay awayway.

6 Earfay ooktay oldhay uponway emthay erethay, [andway] ainpay, asway ofway away omanway inway availtray.

7 Outhay eakestbray ethay ipsshay ofway Arshishtay ithway anway eastway indway.

8 Asway eway avehay eardhay, osay avehay eway eensay inway ethay itycay ofway ethay ORDLAY ofway ostshay, inway ethay itycay ofway ourway Odgay: Odgay illway establishway itway orfay everway. Elahsay.

9 Eway avehay oughtthay ofway thyay ovingkindnesslay, OWAY Odgay, inway ethay idstmay ofway thyay empletay.

10 Accordingway otay thyay amenay, OWAY Odgay, osay [isway] thyay aisepray untoway ethay endsway ofway ethay earthway: thyay ightray andhay isway ullfay ofway ighteousnessray.

11 Etlay ountmay Ionzay ejoiceray, etlay ethay aughtersday ofway Udahjay ebay adglay, ecausebay ofway thyay udgmentsjay.

12 Alkway aboutway Ionzay, andway ogay oundray aboutway erhay: elltay ethay owerstay ereofthay.

13 Arkmay eyay ellway erhay ulwarksbay, onsidercay erhay alacespay; atthay eyay aymay elltay [itway] otay ethay enerationgay ollowingfay.

14 Orfay isthay Odgay [isway] ourway Odgay orfay everway andway everway: ehay illway ebay ourway uidegay [evenway] untoway eathday.

ALMPSAY 49
Otay ethay iefchay Usicianmay, AWAY Almpsay orfay ethay onssay ofway Orahkay.

1 Earhay isthay, allway [eyay] eoplepay; ivegay earway, allway [eyay] inhabitantsway ofway ethay orldway:

2 Othbay owlay andway ighhay, ichray andway oorpay, ogethertay.

3 Myay outhmay allshay eakspay ofway isdomway; andway ethay editationmay ofway myay earthay [allshay ebay] ofway understandingway.

4 IWAY illway inclineway inemay earway otay away arablepay: IWAY illway openway myay arkday ayingsay uponway ethay arphay.

5 Ereforewhay ouldshay IWAY earfay inway ethay aysday ofway evilway, [enwhay] ethay iniquityway ofway myay eelshay allshay ompasscay emay aboutway?

6 Eythay atthay usttray inway eirthay ealthway, andway oastbay emselvesthay inway ethay ultitudemay ofway eirthay ichesray;

7 Onenay [ofway emthay] ancay byay anyway eansmay edeemray ishay otherbray, ornay ivegay otay Odgay away ansomray orfay imhay:

8 (Orfay ethay edemptionray ofway eirthay oulsay [isway] eciouspray, andway itway easethcay orfay everway:)

9 Atthay ehay ouldshay illstay ivelay orfay everway, [andway] otnay eesay orruptioncay.

10 Orfay ehay eethsay [atthay] iseway enmay ieday, ikewiselay ethay oolfay andway ethay utishbray ersonpay erishpay, andway eavelay eirthay ealthway otay othersway.

11 Eirthay inwardway oughtthay [isway, atthay] eirthay ouseshay [allshay ontinuecay] orfay everway, [andway] eirthay ellingdway acesplay otay allway enerationsgay; eythay allcay [eirthay] andslay afterway eirthay ownway amesnay.

12 Everthelessnay anmay [eingbay] inway onourhay abidethway otnay: ehay isway ikelay ethay eastsbay [atthay] erishpay.

13 Isthay eirthay ayway [isway] eirthay ollyfay: etyay eirthay osteritypay approveway eirthay ayingssay. Elahsay.

14 Ikelay eepshay eythay areway aidlay inway ethay avegray; eathday allshay eedfay onway emthay; andway ethay uprightway allshay avehay ominionday overway emthay inway ethay orningmay; andway eirthay eautybay allshay onsumecay inway ethay avegray omfray eirthay ellingdway.

15 Utbay Odgay illway edeemray myay oulsay omfray ethay owerpay ofway ethay avegray: orfay ehay allshay eceiveray emay. Elahsay.

16 Ebay otnay outhay afraidway enwhay oneway isway ademay ichray, enwhay ethay oryglay ofway ishay ousehay isway increasedway;

17 Orfay enwhay ehay iethday ehay allshay arrycay othingnay awayway: ishay oryglay allshay otnay escendday afterway imhay.

18 Oughthay ilewhay ehay ivedlay ehay essedblay ishay oulsay: andway [enmay] illway aisepray eethay, enwhay outhay oestday ellway otay elfthysay.

19 Ehay allshay ogay otay ethay enerationgay ofway ishay athersfay; eythay allshay evernay eesay ightlay.

20 Anmay [atthay isway] inway onourhay, andway understandethway otnay, isway ikelay ethay eastsbay [atthay] erishpay.

ALMPSAY 50
AWAY Almpsay ofway Asaphway.

1 Ethay ightymay Odgay, [evenway] ethay ORDLAY, athhay okenspay, andway alledcay ethay earthway omfray ethay isingray ofway ethay unsay untoway ethay oinggay ownday ereofthay.

2 Outway ofway Ionzay, ethay erfectionpay ofway eautybay, Odgay athhay inedshay.

3 Ourway Odgay allshay omecay, andway allshay otnay eepkay ilencesay: away irefay allshay evourday eforebay imhay, andway itway allshay ebay eryvay empestuoustay oundray aboutway imhay.

4 Ehay allshay allcay otay ethay eavenshay omfray aboveway, andway otay ethay earthway, atthay ehay aymay udgejay ishay eoplepay.

5 Athergay myay aintssay ogethertay untoway emay; osethay atthay avehay ademay away ovenantcay ithway emay byay acrificesay.

6 Andway ethay eavenshay allshay eclareday ishay ighteousnessray: orfay Odgay [isway] udgejay imselfhay. Elahsay.

7 Earhay, OWAY myay eoplepay, andway IWAY illway eakspay; OWAY Israelway, andway IWAY illway estifytay againstway eethay: IWAY [amway] Odgay, [evenway] thyay Odgay.

8 IWAY illway otnay eproveray eethay orfay thyay acrificessay orway thyay urntbay offeringsway, [otay avehay eenbay] ontinuallycay eforebay emay.

9 IWAY illway aketay onay ullockbay outway ofway thyay ousehay, [ornay] ehay oatsgay outway ofway thyay oldsfay.

10 Orfay everyway eastbay ofway ethay orestfay [isway] inemay, [andway] ethay attlecay uponway away ousandthay illshay.

11 IWAY owknay allway ethay owlsfay ofway ethay ountainsmay: andway ethay ildway eastsbay ofway ethay ieldfay [areway] inemay.

12 Ifway IWAY ereway ungryhay, IWAY ouldway otnay elltay eethay: orfay ethay orldway [isway] inemay, andway ethay ulnessfay ereofthay.

13 Illway IWAY eatway ethay eshflay ofway ullsbay, orway inkdray ethay oodblay ofway oatsgay?

14 Offerway untoway Odgay anksgivingthay; andway aypay thyay owsvay untoway ethay ostmay Ighhay:

15 Andway allcay uponway emay inway ethay ayday ofway oubletray: IWAY illway eliverday eethay, andway outhay altshay orifyglay emay.

16 Utbay untoway ethay ickedway Odgay aithsay, Atwhay asthay outhay otay oday otay eclareday myay atutesstay, orway [atthay] outhay ouldestshay aketay myay ovenantcay inway thyay outhmay?

17 Eeingsay outhay atesthay instructionway, andway astestcay myay ordsway ehindbay eethay.

18 Enwhay outhay awestsay away iefthay, enthay outhay onsentedstcay ithway imhay, andway asthay eenbay artakerpay ithway adulterersway.

19 Outhay ivestgay thyay outhmay otay evilway, andway thyay onguetay amethfray eceitday.

20 Outhay ittestsay [andway] eakestspay againstway thyay otherbray; outhay anderestslay inethay ownway othermay'say onsay.

21 Esethay [ingsthay] asthay outhay oneday, andway IWAY eptkay ilencesay; outhay oughtestthay atthay IWAY asway altogetherway [uchsay anway oneway] asway elfthysay: [utbay] IWAY illway eproveray eethay, andway etsay [emthay] inway orderway eforebay inethay eyesway.

22 Ownay onsidercay isthay, eyay atthay orgetfay Odgay, estlay IWAY eartay [ouyay] inway iecespay, andway [erethay ebay] onenay otay eliverday.

23 Osowhay offerethway aisepray orifiethglay emay: andway otay imhay atthay orderethway [ishay] onversationcay [arightway] illway IWAY ewshay ethay alvationsay ofway Odgay.

ALMPSAY 51

Otay ethay iefchay Usicianmay, AWAY Almpsay ofway Avidday, enwhay Athannay ethay ophetpray amecay untoway imhay, afterway ehay adhay onegay inway otay Athbay-ebashay.

1 Avehay ercymay uponway emay, OWAY Odgay, accordingway otay thyay ovingkindnesslay: accordingway untoway ethay ultitudemay ofway thyay endertay erciesmay otblay outway myay ansgressionstray.

2 Ashway emay oughlythray omfray inemay iniquityway, andway eanseclay emay omfray myay insay.

3 Orfay IWAY acknowledgeway myay ansgressionstray: andway myay insay [isway] everway eforebay emay.

4 Againstway eethay, eethay onlyway, avehay IWAY innedsay, andway oneday [isthay] evilway inway thyay ightsay: atthay outhay ightestmay

ebay ustifiedjay enwhay outhay eakestspay, [andway] ebay earclay enwhay outhay udgestjay.

5 Eholdbay, IWAY asway apenshay inway iniquityway; andway inway insay idday myay othermay onceivecay emay.

6 Eholdbay, outhay esirestday uthtray inway ethay inwardway artspay: andway inway ethay iddenhay [artpay] outhay altshay akemay emay otay owknay isdomway.

7 Urgepay emay ithway ophyssay, andway IWAY allshay ebay eanclay: ashway emay, andway IWAY allshay ebay iterwhay anthay owsnay.

8 Akemay emay otay earhay oyjay andway adnessglay; [atthay] ethay onesbay [ichwhay] outhay asthay okenbray aymay ejoiceray.

9 Idehay thyay acefay omfray myay inssay, andway otblay outway allway inemay iniquitiesway.

10 Eatecray inway emay away eanclay earthay, OWAY Odgay; andway enewray away ightray iritspay ithinway emay.

11 Astcay emay otnay awayway omfray thyay esencepray; andway aketay otnay thyay olyhay iritspay omfray emay.

12 Estoreray untoway emay ethay oyjay ofway thyay alvationsay; andway upholdway emay [ithway thyay] eefray iritspay.

13 [Enthay] illway IWAY eachtay ansgressorstray thyay aysway; andway innerssay allshay ebay onvertedcay untoway eethay.

14 Eliverday emay omfray oodguiltinessblay, OWAY Odgay, outhay Odgay ofway myay alvationsay: [andway] myay onguetay allshay ingsay aloudway ofway thyay ighteousnessray.

15 OWAY Ordlay, openway outhay myay ipslay; andway myay outhmay allshay ewshay orthfay thyay aisepray.

16 Orfay outhay esirestday otnay acrificesay; elseway ouldway IWAY ivegay [itway]: outhay elightestday otnay inway urntbay offeringway.

17 Ethay acrificessay ofway Odgay [areway] away okenbray iritspay: away okenbray andway away ontritecay earthay, OWAY Odgay, outhay iltway otnay espiseday.

18 Oday oodgay inway thyay oodgay easureplay untoway Ionzay: uildbay outhay ethay allsway ofway Erusalemjay.

19 Enthay altshay outhay ebay easedplay ithway ethay acrificessay ofway ighteousnessray, ithway urntbay offeringway andway olewhay urntbay offeringway: enthay allshay eythay offerway ullocksbay uponway inethay altarway.

ALMPSAY 52
Otay ethay iefchay Usicianmay, Aschilmay, [AWAY Almpsay] ofway Avidday, enwhay Oegday ethay Edomiteway amecay andway oldtay Aulsay, andway aidsay untoway imhay, Avidday isway omecay otay ethay ousehay ofway Ahimelechway.
1 Whyay oastestbay outhay elfthysay inway ischiefmay, OWAY ightymay anmay? ethay oodnessgay ofway Odgay [endurethway] ontinuallycay.
2 Thyay onguetay evisethday ischiefsmay; ikelay away arpshay azorray, orkingway eceitfullyday.
3 Outhay ovestlay evilway oremay anthay oodgay; [andway] inglyay atherray anthay otay eakspay ighteousnessray. Elahsay.
4 Outhay ovestlay allway evouringday ordsway, OWAY [outhay] eceitfulday onguetay.
5 Odgay allshay ikewiselay estroyday eethay orfay everway, ehay allshay aketay eethay awayway, andway uckplay eethay outway ofway [thyay] ellingdway aceplay, andway ootray eethay outway ofway ethay andlay ofway ethay ivinglay. Elahsay.
6 Ethay ighteousray alsoway allshay eesay, andway earfay, andway allshay aughlay atway imhay:
7 Olay, [isthay isway] ethay anmay [atthay] ademay otnay Odgay ishay engthstray; utbay ustedtray inway ethay abundanceway ofway ishay ichesray, [andway] engthenedstray imselfhay inway ishay ickednessway.
8 Utbay IWAY [amway] ikelay away eengray oliveway eetray inway ethay ousehay ofway Odgay: IWAY usttray inway ethay ercymay ofway Odgay orfay everway andway everway.
9 IWAY illway aisepray eethay orfay everway, ecausebay outhay asthay oneday [itway]: andway IWAY illway aitway onway thyay amenay; orfay [itway isway] oodgay eforebay thyay aintssay.

ALMPSAY 53
Otay ethay iefchay Usicianmay uponway Ahalathmay, Aschilmay, [AWAY Almpsay] ofway Avidday.
1 Ethay oolfay athhay aidsay inway ishay earthay, [Erethay isway] onay Odgay. Orruptcay areway eythay, andway avehay oneday abominableway iniquityway: [erethay isway] onenay atthay oethday oodgay.
2 Odgay ookedlay ownday omfray eavenhay uponway ethay ildrenchay ofway enmay, otay eesay ifway erethay ereway [anyway] atthay idday understandway, atthay idday eeksay Odgay.

3 Everyway oneway ofway emthay isway onegay ackbay: eythay areway altogetherway ecomebay ilthyfay; [erethay isway] onenay atthay oethday oodgay, onay, otnay oneway.

4 Avehay ethay orkersway ofway iniquityway onay owledgeknay? owhay eatway upway myay eoplepay [asway] eythay eatway eadbray: eythay avehay otnay alledcay uponway Odgay.

5 Erethay ereway eythay inway eatgray earfay, [erewhay] onay earfay asway: orfay Odgay athhay atteredscay ethay onesbay ofway imhay atthay encampethway [againstway] eethay: outhay asthay utpay [emthay] otay ameshay, ecausebay Odgay athhay espisedday emthay.

6 Ohway atthay ethay alvationsay ofway Israelway [ereway omecay] outway ofway Ionzay! Enwhay Odgay ingethbray ackbay ethay aptivitycay ofway ishay eoplepay, Acobjay allshay ejoiceray, [andway] Israelway allshay ebay adglay.

ALMPSAY 54
Otay ethay iefchay Usicianmay onway Eginothnay, Aschilmay, [AWAY Almpsay] ofway Avidday, enwhay ethay Iphimszay amecay andway aidsay otay Aulsay, Othday otnay Avidday idehay imselfhay ithway usway?

1 Avesay emay, OWAY Odgay, byay thyay amenay, andway udgejay emay byay thyay engthstray.

2 Earhay myay ayerpray, OWAY Odgay; ivegay earway otay ethay ordsway ofway myay outhmay.

3 Orfay angersstray areway isenray upway againstway emay, andway oppressorsway eeksay afterway myay oulsay: eythay avehay otnay etsay Odgay eforebay emthay. Elahsay.

4 Eholdbay, Odgay [isway] inemay elperhay: ethay Ordlay [isway] ithway emthay atthay upholdway myay oulsay.

5 Ehay allshay ewardray evilway untoway inemay enemiesway: utcay emthay offway inway thyay uthtray.

6 IWAY illway eelyfray acrificesay untoway eethay: IWAY illway aisepray thyay amenay, OWAY ORDLAY; orfay [itway isway] oodgay.

7 Orfay ehay athhay eliveredday emay outway ofway allway oubletray: andway inemay eyeway athhay eensay [ishay esireday] uponway inemay enemiesway.

ALMPSAY 55
Otay ethay iefchay Usicianmay onway Eginothnay, Aschilmay, [AWAY Almpsay] ofway Avidday.

1 Ivegay earway otay myay ayerpray, OWAY Odgay; andway idehay otnay elfthysay omfray myay upplicationsay.

2 Attendway untoway emay, andway earhay emay: IWAY ournmay inway myay omplaintcay, andway akemay away oisenay;

3 Ecausebay ofway ethay oicevay ofway ethay enemyway, ecausebay ofway ethay oppressionway ofway ethay ickedway: orfay eythay astcay iniquityway uponway emay, andway inway athwray eythay atehay emay.

4 Myay earthay isway oresay ainedpay ithinway emay: andway ethay errorstay ofway eathday areway allenfay uponway emay.

5 Earfulnessfay andway emblingtray areway omecay uponway emay, andway orrorhay athhay overwhelmedway emay.

6 Andway IWAY aidsay, Ohway atthay IWAY adhay ingsway ikelay away oveday! [orfay enthay] ouldway IWAY flyay awayway, andway ebay atway estray.

7 Olay, [enthay] ouldway IWAY anderway arfay offway, [andway] emainray inway ethay ildernessway. Elahsay.

8 IWAY ouldway astenhay myay escapeway omfray ethay indyway ormstay [andway] empesttay.

9 Estroyday, OWAY Ordlay, [andway] ivideday eirthay onguestay: orfay IWAY avehay eensay iolencevay andway ifestray inway ethay itycay.

10 Ayday andway ightnay eythay ogay aboutway itway uponway ethay allsway ereofthay: ischiefmay alsoway andway orrowsay [areway] inway ethay idstmay ofway itway.

11 Ickednessway [isway] inway ethay idstmay ereofthay: eceitday andway uilegay epartday otnay omfray erhay eetsstray.

12 Orfay [itway asway] otnay anway enemyway [atthay] eproachedray emay; enthay IWAY ouldcay avehay ornebay [itway]: eithernay [asway itway] ehay atthay atedhay emay [atthay] idday agnifymay [imselfhay] againstway emay; enthay IWAY ouldway avehay idhay elfmysay omfray imhay:

13 Utbay [itway asway] outhay, away anmay inemay equalway, myay uidegay, andway inemay acquaintanceway.

14 Eway ooktay eetsway ounselcay ogethertay, [andway] alkedway untoway ethay ousehay ofway Odgay inway ompanycay.

15 Etlay eathday eizesay uponway emthay, [andway] etlay emthay ogay ownday uickqay intoway ellhay: orfay ickednessway [isway] inway eirthay ellingsdway, [andway] amongway emthay.

16 Asway orfay emay, IWAY illway allcay uponway Odgay; andway ethay ORDLAY allshay avesay emay.

17 Eveningway, andway orningmay, andway atway oonnay, illway IWAY aypray, andway cryay aloudway: andway ehay allshay earhay myay oicevay.

18 Ehay athhay eliveredday myay oulsay inway eacepay omfray ethay attlebay [atthay asway] againstway emay: orfay erethay ereway anymay ithway emay.

19 Odgay allshay earhay, andway afflictway emthay, evenway ehay atthay abidethway ofway oldway. Elahsay. Ecausebay eythay avehay onay angeschay, ereforethay eythay earfay otnay Odgay.

20 Ehay athhay utpay orthfay ishay andshay againstway uchsay asway ebay atway eacepay ithway imhay: ehay athhay okenbray ishay ovenantcay.

21 [Ethay ordsway] ofway ishay outhmay ereway oothersmay anthay utterbay, utbay arway [asway] inway ishay earthay: ishay ordsway ereway oftersay anthay oilway, etyay [ereway] eythay awndray ordssway.

22 Astcay thyay urdenbay uponway ethay ORDLAY, andway ehay allshay ustainsay eethay: ehay allshay evernay uffersay ethay ighteousray otay ebay ovedmay.

23 Utbay outhay, OWAY Odgay, altshay ingbray emthay ownday intoway ethay itpay ofway estructionday: oodyblay andway eceitfulday enmay allshay otnay ivelay outway alfhay eirthay aysday; utbay IWAY illway usttray inway eethay.

ALMPSAY 56
Otay ethay iefchay Usicianmay uponway Onathjay-elemway-echokimray, Ichtammay ofway Avidday, enwhay ethay Ilistinesphay ooktay imhay inway Athgay.

1 Ebay ercifulmay untoway emay, OWAY Odgay: orfay anmay ouldway allowsway emay upway; ehay ightingfay ailyday oppressethway emay.

2 Inemay enemiesway ouldway ailyday allowsway [emay] upway: orfay [eythay ebay] anymay atthay ightfay againstway emay, OWAY outhay ostmay Ighhay.

3 Atwhay imetay IWAY amway afraidway, IWAY illway usttray inway eethay.

4 Inway Odgay IWAY illway aisepray ishay ordway, inway Odgay IWAY avehay utpay myay usttray; IWAY illway otnay earfay atwhay eshflay ancay oday untoway emay.

5 Everyway ayday eythay estwray myay ordsway: allway eirthay oughtsthay [areway] againstway emay orfay evilway.

6 Eythay athergay emselvesthay ogethertay, eythay idehay emselvesthay, eythay arkmay myay epsstay, enwhay eythay aitway orfay myay oulsay.
7 Allshay eythay escapeway byay iniquityway? inway [inethay] angerway astcay ownday ethay eoplepay, OWAY Odgay.
8 Outhay ellesttay myay anderingsway: utpay outhay myay earstay intoway thyay ottlebay: [areway eythay] otnay inway thyay ookbay?
9 Enwhay IWAY cryay [untoway eethay], enthay allshay inemay enemiesway urntay ackbay: isthay IWAY owknay; orfay Odgay [isway] orfay emay.
10 Inway Odgay illway IWAY aisepray [ishay] ordway: inway ethay ORDLAY illway IWAY aisepray [ishay] ordway.
11 Inway Odgay avehay IWAY utpay myay usttray: IWAY illway otnay ebay afraidway atwhay anmay ancay oday untoway emay.
12 Thyay owsvay [areway] uponway emay, OWAY Odgay: IWAY illway enderray aisespray untoway eethay.
13 Orfay outhay asthay eliveredday myay oulsay omfray eathday: [iltway] otnay [outhay eliverday] myay eetfay omfray allingfay, atthay IWAY aymay alkway eforebay Odgay inway ethay ightlay ofway ethay ivinglay?

ALMPSAY 57
Otay ethay iefchay Usicianmay, Alway-aschithtay, Ichtammay ofway Avidday, enwhay ehay edflay omfray Aulsay inway ethay avecay.
1 Ebay ercifulmay untoway emay, OWAY Odgay, ebay ercifulmay untoway emay: orfay myay oulsay usteththray inway eethay: eayay, inway ethay adowshay ofway thyay ingsway illway IWAY akemay myay efugeray, untilway [esethay] alamitiescay ebay overpastway.
2 IWAY illway cryay untoway Odgay ostmay ighhay; untoway Odgay atthay erformethpay [allway ingsthay] orfay emay.
3 Ehay allshay endsay omfray eavenhay, andway avesay emay [omfray] ethay eproachray ofway imhay atthay ouldway allowsway emay upway. Elahsay. Odgay allshay endsay orthfay ishay ercymay andway ishay uthtray.
4 Myay oulsay [isway] amongway ionslay: [andway] IWAY ielay [evenway amongway] emthay atthay areway etsay onway irefay, [evenway] ethay onssay ofway enmay, osewhay eethtay [areway] earsspay andway arrowsway, andway eirthay onguetay away arpshay ordsway.
5 Ebay outhay exaltedway, OWAY Odgay, aboveway ethay eavenshay; [etlay] thyay oryglay [ebay] aboveway allway ethay earthway.
6 Eythay avehay eparedpray away etnay orfay myay epsstay; myay oulsay isway owedbay ownday: eythay avehay iggedday away itpay eforebay

emay, intoway ethay idstmay ereofwhay eythay areway allenfay [emselvesthay]. Elahsay.

7 Myay earthay isway ixedfay, OWAY Odgay, myay earthay isway ixedfay: IWAY illway ingsay andway ivegay aisepray.

8 Awakeway upway, myay oryglay; awakeway, alterypsay andway arphay: IWAY [elfmysay] illway awakeway earlyway.

9 IWAY illway aisepray eethay, OWAY Ordlay, amongway ethay eoplepay: IWAY illway ingsay untoway eethay amongway ethay ationsnay.

10 Orfay thyay ercymay [isway] eatgray untoway ethay eavenshay, andway thyay uthtray untoway ethay oudsclay.

11 Ebay outhay exaltedway, OWAY Odgay, aboveway ethay eavenshay: [etlay] thyay oryglay [ebay] aboveway allway ethay earthway.

ALMPSAY 58

Otay ethay iefchay Usicianmay, Alway-aschithtay, Ichtammay ofway Avidday.

1 Oday eyay indeedway eakspay ighteousnessray, OWAY ongregationcay? oday eyay udgejay uprightlyway, OWAY eyay onssay ofway enmay?

2 Eayay, inway earthay eyay orkway ickednessway; eyay eighway ethay iolencevay ofway ouryay andshay inway ethay earthway.

3 Ethay ickedway areway estrangedway omfray ethay ombway: eythay ogay astrayway asway oonsay asway eythay ebay ornbay, eakingspay ieslay.

4 Eirthay oisonpay [isway] ikelay ethay oisonpay ofway away erpentsay: [eythay areway] ikelay ethay eafday adderway [atthay] oppethstay erhay earway;

5 Ichwhay illway otnay earkenhay otay ethay oicevay ofway armerschay, armingchay evernay osay iselyway.

6 Eakbray eirthay eethtay, OWAY Odgay, inway eirthay outhmay: eakbray outway ethay eatgray eethtay ofway ethay oungyay ionslay, OWAY ORDLAY.

7 Etlay emthay eltmay awayway asway atersway [ichwhay] unray ontinuallycay: [enwhay] ehay endethbay [ishay owbay otay ootshay] ishay arrowsway, etlay emthay ebay asway utcay inway iecespay.

8 Asway away ailsnay [ichwhay] eltethmay, etlay [everyway oneway ofway emthay] asspay awayway: [ikelay] ethay untimelyway irthbay ofway away omanway, [atthay] eythay aymay otnay eesay ethay unsay.

9 Eforebay ouryay otspay ancay eelfay ethay ornsthay, ehay allshay aketay emthay awayway asway ithway away irlwindwhay, othbay ivinglay, andway inway [ishay] athwray.

10 Ethay ighteousray allshay ejoiceray enwhay ehay eethsay ethay engeancevay: ehay allshay ashway ishay eetfay inway ethay oodblay ofway ethay ickedway.

11 Osay atthay away anmay allshay aysay, Erilyvay [erethay isway] away ewardray orfay ethay ighteousray: erilyvay ehay isway away Odgay atthay udgethjay inway ethay earthway.

ALMPSAY 59

Otay ethay iefchay Usicianmay, Alway-aschithtay, Ichtammay ofway Avidday; enwhay Aulsay entsay, andway eythay atchedway ethay ousehay otay illkay imhay.

1 Eliverday emay omfray inemay enemiesway, OWAY myay Odgay: efendday emay omfray emthay atthay iseray upway againstway emay.

2 Eliverday emay omfray ethay orkersway ofway iniquityway, andway avesay emay omfray oodyblay enmay.

3 Orfay, olay, eythay ielay inway aitway orfay myay oulsay: ethay ightymay areway atheredgay againstway emay; otnay [orfay] myay ansgressiontray, ornay [orfay] myay insay, OWAY ORDLAY.

4 Eythay unray andway eparepray emselvesthay ithoutway [myay] aultfay: awakeway otay elphay emay, andway eholdbay.

5 Outhay ereforethay, OWAY ORDLAY Odgay ofway ostshay, ethay Odgay ofway Israelway, awakeway otay isitvay allway ethay eathenhay: ebay otnay ercifulmay otay anyway ickedway ansgressorstray. Elahsay.

6 Eythay eturnray atway eveningway: eythay akemay away oisenay ikelay away ogday, andway ogay oundray aboutway ethay itycay.

7 Eholdbay, eythay elchbay outway ithway eirthay outhmay: ordssway [areway] inway eirthay ipslay: orfay owhay, [aysay eythay], othday earhay?

8 Utbay outhay, OWAY ORDLAY, altshay aughlay atway emthay; outhay altshay avehay allway ethay eathenhay inway erisionday.

9 [Ecausebay ofway] ishay engthstray illway IWAY aitway uponway eethay: orfay Odgay [isway] myay efenceday.

10 Ethay Odgay ofway myay ercymay allshay eventpray emay: Odgay allshay etlay emay eesay [myay esireday] uponway inemay enemiesway.

11 Ayslay emthay otnay, estlay myay eoplepay orgetfay: atterscay emthay byay thyay owerpay; andway ingbray emthay ownday, OWAY Ordlay ourway ieldshay.

12 [Orfay] ethay insay ofway eirthay outhmay [andway] ethay ordsway ofway eirthay ipslay etlay emthay evenway ebay akentay inway eirthay idepray: andway orfay ursingcay andway inglyay [ichwhay] eythay eakspay.

13 Onsumecay [emthay] inway athwray, onsumecay [emthay], atthay eythay [aymay] otnay [ebay]: andway etlay emthay owknay atthay Odgay ulethray inway Acobjay untoway ethay endsway ofway ethay earthway. Elahsay.

14 Andway atway eveningway etlay emthay eturnray; [andway] etlay emthay akemay away oisenay ikelay away ogday, andway ogay oundray aboutway ethay itycay.

15 Etlay emthay anderway upway andway ownday orfay eatmay, andway udgegray ifway eythay ebay otnay atisfiedsay.

16 Utbay IWAY illway ingsay ofway thyay owerpay; eayay, IWAY illway ingsay aloudway ofway thyay ercymay inway ethay orningmay: orfay outhay asthay eenbay myay efenceday andway efugeray inway ethay ayday ofway myay oubletray.

17 Untoway eethay, OWAY myay engthstray, illway IWAY ingsay: orfay Odgay [isway] myay efenceday, [andway] ethay Odgay ofway myay ercymay.

ALMPSAY 60

Otay ethay iefchay Usicianmay uponway Ushanshay-eduthway, Ichtammay ofway Avidday, otay eachtay; enwhay ehay ovestray ithway Aramway-aharaimnay andway ithway Aramway-obahzay, enwhay Oabjay eturnedray, andway otesmay ofway Edomway inway ethay alleyvay ofway altsay elvetway ousandthay.

1 OWAY Odgay, outhay asthay astcay usway offway, outhay asthay atteredscay usway, outhay asthay eenbay ispleasedday; OWAY urntay elfthysay otay usway againway.

2 Outhay asthay ademay ethay earthway otay embletray; outhay asthay okenbray itway: ealhay ethay eachesbray ereofthay; orfay itway akethshay.

3 Outhay asthay ewedshay thyay eoplepay ardhay ingsthay: outhay asthay ademay usway otay inkdray ethay ineway ofway astonishmentway.

4 Outhay asthay ivengay away annerbay otay emthay atthay earfay eethay, atthay itway aymay ebay isplayedday ecausebay ofway ethay uthtray. Elahsay.

5 Atthay thyay elovedbay aymay ebay eliveredday; avesay [ithway] thyay ightray andhay, andway earhay emay.

6 Odgay athhay okenspay inway ishay olinesshay; IWAY illway ejoiceray, IWAY illway ivideday Echemshay, andway etemay outway ethay alleyvay ofway Uccothsay.

7 Ileadgay [isway] inemay, andway Anassehmay [isway] inemay; Ephraimway alsoway [isway] ethay engthstray ofway inemay eadhay; Udahjay [isway] myay awgiverlay;

8 Oabmay [isway] myay ashpotway; overway Edomway illway IWAY astcay outway myay oeshay: Ilistiaphay, iumphtray outhay ecausebay ofway emay.

9 Owhay illway ingbray emay [intoway] ethay ongstray itycay? owhay illway eadlay emay intoway Edomway?

10 [Iltway] otnay outhay, OWAY Odgay, [ichwhay] adsthay astcay usway offway? andway [outhay], OWAY Odgay, [ichwhay] idstday otnay ogay outway ithway ourway armiesway?

11 Ivegay usway elphay omfray oubletray: orfay ainvay [isway] ethay elphay ofway anmay.

12 Oughthray Odgay eway allshay oday aliantlyvay: orfay ehay [itway isway atthay] allshay eadtray ownday ourway enemiesway.

ALMPSAY 61

Otay ethay iefchay Usicianmay uponway Eginahnay, [AWAY Almpsay] ofway Avidday.

1 Earhay myay cryay, OWAY Odgay; attendway untoway myay ayerpray.

2 Omfray ethay endway ofway ethay earthway illway IWAY cryay untoway eethay, enwhay myay earthay isway overwhelmedway: eadlay emay otay ethay ockray [atthay] isway igherhay anthay IWAY.

3 Orfay outhay asthay eenbay away eltershay orfay emay, [andway] away ongstray owertay omfray ethay enemyway.

4 IWAY illway abideway inway thyay abernacletay orfay everway: IWAY illway usttray inway ethay overtcay ofway thyay ingsway. Elahsay.

5 Orfay outhay, OWAY Odgay, asthay eardhay myay owsvay: outhay asthay ivengay [emay] ethay eritagehay ofway osethay atthay earfay thyay amenay.

6 Outhay iltway olongpray ethay ingkay'say ifelay: [andway] ishay earsyay asway anymay enerationsgay.

7 Ehay allshay abideway eforebay Odgay orfay everway: OWAY eparepray ercymay andway uthtray, [ichwhay] aymay eservepray imhay.

8 Osay illway IWAY ingsay aisepray untoway thyay amenay orfay everway, atthay IWAY aymay ailyday erformpay myay owsvay.

ALMPSAY 62

Otay ethay iefchay Usicianmay, otay Eduthunjay, AWAY Almpsay ofway Avidday.

1 Ulytray myay oulsay aitethway uponway Odgay: omfray imhay [omethcay] myay alvationsay.

2 Ehay onlyway [isway] myay ockray andway myay alvationsay; [ehay isway] myay efenceday; IWAY allshay otnay ebay eatlygray ovedmay.

3 Owhay onglay illway eyay imagineway ischiefmay againstway away anmay? eyay allshay ebay ainslay allway ofway ouyay: asway away owingbay allway [allshay eyay ebay, andway asway] away otteringtay encefay.

4 Eythay onlyway onsultcay otay astcay [imhay] ownday omfray ishay excellencyway: eythay elightday inway ieslay: eythay essblay ithway eirthay outhmay, utbay eythay ursecay inwardlyway. Elahsay.

5 Myay oulsay, aitway outhay onlyway uponway Odgay; orfay myay expectationway [isway] omfray imhay.

6 Ehay onlyway [isway] myay ockray andway myay alvationsay: [ehay isway] myay efenceday; IWAY allshay otnay ebay ovedmay.

7 Inway Odgay [isway] myay alvationsay andway myay oryglay: ethay ockray ofway myay engthstray, [andway] myay efugeray, [isway] inway Odgay.

8 Usttray inway imhay atway allway imestay; [eyay] eoplepay, ourpay outway ouryay earthay eforebay imhay: Odgay [isway] away efugeray orfay usway. Elahsay.

9 Urelysay enmay ofway owlay egreeday [areway] anityvay, [andway] enmay ofway ighhay egreeday [areway] away ielay: otay ebay aidlay inway ethay alancebay, eythay [areway] altogetherway [ighterlay] anthay anityvay.

10 Usttray otnay inway oppressionway, andway ecomebay otnay ainvay inway obberyray: ifway ichesray increaseway, etsay otnay ouryay earthay [uponway emthay].

11 Odgay athhay okenspay onceway; icetway avehay IWAY eardhay isthay; atthay owerpay [elongethbay] untoway Odgay.

12 Alsoway untoway eethay, OWAY Ordlay, [elongethbay] ercymay: orfay outhay enderestray otay everyway anmay accordingway otay ishay orkway.

ALMPSAY 63

AWAY Almpsay ofway Avidday, enwhay ehay asway inway ethay ildernessway ofway Udahjay.

1 OWAY Odgay, outhay [artway] myay Odgay; earlyway illway IWAY eeksay eethay: myay oulsay irsteththay orfay eethay, myay eshflay ongethlay orfay eethay inway away dryay andway irstythay andlay, erewhay onay aterway isway;

2 Otay eesay thyay owerpay andway thyay oryglay, osay [asway] IWAY avehay eensay eethay inway ethay anctuarysay.

3 Ecausebay thyay ovingkindnesslay [isway] etterbay anthay ifelay, myay ipslay allshay aisepray eethay.

4 Usthay illway IWAY essblay eethay ilewhay IWAY ivelay: IWAY illway iftlay upway myay andshay inway thyay amenay.

5 Myay oulsay allshay ebay atisfiedsay asway [ithway] arrowmay andway atnessfay; andway myay outhmay allshay aisepray [eethay] ithway oyfuljay ipslay:

6 Enwhay IWAY ememberray eethay uponway myay edbay, [andway] editatemay onway eethay inway ethay [ightnay] atchesway.

7 Ecausebay outhay asthay eenbay myay elphay, ereforethay inway ethay adowshay ofway thyay ingsway illway IWAY ejoiceray.

8 Myay oulsay ollowethfay ardhay afterway eethay: thyay ightray andhay upholdethway emay.

9 Utbay osethay [atthay] eeksay myay oulsay, otay estroyday [itway], allshay ogay intoway ethay owerlay artspay ofway ethay earthway.

10 Eythay allshay allfay byay ethay ordsway: eythay allshay ebay away ortionpay orfay oxesfay.

11 Utbay ethay ingkay allshay ejoiceray inway Odgay; everyway oneway atthay earethsway byay imhay allshay oryglay: utbay ethay outhmay ofway emthay atthay eakspay ieslay allshay ebay oppedstay.

ALMPSAY 64

Otay ethay iefchay Usicianmay, AWAY Almpsay ofway Avidday.

1 Earhay myay oicevay, OWAY Odgay, inway myay ayerpray: eservepray myay ifelay omfray earfay ofway ethay enemyway.

2 Idehay emay omfray ethay ecretsay ounselcay ofway ethay ickedway; omfray ethay insurrectionway ofway ethay orkersway ofway iniquityway:

3 Owhay etwhay eirthay onguetay ikelay away ordsway, [andway] endbay [eirthay owsbay otay ootshay] eirthay arrowsway, [evenway] itterbay ordsway:

4 Atthay eythay aymay ootshay inway ecretsay atway ethay erfectpay: uddenlysay oday eythay ootshay atway imhay, andway earfay otnay.

5 Eythay encourageway emselvesthay [inway] anway evilway attermay: eythay ommunecay ofway ayinglay aressnay ivilypray; eythay aysay, Owhay allshay eesay emthay?

6 Eythay earchsay outway iniquitiesway; eythay accomplishway away iligentday earchsay: othbay ethay inwardway [oughtthay] ofway everyway oneway [ofway emthay], andway ethay earthay, [isway] eepday.

7 Utbay Odgay allshay ootshay atway emthay [ithway] anway arrowway; uddenlysay allshay eythay ebay oundedway.

8 Osay eythay allshay akemay eirthay ownway onguetay otay allfay uponway emselvesthay: allway atthay eesay emthay allshay eeflay awayway.

9 Andway allway enmay allshay earfay, andway allshay eclareday ethay orkway ofway Odgay; orfay eythay allshay iselyway onsidercay ofway ishay oingday.

10 Ethay ighteousray allshay ebay adglay inway ethay ORDLAY, andway allshay usttray inway imhay; andway allway ethay uprightway inway earthay allshay oryglay.

ALMPSAY 65
Otay ethay iefchay Usicianmay, AWAY Almpsay [andway] Ongsay ofway Avidday.

1 Aisepray aitethway orfay eethay, OWAY Odgay, inway Ionsay: andway untoway eethay allshay ethay owvay ebay erformedpay.

2 OWAY outhay atthay earesthay ayerpray, untoway eethay allshay allway eshflay omecay.

3 Iniquitiesway evailpray againstway emay: [asway orfay] ourway ansgressionstray, outhay altshay urgepay emthay awayway.

4 Essedblay [isway ethay anmay omwhay] outhay oosestchay, andway ausestcay otay approachway [untoway eethay, atthay] ehay aymay elldway inway thyay ourtscay: eway allshay ebay atisfiedsay ithway ethay oodnessgay ofway thyay ousehay, [evenway] ofway thyay olyhay empletay.

5 [Byay] erribletay ingsthay inway ighteousnessray iltway outhay answerway usway, OWAY Odgay ofway ourway alvationsay; [owhay artway] ethay onfidencecay ofway allway ethay endsway ofway ethay earthway, andway ofway emthay atthay areway afarway offway [uponway] ethay easay:

6 Ichwhay byay ishay engthstray ettethsay astfay ethay ountainsmay; [eingbay] irdedgay ithway owerpay:
7 Ichwhay illethstay ethay oisenay ofway ethay eassay, ethay oisenay ofway eirthay avesway, andway ethay umulttay ofway ethay eoplepay.
8 Eythay alsoway atthay elldway inway ethay uttermostway artspay areway afraidway atway thyay okenstay: outhay akestmay ethay outgoingsway ofway ethay orningmay andway eveningway otay ejoiceray.
9 Outhay isitestvay ethay earthway, andway aterestway itway: outhay eatlygray enrichestway itway ithway ethay iverray ofway Odgay, [ichwhay] isway ullfay ofway aterway: outhay eparestpray emthay orncay, enwhay outhay asthay osay ovidedpray orfay itway.
10 Outhay aterestway ethay idgesray ereofthay abundantlyway: outhay ettlestsay ethay urrowsfay ereofthay: outhay akestmay itway oftsay ithway owersshay: outhay essestblay ethay ingingspray ereofthay.
11 Outhay ownestcray ethay earyay ithway thyay oodnessgay; andway thyay athspay opdray atnessfay.
12 Eythay opdray [uponway] ethay asturespay ofway ethay ildernessway: andway ethay ittlelay illshay ejoiceray onway everyway idesay.
13 Ethay asturespay areway othedclay ithway ocksflay; ethay alleysvay alsoway areway overedcay overway ithway orncay; eythay outshay orfay oyjay, eythay alsoway ingsay.

ALMPSAY 66
Otay ethay iefchay Usicianmay, AWAY Ongsay [orway] Almpsay.
1 Akemay away oyfuljay oisenay untoway Odgay, allway eyay andslay:
2 Ingsay orthfay ethay onourhay ofway ishay amenay: akemay ishay aisepray oriousglay.
3 Aysay untoway Odgay, Owhay erribletay [artway outhay inway] thyay orksway! oughthray ethay eatnessgray ofway thyay owerpay allshay inethay enemiesway ubmitsay emselvesthay untoway eethay.
4 Allway ethay earthway allshay orshipway eethay, andway allshay ingsay untoway eethay; eythay allshay ingsay [otay] thyay amenay. Elahsay.
5 Omecay andway eesay ethay orksway ofway Odgay: [ehay isway] erribletay [inway ishay] oingday owardtay ethay ildrenchay ofway enmay.
6 Ehay urnedtay ethay easay intoway dryay [andlay]: eythay entway oughthray ethay oodflay onway ootfay: erethay idday eway ejoiceray inway imhay.
7 Ehay ulethray byay ishay owerpay orfay everway; ishay eyesway eholdbay ethay ationsnay: etlay otnay ethay ebelliousray exaltway emselvesthay. Elahsay.

8 OWAY essblay ourway Odgay, eyay eoplepay, andway akemay ethay oicevay ofway ishay aisepray otay ebay eardhay:
9 Ichwhay oldethhay ourway oulsay inway ifelay, andway ufferethsay otnay ourway eetfay otay ebay ovedmay.
10 Orfay outhay, OWAY Odgay, asthay ovedpray usway: outhay asthay iedtray usway, asway ilversay isway iedtray.
11 Outhay oughtestbray usway intoway ethay etnay; outhay aidstlay afflictionway uponway ourway oinslay.
12 Outhay asthay ausedcay enmay otay ideray overway ourway eadshay; eway entway oughthray irefay andway oughthray aterway: utbay outhay oughtestbray usway outway intoway away ealthyway [aceplay].
13 IWAY illway ogay intoway thyay ousehay ithway urntbay offeringsway: IWAY illway aypay eethay myay owsvay,
14 Ichwhay myay ipslay avehay utteredway, andway myay outhmay athhay okenspay, enwhay IWAY asway inway oubletray.
15 IWAY illway offerway untoway eethay urntbay acrificessay ofway atlingsfay, ithway ethay incenseway ofway amsray; IWAY illway offerway ullocksbay ithway oatsgay. Elahsay.
16 Omecay [andway] earhay, allway eyay atthay earfay Odgay, andway IWAY illway eclareday atwhay ehay athhay oneday orfay myay oulsay.
17 IWAY iedcray untoway imhay ithway myay outhmay, andway ehay asway extolledway ithway myay onguetay.
18 Ifway IWAY egardray iniquityway inway myay earthay, ethay Ordlay illway otnay earhay [emay]:
19 [Utbay] erilyvay Odgay athhay eardhay [emay]; ehay athhay attendedway otay ethay oicevay ofway myay ayerpray.
20 Essedblay [ebay] Odgay, ichwhay athhay otnay urnedtay awayway myay ayerpray, ornay ishay ercymay omfray emay.

ALMPSAY 67
Otay ethay iefchay Usicianmay onway Eginothnay, AWAY Almpsay [orway] Ongsay.
1 Odgay ebay ercifulmay untoway usway, andway essblay usway; [andway] ausecay ishay acefay otay ineshay uponway usway; Elahsay.
2 Atthay thyay ayway aymay ebay ownknay uponway earthway, thyay avingsay ealthhay amongway allway ationsnay.
3 Etlay ethay eoplepay aisepray eethay, OWAY Odgay; etlay allway ethay eoplepay aisepray eethay.

4 OWAY etlay ethay ationsnay ebay adglay andway ingsay orfay oyjay: orfay outhay altshay udgejay ethay eoplepay ighteouslyray, andway overngay ethay ationsnay uponway earthway. Elahsay.

5 Etlay ethay eoplepay aisepray eethay, OWAY Odgay; etlay allway ethay eoplepay aisepray eethay.

6 [Enthay] allshay ethay earthway ieldyay erhay increaseway; [andway] Odgay, [evenway] ourway ownway Odgay, allshay essblay usway.

7 Odgay allshay essblay usway; andway allway ethay endsway ofway ethay earthway allshay earfay imhay.

ALMPSAY 68

Otay ethay iefchay Usicianmay, AWAY Almpsay [orway] Ongsay ofway Avidday.

1 Etlay Odgay ariseway, etlay ishay enemiesway ebay atteredscay: etlay emthay alsoway atthay atehay imhay eeflay eforebay imhay.

2 Asway okesmay isway ivendray awayway, [osay] ivedray [emthay] awayway: asway axway eltethmay eforebay ethay irefay, [osay] etlay ethay ickedway erishpay atway ethay esencepray ofway Odgay.

3 Utbay etlay ethay ighteousray ebay adglay; etlay emthay ejoiceray eforebay Odgay: eayay, etlay emthay exceedinglyway ejoiceray.

4 Ingsay untoway Odgay, ingsay aisespray otay ishay amenay: extolway imhay atthay idethray uponway ethay eavenshay byay ishay amenay AHJAY, andway ejoiceray eforebay imhay.

5 AWAY atherfay ofway ethay atherlessfay, andway away udgejay ofway ethay idowsway, [isway] Odgay inway ishay olyhay abitationhay.

6 Odgay ettethsay ethay olitarysay inway amiliesfay: ehay ingethbray outway osethay ichwhay areway oundbay ithway ainschay: utbay ethay ebelliousray elldway inway away dryay [andlay].

7 OWAY Odgay, enwhay outhay entestway orthfay eforebay thyay eoplepay, enwhay outhay idstday archmay oughthray ethay ildernessway; Elahsay:

8 Ethay earthway ookshay, ethay eavenshay alsoway oppeddray atway ethay esencepray ofway Odgay: [evenway] Inaisay itselfway [asway ovedmay] atway ethay esencepray ofway Odgay, ethay Odgay ofway Israelway.

9 Outhay, OWAY Odgay, idstday endsay away entifulplay ainray, erebywhay outhay idstday onfirmcay inethay inheritanceway, enwhay itway asway earyway.

10 Thyay ongregationcay athhay eltdway ereinthay: outhay, OWAY Odgay, asthay eparedpray ofway thyay oodnessgay orfay ethay oorpay.

11 Ethay Ordlay avegay ethay ordway: eatgray [asway] ethay ompanycay ofway osethay atthay ublishedpay [itway].

12 Ingskay ofway armiesway idday eeflay apaceway: andway eshay atthay arriedtay atway omehay ividedday ethay oilspay.

13 Oughthay eyay avehay ienlay amongway ethay otspay, [etyay allshay eyay ebay asway] ethay ingsway ofway away oveday overedcay ithway ilversay, andway erhay eathersfay ithway ellowyay oldgay.

14 Enwhay ethay Almightyway atteredscay ingskay inway itway, itway asway [itewhay] asway owsnay inway Almonsay.

15 Ethay illhay ofway Odgay [isway asway] ethay illhay ofway Ashanbay; anway ighhay illhay [asway] ethay illhay ofway Ashanbay.

16 Whyay eaplay eyay, eyay ighhay illshay? [isthay isway] ethay illhay [ichwhay] Odgay esirethday otay elldway inway; eayay, ethay ORDLAY illway elldway [inway itway] orfay everway.

17 Ethay ariotschay ofway Odgay [areway] entytway ousandthay, [evenway] ousandsthay ofway angelsway: ethay Ordlay [isway] amongway emthay, [asway inway] Inaisay, inway ethay olyhay [aceplay].

18 Outhay asthay ascendedway onway ighhay, outhay asthay edlay aptivitycay aptivecay: outhay asthay eceivedray iftsgay orfay enmay; eayay, [orfay] ethay ebelliousray alsoway, atthay ethay ORDLAY Odgay ightmay elldway [amongway emthay].

19 Essedblay [ebay] ethay Ordlay, [owhay] ailyday oadethlay usway [ithway enefitsbay, evenway] ethay Odgay ofway ourway alvationsay. Elahsay.

20 [Ehay atthay isway] ourway Odgay [isway] ethay Odgay ofway alvationsay; andway untoway ODGAY ethay Ordlay [elongbay] ethay issuesway omfray eathday.

21 Utbay Odgay allshay oundway ethay eadhay ofway ishay enemiesway, [andway] ethay airyhay alpscay ofway uchsay anway oneway asway oethgay onway illstay inway ishay espassestray.

22 Ethay Ordlay aidsay, IWAY illway ingbray againway omfray Ashanbay, IWAY illway ingbray [myay eoplepay] againway omfray ethay epthsday ofway ethay easay:

23 Atthay thyay ootfay aymay ebay ippedday inway ethay oodblay ofway [inethay] enemiesway, [andway] ethay onguetay ofway thyay ogsday inway ethay amesay.

24 Eythay avehay eensay thyay oingsgay, OWAY Odgay; [evenway] ethay oingsgay ofway myay Odgay, myay Ingkay, inway ethay anctuarysay.

25 Ethay ingerssay entway eforebay, ethay ayersplay onway instrumentsway [ollowedfay] afterway; amongway [emthay ereway] ethay amselsday ayingplay ithway imbrelstay.
26 Essblay eyay Odgay inway ethay ongregationscay, [evenway] ethay Ordlay, omfray ethay ountainfay ofway Israelway.
27 Erethay [isway] ittlelay Enjaminbay [ithway] eirthay ulerray, ethay incespray ofway Udahjay [andway] eirthay ouncilcay, ethay incespray ofway Ebulunzay, [andway] ethay incespray ofway Aphtalinay.
28 Thyay Odgay athhay ommandedcay thyay engthstray: engthenstray, OWAY Odgay, atthay ichwhay outhay asthay oughtwray orfay usway.
29 Ecausebay ofway thyay empletay atway Erusalemjay allshay ingskay ingbray esentspray untoway eethay.
30 Ebukeray ethay ompanycay ofway earmenspay, ethay ultitudemay ofway ethay ullsbay, ithway ethay alvescay ofway ethay eoplepay, [illtay everyway oneway] ubmitsay imselffhay ithway iecespay ofway ilversay: atterscay outhay ethay eoplepay [atthay] elightday inway arway.
31 Incespray allshay omecay outway ofway Egyptway; Ethiopiaway allshay oonsay etchstray outway erhay andshay untoway Odgay.
32 Ingsay untoway Odgay, eyay ingdomskay ofway ethay earthway; OWAY ingsay aisespray untoway ethay Ordlay; Elahsay:
33 Otay imhay atthay idethray uponway ethay eavenshay ofway eavenshay, [ichwhay ereway] ofway oldway; olay, ehay othday endsay outway ishay oicevay, [andway atthay] away ightymay oicevay.
34 Ascribeway eyay engthstray untoway Odgay: ishay excellencyway [isway] overway Israelway, andway ishay engthstray [isway] inway ethay oudsclay.
35 OWAY Odgay, [outhay artway] erribletay outway ofway thyay olyhay acesplay: ethay Odgay ofway Israelway [isway] ehay atthay ivethgay engthstray andway owerpay untoway [ishay] eoplepay. Essedblay [ebay] Odgay.

ALMPSAY 69
Otay ethay iefchay Usicianmay uponway Oshannimshay, [AWAY Almpsay] ofway Avidday.
1 Avesay emay, OWAY Odgay; orfay ethay atersway areway omecay inway untoway [myay] oulsay.
2 IWAY inksay inway eepday iremay, erewhay [erethay isway] onay andingstay: IWAY amway omecay intoway eepday atersway, erewhay ethay oodsflay overflowway emay.

3 IWAY amway earyway ofway myay ingcryay: myay oatthray isway ieddray: inemay eyesway ailfay ilewhay IWAY aitway orfay myay Odgay.

4 Eythay atthay atehay emay ithoutway away ausecay areway oremay anthay ethay airshay ofway inemay eadhay: eythay atthay ouldway estroyday emay, [eingbay] inemay enemiesway ongfullywray, areway ightymay: enthay IWAY estoredray [atthay] ichwhay IWAY ooktay otnay awayway.

5 OWAY Odgay, outhay owestknay myay oolishnessfay; andway myay inssay areway otnay idhay omfray eethay.

6 Etlay otnay emthay atthay aitway onway eethay, OWAY Ordlay ODGAY ofway ostshay, ebay ashamedway orfay myay akesay: etlay otnay osethay atthay eeksay eethay ebay onfoundedcay orfay myay akesay, OWAY Odgay ofway Israelway.

7 Ecausebay orfay thyay akesay IWAY avehay ornebay eproachray; ameshay athhay overedcay myay acefay.

8 IWAY amway ecomebay away angerstray untoway myay ethrenbray, andway anway alienway untoway myay othermay'say ildrenchay.

9 Orfay ethay ealzay ofway inethay ousehay athhay eatenway emay upway; andway ethay eproachesray ofway emthay atthay eproachedray eethay areway allenfay uponway emay.

10 Enwhay IWAY eptway, [andway astenedchay] myay oulsay ithway astingfay, atthay asway otay myay eproachray.

11 IWAY ademay ackclothsay alsoway myay armentgay; andway IWAY ecamebay away overbpray otay emthay.

12 Eythay atthay itsay inway ethay ategay eakspay againstway emay; andway IWAY [asway] ethay ongsay ofway ethay unkardsdray.

13 Utbay asway orfay emay, myay ayerpray [isway] untoway eethay, OWAY ORDLAY, [inway] anway acceptableway imetay: OWAY Odgay, inway ethay ultitudemay ofway thyay ercymay earhay emay, inway ethay uthtray ofway thyay alvationsay.

14 Eliverday emay outway ofway ethay iremay, andway etlay emay otnay inksay: etlay emay ebay eliveredday omfray emthay atthay atehay emay, andway outway ofway ethay eepday aterssway.

15 Etlay otnay ethay aterfloodway overflowway emay, eithernay etlay ethay eepday allowsway emay upway, andway etlay otnay ethay itpay utshay erhay outhmay uponway emay.

16 Earhay emay, OWAY ORDLAY; orfay thyay ovingkindnesslay [isway] oodgay: urntay untoway emay accordingway otay ethay ultitudemay ofway thyay endertay erciesmay.

17 Andway idehay otnay thyay acefay omfray thyay ervantsay; orfay IWAY amway inway oubletray: earhay emay eedilyspay.

18 Awdray ighnay untoway myay oulsay, [andway] edeemray itway: eliverday emay ecausebay ofway inemay enemiesway.

19 Outhay asthay ownknay myay eproachray, andway myay ameshay, andway myay ishonourday: inemay adversariesway [areway] allway eforebay eethay.

20 Eproachray athhay okenbray myay earthay; andway IWAY amway ullfay ofway eavinesshay: andway IWAY ookedlay [orfay omesay] otay aketay itypay, utbay [erethay asway] onenay; andway orfay omforterscay, utbay IWAY oundfay onenay.

21 Eythay avegay emay alsoway allgay orfay myay eatmay; andway inway myay irstthay eythay avegay emay inegarvay otay inkdray.

22 Etlay eirthay abletay ecomebay away aresnay eforebay emthay: andway [atthay ichwhay ouldshay avehay eenbay] orfay [eirthay] elfareway, [etlay itway ecomebay] away aptray.

23 Etlay eirthay eyesway ebay arkenedday, atthay eythay eesay otnay; andway akemay eirthay oinslay ontinuallycay otay akeshay.

24 Ourpay outway inethay indignationway uponway emthay, andway etlay thyay athfulwray angerway aketay oldhay ofway emthay.

25 Etlay eirthay abitationhay ebay esolateday; [andway] etlay onenay elldway inway eirthay entstay.

26 Orfay eythay ersecutepay [imhay] omwhay outhay asthay ittensmay; andway eythay alktay otay ethay iefgray ofway osethay omwhay outhay asthay oundedway.

27 Addway iniquityway untoway eirthay iniquityway: andway etlay emthay otnay omecay intoway thyay ighteousnessray.

28 Etlay emthay ebay ottedblay outway ofway ethay ookbay ofway ethay ivinglay, andway otnay ebay ittenwray ithway ethay ighteousray.

29 Utbay IWAY [amway] oorpay andway orrowfulsay: etlay thyay alvationsay, OWAY Odgay, etsay emay upway onway ighhay.

30 IWAY illway aisepray ethay amenay ofway Odgay ithway away ongsay, andway illway agnifymay imhay ithway anksgivingthay.

31 [Isthay] alsoway allshay easeplay ethay ORDLAY etterbay anthay anway oxway [orway] ullockbay atthay athhay ornshay andway oofshay.

32 Ethay umblehay allshay eesay [isthay, andway] ebay adglay: andway ouryay earthay allshay ivelay atthay eeksay Odgay.

33 Orfay ethay ORDLAY earethhay ethay oorpay, andway espisethday otnay ishay isonerspray.

34 Etlay ethay eavenhay andway earthway aisepray imhay, ethay eassay, andway everyway ingthay atthay ovethmay ereinthay.

35 Orfay Odgay illway avesay Ionzay, andway illway uildbay ethay itiescay ofway Udahjay: atthay eythay aymay elldway erethay, andway avehay itway inway ossessionpay.

36 Ethay eedsay alsoway ofway ishay ervantssay allshay inheritway itway: andway eythay atthay ovelay ishay amenay allshay elldway ereinthay.

ALMPSAY 70
Otay ethay iefchay Usicianmay, [AWAY Almpsay] ofway Avidday, otay ingbray otay emembranceray.

1 [Akemay astehay], OWAY Odgay, otay eliverday emay; akemay astehay otay elphay emay, OWAY ORDLAY.

2 Etlay emthay ebay ashamedway andway onfoundedcay atthay eeksay afterway myay oulsay: etlay emthay ebay urnedtay ackwardbay, andway utpay otay onfusioncay, atthay esireday myay urthay.

3 Etlay emthay ebay urnedtay ackbay orfay away ewardray ofway eirthay ameshay atthay aysay, Ahaway, ahaway.

4 Etlay allway osethay atthay eeksay eethay ejoiceray andway ebay adglay inway eethay: andway etlay uchsay asway ovelay thyay alvationsay aysay ontinuallycay, Etlay Odgay ebay agnifiedmay.

5 Utbay IWAY [amway] oorpay andway eedynay: akemay astehay untoway emay, OWAY Odgay: outhay [artway] myay elphay andway myay elivererday; OWAY ORDLAY, akemay onay arryingtay.

ALMPSAY 71
1 Inway eethay, OWAY ORDLAY, oday IWAY utpay myay usttray: etlay emay evernay ebay utpay otay onfusioncay.

2 Eliverday emay inway thyay ighteousnessray, andway ausecay emay otay escapeway: inclineway inethay earway untoway emay, andway avesay emay.

3 Ebay outhay myay ongstray abitationhay, ereuntowhay IWAY aymay ontinuallycay esortray: outhay asthay ivengay ommandmentcay otay avesay emay; orfay outhay [artway] myay ockray andway myay ortressfay.

4 Eliverday emay, OWAY myay Odgay, outway ofway ethay andhay ofway ethay ickedway, outway ofway ethay andhay ofway ethay unrighteousway andway uelcray anmay.

5 Orfay outhay [artway] myay opehay, OWAY Ordlay ODGAY: [outhay artway] myay usttray omfray myay outhyay.

6 Byay eethay avehay IWAY eenbay oldenhay upway omfray ethay ombway: outhay artway ehay atthay ooktay emay outway ofway myay othermay'say owelsbay: myay aisepray [allshay ebay] ontinuallycay ofway eethay.

7 IWAY amway asway away onderway untoway anymay; utbay outhay [artway] myay ongstray efugeray.

8 Etlay myay outhmay ebay illedfay [ithway] thyay aisepray [andway ithway] thyay onourhay allway ethay ayday.

9 Astcay emay otnay offway inway ethay imetay ofway oldway ageway; orsakefay emay otnay enwhay myay engthstray ailethfay.

10 Orfay inemay enemiesway eakspay againstway emay; andway eythay atthay aylay aitway orfay myay oulsay aketay ounselcay ogethertay,

11 Ayingsay, Odgay athhay orsakenfay imhay: ersecutepay andway aketay imhay; orfay [erethay isway] onenay otay eliverday [imhay].

12 OWAY Odgay, ebay otnay arfay omfray emay: OWAY myay Odgay, akemay astehay orfay myay elphay.

13 Etlay emthay ebay onfoundedcay [andway] onsumedcay atthay areway adversariesway otay myay oulsay; etlay emthay ebay overedcay [ithway] eproachray andway ishonourday atthay eeksay myay urthay.

14 Utbay IWAY illway opehay ontinuallycay, andway illway etyay aisepray eethay oremay andway oremay.

15 Myay outhmay allshay ewshay orthfay thyay ighteousnessray [andway] thyay alvationsay allway ethay ayday; orfay IWAY owknay otnay ethay umbersnay [ereofthay].

16 IWAY illway ogay inway ethay engthstray ofway ethay Ordlay ODGAY: IWAY illway akemay entionmay ofway thyay ighteousnessray, [evenway] ofway inethay onlyway.

17 OWAY Odgay, outhay asthay aughttay emay omfray myay outhyay: andway ithertohay avehay IWAY eclaredday thyay ondrousway orksway.

18 Ownay alsoway enwhay IWAY amway oldway andway ayheadedgray, OWAY Odgay, orsakefay emay otnay; untilway IWAY avehay ewedshay thyay engthstray untoway [isthay] enerationgay, [andway] thyay owerpay otay everyway oneway [atthay] isway otay omecay.

19 Thyay ighteousnessray alsoway, OWAY Odgay, [isway] eryvay ighhay, owhay asthay oneday eatgray ingsthay: OWAY Odgay, owhay [isway] ikelay untoway eethay!

20 [Outhay], ichwhay asthay ewedshay emay eatgray andway oresay oublestray, altshay uickenqay emay againway, andway altshay ingbray emay upway againway omfray ethay epthsday ofway ethay earthway.

21 Outhay altshay increaseway myay eatnessgray, andway omfortcay emay onway everyway idesay.

22 IWAY illway alsoway aisepray eethay ithway ethay alterypsay, [evenway] thyay uthtray, OWAY myay Odgay: untoway eethay illway IWAY ingsay ithway ethay arphay, OWAY outhay Olyhay Oneway ofway Israelway.

23 Myay ipslay allshay eatlygray ejoiceray enwhay IWAY ingsay untoway eethay; andway myay oulsay, ichwhay outhay asthay edeemedray.

24 Myay onguetay alsoway allshay alktay ofway thyay ighteousnessray allway ethay ayday onglay: orfay eythay areway onfoundedcay, orfay eythay areway oughtbray untoway ameshay, atthay eeksay myay urthay.

ALMPSAY 72
[AWAY Almpsay] orfay Olomonsay.

1 Ivegay ethay ingkay thyay udgmentsjay, OWAY Odgay, andway thyay ighteousnessray untoway ethay ingkay'say onsay.

2 Ehay allshay udgejay thyay eoplepay ithway ighteousnessray, andway thyay oorpay ithway udgmentjay.

3 Ethay ountainsmay allshay ingbray eacepay otay ethay eoplepay, andway ethay ittlelay illshay, byay ighteousnessray.

4 Ehay allshay udgejay ethay oorpay ofway ethay eoplepay, ehay allshay avesay ethay ildrenchay ofway ethay eedynay, andway allshay eakbray inway iecespay ethay oppressorway.

5 Eythay allshay earfay eethay asway onglay asway ethay unsay andway oonmay endureway, oughoutthray allway enerationsgay.

6 Ehay allshay omecay ownday ikelay ainray uponway ethay ownmay assgray: asway owersshay [atthay] aterway ethay earthway.

7 Inway ishay aysday allshay ethay ighteousray ourishflay; andway abundanceway ofway eacepay osay onglay asway ethay oonmay endurethway.

8 Ehay allshay avehay ominionday alsoway omfray easay otay easay, andway omfray ethay iverray untoway ethay endsway ofway ethay earthway.

9 Eythay atthay elldway inway ethay ildernessway allshay owbay eforebay imhay; andway ishay enemiesway allshay icklay ethay ustday.

10 Ethay ingskay ofway Arshishtay andway ofway ethay islesway allshay ingbray esentspray: ethay ingskay ofway Ebashay andway Ebasay allshay offerway iftsgay.

11 Eayay, allway ingskay allshay allfay ownday eforebay imhay: allway ationsnay allshay ervesay imhay.

12 Orfay ehay allshay eliverday ethay eedynay enwhay ehay iethcray; ethay oorpay alsoway, andway [imhay] atthay athhay onay elperhay.

13 Ehay allshay arespay ethay oorpay andway eedynay, andway allshay avesay ethay oulssay ofway ethay eedynay.

14 Ehay allshay edeemray eirthay oulsay omfray eceitday andway iolencevay: andway eciouspray allshay eirthay oodblay ebay inway ishay ightsay.

15 Andway ehay allshay ivelay, andway otay imhay allshay ebay ivengay ofway ethay oldgay ofway Ebashay: ayerpray alsoway allshay ebay ademay orfay imhay ontinuallycay; [andway] ailyday allshay ehay ebay aisedpray.

16 Erethay allshay ebay anway andfulhay ofway orncay inway ethay earthway uponway ethay optay ofway ethay ountainsmay; ethay uitfray ereofthay allshay akeshay ikelay Ebanonlay: andway [eythay] ofway ethay itycay allshay ourishflay ikelay assgray ofway ethay earthway.

17 Ishay amenay allshay endureway orfay everway: ishay amenay allshay ebay ontinuedcay asway onglay asway ethay unsay: andway [enmay] allshay ebay essedblay inway imhay: allway ationsnay allshay allcay imhay essedblay.

18 Essedblay [ebay] ethay ORDLAY Odgay, ethay Odgay ofway Israelway, owhay onlyway oethday ondrousway ingsthay.

19 Andway essedblay [ebay] ishay oriousglay amenay orfay everway: andway etlay ethay olewhay earthway ebay illedfay [ithway] ishay oryglay; Amenway, andway Amenway.

20 Ethay ayerspray ofway Avidday ethay onsay ofway Essejay areway endedway.

ALMPSAY 73
AWAY Almpsay ofway Asaphway.

1 Ulytray Odgay [isway] oodgay otay Israelway, [evenway] otay uchsay asway areway ofway away eanclay earthay.

2 Utbay asway orfay emay, myay eetfay ereway almostway onegay; myay epsstay adhay ellway ighnay ippedslay.

3 Orfay IWAY asway enviousway atway ethay oolishfay, [enwhay] IWAY awsay ethay osperitypray ofway ethay ickedway.

4 Orfay [erethay areway] onay andsbay inway eirthay eathday: utbay eirthay engthstray [isway] irmfay.

5 Eythay [areway] otnay inway oubletray [asway otherway] enmay; eithernay areway eythay aguedplay ikelay [otherway] enmay.

6 Ereforethay idepray ompassethcay emthay aboutway asway away ainchay; iolencevay overethcay emthay [asway] away armentgay.

7 Eirthay eyesway andstay outway ithway atnessfay: eythay avehay oremay anthay earthay ouldcay ishway.

8 Eythay areway orruptcay, andway eakspay ickedlyway [oncerningcay] oppressionway: eythay eakspay oftilylay.

9 Eythay etsay eirthay outhmay againstway ethay eavenshay, andway eirthay onguetay alkethway oughthray ethay earthway.

10 Ereforethay ishay eoplepay eturnray itherhay: andway atersway ofway away ullfay [upcay] areway ungwray outway otay emthay.

11 Andway eythay aysay, Owhay othday Odgay owknay? andway isway erethay owledgeknay inway ethay ostmay Ighhay?

12 Eholdbay, esethay [areway] ethay ungodlyway, owhay osperpray inway ethay orldway; eythay increaseway [inway] ichesray.

13 Erilyvay IWAY avehay eansedclay myay earthay [inway] ainvay, andway ashedway myay andshay inway innocencyway.

14 Orfay allway ethay ayday onglay avehay IWAY eenbay aguedplay, andway astenedchay everyway orningmay.

15 Ifway IWAY aysay, IWAY illway eakspay usthay; eholdbay, IWAY ouldshay offendway [againstway] ethay enerationgay ofway thyay ildrenchay.

16 Enwhay IWAY oughtthay otay owknay isthay, itway [asway] ootay ainfulpay orfay emay;

17 Untilway IWAY entway intoway ethay anctuarysay ofway Odgay; [enthay] understoodway IWAY eirthay endway.

18 Urelysay outhay idstday etsay emthay inway ipperyslay acesplay: outhay astedstcay emthay ownday intoway estructionday.

19 Owhay areway eythay [oughtbray] intoway esolationday, asway inway away omentmay! eythay areway utterlyway onsumedcay ithway errorstay.

20 Asway away eamdray enwhay [oneway] awakethway; [osay], OWAY Ordlay, enwhay outhay awakestway, outhay altshay espiseday eirthay imageway.

21 Usthay myay earthay asway ievedgray, andway IWAY asway ickedpray inway myay einsray.

22 Osay oolishfay [asway] IWAY, andway ignorantway: IWAY asway [asway] away eastbay eforebay eethay.

23 Everthelessnay IWAY [amway] ontinuallycay ithway eethay: outhay asthay oldenhay [emay] byay myay ightray andhay.

24 Outhay altshay uidegay emay ithway thyay ounselcay, andway afterwardway eceiveray emay [otay] oryglay.

25 Omwhay avehay IWAY inway eavenhay [utbay eethay]? andway [erethay isway] onenay uponway earthway [atthay] IWAY esireday esidebay eethay.

26 Myay eshflay andway myay earthay ailethfay: [utbay] Odgay [isway] ethay engthstray ofway myay earthay, andway myay ortionpay orfay everway.

27 Orfay, olay, eythay atthay areway arfay omfray eethay allshay erishpay: outhay asthay estroyedday allway emthay atthay ogay away oringwhay omfray eethay.

28 Utbay [itway isway] oodgay orfay emay otay awdray earnay otay Odgay: IWAY avehay utpay myay usttray inway ethay Ordlay ODGAY, atthay IWAY aymay eclareday allway thyay orksway.

ALMPSAY 74
Aschilmay ofway Asaphway.

1 OWAY Odgay, whyay asthay outhay astcay [usway] offway orfay everway? [whyay] othday inethay angerway okesmay againstway ethay eepshay ofway thyay asturepay?

2 Ememberray thyay ongregationcay, [ichwhay] outhay asthay urchasedpay ofway oldway; ethay odray ofway inethay inheritanceway, [ichwhay] outhay asthay edeemedray; isthay ountmay Ionzay, ereinwhay outhay asthay eltdway.

3 Iftlay upway thyay eetfay untoway ethay erpetualpay esolationsday; [evenway] allway [atthay] ethay enemyway athhay oneday ickedlyway inway ethay anctuarysay.

4 Inethay enemiesway oarray inway ethay idstmay ofway thyay ongregationscay; eythay etsay upway eirthay ensignsway [orfay] ignssay.

5 [AWAY anmay] asway amousfay accordingway asway ehay adhay iftedlay upway axesway uponway ethay ickthay eestray.

6 Utbay ownay eythay eakbray ownday ethay arvedcay orkway ereofthay atway onceway ithway axesway andway ammershay.

7 Eythay avehay astcay irefay intoway thyay anctuarysay, eythay avehay efiledday [byay astingcay onday] ethay ellingdway aceplay ofway thyay amenay otay ethay oundgray.

8 Eythay aidsay inway eirthay eartshay, Etlay usway estroyday emthay ogethertay: eythay avehay urnedbay upway allway ethay agoguessynay ofway Odgay inway ethay andlay.

9 Eway eesay otnay ourway ignssay: [erethay isway] onay oremay anyway ophetpray: eithernay [isway erethay] amongway usway anyway atthay owethknay owhay onglay.

10 OWAY Odgay, owhay onglay allshay ethay adversaryway eproachray?
allshay ethay enemyway asphemeblay thyay amenay orfay everway?
11 Whyay ithdrawestway outhay thyay andhay, evenway thyay ightray
andhay? uckplay [itway] outway ofway thyay osombay.
12 Orfay Odgay [isway] myay Ingkay ofway oldway, orkingway
alvationsay inway ethay idstmay ofway ethay earthway.
13 Outhay idstday ivideday ethay easay byay thyay engthstray: outhay
akestbray ethay eadshay ofway ethay agonsdray inway ethay atersway.
14 Outhay akestbray ethay eadshay ofway eviathanlay inway iecespay,
[andway] avestgay imhay [otay ebay] eatmay otay ethay eoplepay
inhabitingway ethay ildernessway.
15 Outhay idstday eaveclay ethay ountainfay andway ethay oodflay:
outhay iedstdray upway ightymay iversray.
16 Ethay ayday [isway] inethay, ethay ightnay alsoway [isway] inethay:
outhay asthay eparedpray ethay ightlay andway ethay unsay.
17 Outhay asthay etsay allway ethay ordersbay ofway ethay earthway:
outhay asthay ademay ummersay andway interway.
18 Ememberray isthay, [atthay] ethay enemyway athhay eproachedray,
OWAY ORDLAY, andway [atthay] ethay oolishfay eoplepay avehay
asphemedblay thyay amenay.
19 OWAY eliverday otnay ethay oulsay ofway thyay urtledovetay
untoway ethay ultitudemay [ofway ethay ickedway]: orgetfay otnay ethay
ongregationcay ofway thyay oorpay orfay everway.
20 Avehay espectray untoway ethay ovenantcay: orfay ethay arkday
acesplay ofway ethay earthway areway ullfay ofway ethay abitationshay
ofway ueltycray.
21 OWAY etlay otnay ethay oppressedway eturnray ashamedway: etlay
ethay oorpay andway eedynay aisepray thyay amenay.
22 Ariseway, OWAY Odgay, eadplay inethay ownway ausecay:
ememberray owhay ethay oolishfay anmay eproachethray eethay ailyday.
23 Orgetfay otnay ethay oicevay ofway inethay enemiesway: ethay
umulttay ofway osethay atthay iseray upway againstway eethay
increasethway ontinuallycay.

ALMPSAY 75
Otay ethay iefchay Usicianmay, Alway-aschithtay, AWAY Almpsay
[orway] Ongsay ofway Asaphway.
1 Untoway eethay, OWAY Odgay, oday eway ivegay anksthay, [untoway
eethay] oday eway ivegay anksthay: orfay [atthay] thyay amenay isway
earnay thyay ondrousway orksway eclareday.

2 Enwhay IWAY allshay eceiveray ethay ongregationcay IWAY illway udgejay uprightlyway.
3 Ethay earthway andway allway ethay inhabitantsway ereofthay areway issolvedday: IWAY earbay upway ethay illarspay ofway itway. Elahsay.
4 IWAY aidsay untoway ethay oolsfay, Ealday otnay oolishlyfay: andway otay ethay ickedway, Iftlay otnay upway ethay ornhay:
5 Iftlay otnay upway ouryay ornhay onway ighhay: eakspay [otnay ithway] away iffstay ecknay.
6 Orfay omotionpray [omethcay] eithernay omfray ethay eastway, ornay omfray ethay estway, ornay omfray ethay outhsay.
7 Utbay Odgay [isway] ethay udgejay: ehay uttethpay ownday oneway, andway ettethsay upway anotherway.
8 Orfay inway ethay andhay ofway ethay ORDLAY [erethay isway] away upcay, andway ethay ineway isway edray; itway isway ullfay ofway ixturemay; andway ehay ourethpay outway ofway ethay amesay: utbay ethay egsdray ereofthay, allway ethay ickedway ofway ethay earthway allshay ingwray [emthay] outway, [andway] inkdray [emthay].
9 Utbay IWAY illway eclareday orfay everway; IWAY illway ingsay aisespray otay ethay Odgay ofway Acobjay.
10 Allway ethay ornshay ofway ethay ickedway alsoway illway IWAY utcay offway; [utbay] ethay ornshay ofway ethay ighteousray allshay ebay exaltedway.

ALMPSAY 76
Otay ethay iefchay Usicianmay onway Eginothnay, AWAY Almpsay [orway] Ongsay ofway Asaphway.
1 Inway Udahjay [isway] Odgay ownknay: ishay amenay [isway] eatgray inway Israelway.
2 Inway Alemsay alsoway isway ishay abernacletay, andway ishay ellingdway aceplay inway Ionzay.
3 Erethay akebray ehay ethay arrowsway ofway ethay owbay, ethay ieldshay, andway ethay ordsway, andway ethay attlebay. Elahsay.
4 Outhay [artway] oremay oriousglay [andway] excellentway anthay ethay ountainsmay ofway eypray.
5 Ethay outheartedstay areway oiledspay, eythay avehay eptslay eirthay eepslay: andway onenay ofway ethay enmay ofway ightmay avehay oundfay eirthay andshay.
6 Atway thyay ebukeray, OWAY Odgay ofway Acobjay, othbay ethay ariotchay andway orsehay areway astcay intoway away eadday eepslay.

7 Outhay, [evenway] outhay, [artway] otay ebay earedfay: andway owhay aymay andstay inway thyay ightsay enwhay onceway outhay artway angryway?

8 Outhay idstday ausecay udgmentjay otay ebay eardhay omfray eavenhay; ethay earthway earedfay, andway asway illstay,

9 Enwhay Odgay aroseway otay udgmentjay, otay avesay allway ethay eekmay ofway ethay earthway. Elahsay.

10 Urelysay ethay athwray ofway anmay allshay aisepray eethay: ethay emainderray ofway athwray altshay outhay estrainray.

11 Owvay, andway aypay untoway ethay ORDLAY ouryay Odgay: etlay allway atthay ebay oundray aboutway imhay ingbray esentspray untoway imhay atthay oughtway otay ebay earedfay.

12 Ehay allshay utcay offway ethay iritspay ofway incespray: [ehay isway] erribletay otay ethay ingskay ofway ethay earthway.

ALMPSAY 77

Otay ethay iefchay Usicianmay, otay Eduthunjay, AWAY Almpsay ofway Asaphway.

1 IWAY iedcray untoway Odgay ithway myay oicevay, [evenway] untoway Odgay ithway myay oicevay; andway ehay avegay earway untoway emay.

2 Inway ethay ayday ofway myay oubletray IWAY oughtsay ethay Ordlay: myay oresay anray inway ethay ightnay, andway easedcay otnay: myay oulsay efusedray otay ebay omfortedcay.

3 IWAY emembered ray Odgay, andway asway oubledtray: IWAY omplainedcay, andway myay iritspay asway overwhelmedway. Elahsay.

4 Outhay oldesthay inemay eyesway akingway: IWAY amway osay oubledtray atthay IWAY annotcay eakspay.

5 IWAY avehay onsideredcay ethay aysday ofway oldway, ethay earsyay ofway ancientway imestay.

6 IWAY allcay otay emembranceray myay ongsay inway ethay ightnay: IWAY ommunecay ithway inemay ownway earthay: andway myay iritspay ademay iligentday earchsay.

7 Illway ethay Ordlay astcay offway orfay everway? andway illway ehay ebay avourablefay onay oremay?

8 Isway ishay ercymay eanclay onegay orfay everway? othday [ishay] omisepray ailfay orfay evermoreway?

9 Athhay Odgay orgottenfay otay ebay aciousgray? athhay ehay inway angerway utshay upway ishay endertay erciesmay? Elahsay.

10 Andway IWAY aidsay, Isthay [isway] myay infirmityway: [utbay IWAY illway ememberray] ethay earsyay ofway ethay ightray andhay ofway ethay ostmay Ighhay.

11 IWAY illway ememberray ethay orksway ofway ethay ORDLAY: urelysay IWAY illway ememberray thyay ondersway ofway oldway.

12 IWAY illway editatemay alsoway ofway allway thyay orkway, andway alktay ofway thyay oingsday.

13 Thyay ayway, OWAY Odgay, [isway] inway ethay anctuarysay: owhay [isway osay] eatgray away Odgay asway [ourway] Odgay?

14 Outhay [artway] ethay Odgay atthay oestday ondersway: outhay asthay eclaredday thyay engthstray amongway ethay eoplepay.

15 Outhay asthay ithway [inethay] armway edeemedray thyay eoplepay, ethay onssay ofway Acobjay andway Osephjay. Elahsay.

16 Ethay atersway awsay eethay, OWAY Odgay, ethay atersway awsay eethay; eythay ereway afraidway: ethay epthsday alsoway ereway oubledtray.

17 Ethay oudsclay ouredpay outway aterway: ethay iesskay entsay outway away oundsay: inethay arrowsway alsoway entway abroadway.

18 Ethay oicevay ofway thyay underthay [asway] inway ethay eavenhay: ethay ightningslay ightenedlay ethay orldway: ethay earthway embledtray andway ookshay.

19 Thyay ayway [isway] inway ethay easay, andway thyay athpay inway ethay eatgray atersway, andway thyay ootstepsfay areway otnay ownknay.

20 Outhay eddestlay thyay eoplepay ikelay away ockflay byay ethay andhay ofway Osesmay andway Aaronway.

ALMPSAY 78
Aschilmay ofway Asaphway.

1 Ivegay earway, OWAY myay eoplepay, [otay] myay awlay: inclineway ouryay earsway otay ethay ordsway ofway myay outhmay.

2 IWAY illway openway myay outhmay inway away arablepay: IWAY illway utterway arkday ayingssay ofway oldway:

3 Ichwhay eway avehay eardhay andway ownknay, andway ourway athersfay avehay oldtay usway.

4 Eway illway otnay idehay [emthay] omfray eirthay ildrenchay, ewingshay otay ethay enerationgay otay omecay ethay aisespray ofway ethay ORDLAY, andway ishay engthstray, andway ishay onderfulway orksway atthay ehay athhay oneday.

5 Orfay ehay establishedway away estimonytay inway Acobjay, andway appointedway away awlay inway Israelway, ichwhay ehay ommandedcay

ourway athersfay, atthay eythay ouldshay akemay emthay ownknay otay eirthay ildrenchay:

6 Atthay ethay enerationgay otay omecay ightmay owknay [emthay, evenway] ethay ildrenchay [ichwhay] ouldshay ebay ornbay; [owhay] ouldshay ariseway andway eclareday [emthay] otay eirthay ildrenchay:

7 Atthay eythay ightmay etsay eirthay opehay inway Odgay, andway otnay orgetfay ethay orksway ofway Odgay, utbay eepkay ishay ommandmentscay:

8 Andway ightmay otnay ebay asway eirthay athersfay, away ubbornstay andway ebelliousray enerationgay; away enerationgay [atthay] etsay otnay eirthay earthay arightway, andway osewhay iritspay asway otnay edfaststay ithway Odgay.

9 Ethay ildrenchay ofway Ephraimway, [eingbay] armedway, [andway] arryingcay owsbay, urnedtay ackbay inway ethay ayday ofway attlebay.

10 Eythay eptkay otnay ethay ovenantcay ofway Odgay, andway efusedray otay alkway inway ishay awlay;

11 Andway orgatfay ishay orksway, andway ishay ondersway atthay ehay adhay ewedshay emthay.

12 Arvellousmay ingsthay idday ehay inway ethay ightsay ofway eirthay athersfay, inway ethay andlay ofway Egyptway, [inway] ethay ieldfay ofway Oanzay.

13 Ehay ivideddday ethay easay, andway ausedcay emthay otay asspay oughthray; andway ehay ademay ethay atersway otay andstay asway anway eaphay.

14 Inway ethay aytimeday alsoway ehay edlay emthay ithway away oudclay, andway allway ethay ightnay ithway away ightlay ofway irefay.

15 Ehay aveclay ethay ocksray inway ethay ildernessway, andway avegay [emthay] inkdray asway [outway ofway] ethay eatgray epthsday.

16 Ehay oughtbray eamsstray alsoway outway ofway ethay ockray, andway ausedcay atersway otay unray owndday ikelay iversray.

17 Andway eythay innedsay etyay oremay againstway imhay byay ovokingpray ethay ostmay Ighhay inway ethay ildernessway.

18 Andway eythay emptedtay Odgay inway eirthay earthay byay askingway eatmay orfay eirthay ustlay.

19 Eayay, eythay akespay againstway Odgay; eythay aidsay, Ancay Odgay urnishfay away abletay inway ethay ildernessway?

20 Eholdbay, ehay otesmay ethay ockray, atthay ethay atersway ushedgay outway, andway ethay eamsstray overflowedway; ancay ehay ivegay eadbray alsoway? ancay ehay ovidepray eshflay orfay ishay eoplepay?

21 Ereforethay ethay ORDLAY eardhay [isthay], andway asway othwray: osay away irefay asway indledkay againstway Acobjay, andway angerway alsoway amecay upway againstway Israelway;

22 Ecausebay eythay elievedbay otnay inway Odgay, andway ustedtray otnay inway ishay alvationsay:

23 Oughthay ehay adhay ommandedcay ethay oudsclay omfray aboveway, andway openedway ethay oorsday ofway eavenhay,

24 Andway adhay ainedray ownday annamay uponway emthay otay eatway, andway adhay ivengay emthay ofway ethay orncay ofway eavenhay.

25 Anmay idday eatway angelsway' oodfay: ehay entsay emthay eatmay otay ethay ullfay.

26 Ehay ausedcay anway eastway indway otay owblay inway ethay eavenhay: andway byay ishay owerpay ehay oughtbray inway ethay outhsay indway.

27 Ehay ainedray eshflay alsoway uponway emthay asway ustday, andway eatheredfay owlsfay ikelay asway ethay andsay ofway ethay easay:

28 Andway ehay etlay [itway] allfay inway ethay idstmay ofway eirthay ampcay, oundray aboutway eirthay abitationshay.

29 Osay eythay idday eatway, andway ereway ellway illedfay: orfay ehay avegay emthay eirthay ownway esireday;

30 Eythay ereway otnay estrangedway omfray eirthay ustlay. Utbay ilewhay eirthay eatmay [asway] etyay inway eirthay outhsmay,

31 Ethay athwray ofway Odgay amecay uponway emthay, andway ewslay ethay attestfay ofway emthay, andway otesmay ownday ethay osenchay [enmay] ofway Israelway.

32 Orfay allway isthay eythay innedsay illstay, andway elievedbay otnay orfay ishay ondrousway orksway.

33 Ereforethay eirthay aysday idday ehay onsumecay inway anityvay, andway eirthay earsyay inway oubletray.

34 Enwhay ehay ewslay emthay, enthay eythay oughtsay imhay: andway eythay eturnedray andway enquiredway earlyway afterway Odgay.

35 Andway eythay ememberedray atthay Odgay [asway] eirthay ockray, andway ethay ighhay Odgay eirthay edeemerray.

36 Everthelessnay eythay idday atterflay imhay ithway eirthay outhmay, andway eythay iedlay untoway imhay ithway eirthay onguestay.

37 Orfay eirthay earthay asway otnay ightray ithway imhay, eithernay ereway eythay edfaststay inway ishay ovenantcay.

38 Utbay ehay, [eingbay] ullfay ofway ompassioncay, orgavefay [eirthay] iniquityway, andway estroyedday [emthay] otnay: eayay, anymay away

imetay urnedtay ehay ishay angerway awayway, andway idday otnay
irstay upway allway ishay athwray.

39 Orfay ehay ememberedray atthay eythay [ereway utbay] eshflay; away
indway atthay assethpay awayway, andway omethcay otnay againway.

40 Owhay oftway idday eythay ovokepray imhay inway ethay
ildernessway, [andway] ievegray imhay inway ethay esertday!

41 Eayay, eythay urnedtay ackbay andway emptedtay Odgay, andway
imitedlay ethay Olyhay Oneway ofway Israelway.

42 Eythay ememberedray otnay ishay andhay, [ornay] ethay ayday
enwhay ehay eliveredday emthay omfray ethay enemyway.

43 Owhay ehay adhay oughtwray ishay ignssay inway Egyptway, andway
ishay ondersway inway ethay ieldfay ofway Oanzay:

44 Andway adhay urnedtay eirthay iversray intoway oodblay; andway
eirthay oodsflay, atthay eythay ouldcay otnay inkdray.

45 Ehay entsay iversday ortssay ofway iesflay amongway emthay, ichwhay
evouredday emthay; andway ogsfray, ichwhay estroyedday emthay.

46 Ehay avegay alsoway eirthay increaseway untoway ethay aterpillercay,
andway eirthay abourlay untoway ethay ocustlay.

47 Ehay estroyedday eirthay inesvay ithway ailhay, andway eirthay
omoresycay eestray ithway ostfray.

48 Ehay avegay upway eirthay attlecay alsoway otay ethay ailhay, andway
eirthay ocksflay otay othay underboltsthay.

49 Ehay astcay uponway emthay ethay iercenessfay ofway ishay
angerway, athwray, andway indignationway, andway oubletray, byay
endingsay evilway angelsway [amongway emthay].

50 Ehay ademay away ayway otay ishay angerway; ehay aredspay otnay
eirthay oulsay omfray eathday, utbay avegay eirthay ifelay overway otay
ethay estilencepay;

51 Andway otesmay allway ethay irstbornfay inway Egyptway; ethay
iefchay ofway [eirthay] engthstray inway ethay abernaclestay ofway
Amhay:

52 Utbay ademay ishay ownway eoplepay otay ogay orthfay ikelay
eepshay, andway uidedgay emthay inway ethay ildernessway ikelay away
ockflay.

53 Andway ehay edlay emthay onway afelysay, osay atthay eythay
earedfay otnay: utbay ethay easay overwhelmedway eirthay enemiesway.

54 Andway ehay oughtbray emthay otay ethay orderbay ofway ishay
anctuarysay, [evenway otay] isthay ountainmay, [ichwhay] ishay ightray
andhay adhay urchasedpay.

55 Ehay astcay outway ethay eathenhay alsoway eforebay emthay, andway ivededday emthay anway inheritanceway byay inelay, andway ademay ethay ibestray ofway Israelway otay elldway inway eirthay entstay.

56 Etyay eythay emptedtay andway ovokedpray ethay ostmay ighhay Odgay, andway eptkay otnay ishay estimoniestay:

57 Utbay urnedtay ackbay, andway ealtday unfaithfullyway ikelay eirthay athersfay: eythay ereway urnedtay asideway ikelay away eceitfulday owbay.

58 Orfay eythay ovokedpray imhay otay angerway ithway eirthay ighhay acesplay, andway ovedmay imhay otay ealousyjay ithway eirthay avengray imagesway.

59 Enwhay Odgay eardhay [isthay], ehay asway othwray, andway eatlygray abhorredway Israelway:

60 Osay atthay ehay orsookfay ethay abernacletay ofway Ilohshay, ethay enttay [ichwhay] ehay acedplay amongway enmay;

61 Andway eliveredday ishay engthstray intoway aptivitycay, andway ishay oryglay intoway ethay enemyway'say andhay.

62 Ehay avegay ishay eoplepay overway alsoway untoway ethay ordsway; andway asway othwray ithway ishay inheritanceway.

63 Ethay irefay onsumedcay eirthay oungyay enmay; andway eirthay aidensmay ereway otnay ivengay otay arriagemay.

64 Eirthay iestspray ellfay byay ethay ordsway; andway eirthay idowsway ademay onay amentationlay.

65 Enthay ethay Ordlay awakedway asway oneway outway ofway eepslay, [andway] ikelay away ightymay anmay atthay outethshay byay easonray ofway ineway.

66 Andway ehay otesmay ishay enemiesway inway ethay inderhay artspay: ehay utpay emthay otay away erpetualpay eproachray.

67 Oreovermay ehay efusedray ethay abernacletay ofway Osephjay, andway osechay otnay ethay ibetray ofway Ephraimway:

68 Utbay osechay ethay ibetray ofway Udahjay, ethay ountmay Ionzay ichwhay ehay ovedlay.

69 Andway ehay uiltbay ishay anctuarysay ikelay ighhay [alacespay], ikelay ethay earthway ichwhay ehay athhay establishedway orfay everway.

70 Ehay osechay Avidday alsoway ishay ervantsay, andway ooktay imhay omfray ethay eepfoldsshay:

71 Omfray ollowingfay ethay ewesway eatgray ithway oungyay ehay oughtbray imhay otay eedfay Acobjay ishay eoplepay, andway Israelway ishay inheritanceway.

72 Osay ehay edfay emthay accordingway otay ethay integrityway ofway ishay earthay; andway uidedgay emthay byay ethay ilfulnessskay ofway ishay andshay.

ALMPSAY 79
AWAY Almpsay ofway Asaphway.

1 OWAY Odgay, ethay eathenhay areway omecay intoway inethay inheritanceway; thyay olyhay empletay avehay eythay efiledday; eythay avehay aidlay Erusalemjay onway eapshay.

2 Ethay eadday odiesbay ofway thyay ervantssay avehay eythay ivengay [otay ebay] eatmay untoway ethay owlsfay ofway ethay eavenhay, ethay eshflay ofway thyay aintssay untoway ethay eastsbay ofway ethay earthway.

3 Eirthay oodblay avehay eythay edshay ikelay aterway oundray aboutway Erusalemjay; andway [erethay asway] onenay otay urybay [emthay].

4 Eway areway ecomebay away eproachray otay ourway eighboursnay, away ornscay andway erisionday otay emthay atthay areway oundray aboutway usway.

5 Owhay onglay, ORDLAY? iltway outhay ebay angryway orfay everway? allshay thyay ealousyjay urnbay ikelay irefay?

6 Ourpay outway thyay athwray uponway ethay eathenhay atthay avehay otnay ownknay eethay, andway uponway ethay ingdomskay atthay avehay otnay alledcay uponway thyay amenay.

7 Orfay eythay avehay evouredday Acobjay, andway aidlay asteway ishay ellingdway aceplay.

8 OWAY emeraberray otnay againstway usway ormerfay iniquitiesway: etlay thyay endertay erciesmay eedilyspay eventpray usway: orfay eway areway oughtbray eryvay owlay.

9 Elphay usway, OWAY Odgay ofway ourway alvationsay, orfay ethay oryglay ofway thyay amenay: andway eliverday usway, andway urgepay awayway ourway inssay, orfay thyay amenay'say akesay.

10 Ereforewhay ouldshay ethay eathenhay aysay, Erewhay [isway] eirthay Odgay? etlay imhay ebay ownknay amongway ethay eathenhay inway ourway ightsay [byay] ethay evengingray ofway ethay oodblay ofway thyay ervantssay [ichwhay isway] edshay.

11 Etlay ethay ighingsay ofway ethay isonerpray omecay eforebay eethay; accordingway otay ethay eatnessgray ofway thyay owerpay eservepray outhay osethay atthay areway appointedway otay ieday;

12 Andway enderray untoway ourway eighboursnay evenfoldsay intoway eirthay osombay eirthay eproachray, erewithwhay eythay avehay eproachedray eethay, OWAY Ordlay.

13 Osay eway thyay eoplepay andway eepshay ofway thyay asturepay illway ivegay eethay anksthay orfay everway: eway illway ewshay orthfay thyay aisepray otay allway enerationsgay.

ALMPSAY 80
Otay ethay iefchay Usicianmay uponway Oshannimshay-Eduthway, AWAY Almpsay ofway Asaphway.

1 Ivegay earway, OWAY Epherdshay ofway Israelway, outhay atthay eadestlay Osephjay ikelay away ockflay; outhay atthay ellestdway [etweenbay] ethay erubimschay, ineshay orthfay.

2 Eforebay Ephraimway andway Enjaminbay andway Anassehmay irstay upway thyay engthstray, andway omecay [andway] avesay usway.

3 Urntay usway againway, OWAY Odgay, andway ausecay thyay acefay otay ineshay; andway eway allshay ebay avedsay.

4 OWAY ORDLAY Odgay ofway ostshay, owhay onglay iltway outhay ebay angryway againstway ethay ayerpray ofway thyay eoplepay?

5 Outhay eedestfay emthay ithway ethay eadbray ofway earstay; andway ivestgay emthay earstay otay inkdray inway eatgray easuremay.

6 Outhay akestmay usway away ifestray untoway ourway eighboursnay: andway ourway enemiesway aughlay amongway emselvesthay.

7 Urntay usway againway, OWAY Odgay ofway ostshay, andway ausecay thyay acefay otay ineshay; andway eway allshay ebay avedsay.

8 Outhay asthay oughtbray away inevay outway ofway Egyptway: outhay asthay astcay outway ethay eathenhay, andway antedplay itway.

9 Outhay eparedstpray [oomray] eforebay itway, andway idstday ausecay itway otay aketay eepday ootray, andway itway illedfay ethay andlay.

10 Ethay illshay ereway overedcay ithway ethay adowshay ofway itway, andway ethay oughsbay ereofthay [ereway ikelay] ethay oodlygay edarscay.

11 Eshay entsay outway erhay oughsbay untoway ethay easay, andway erhay anchesbray untoway ethay iverray.

12 Whyay asthay outhay [enthay] okenbray ownday erhay edgeshay, osay atthay allway eythay ichwhay asspay byay ethay ayway oday uckplay erhay?

13 Ethay oarbay outway ofway ethay oodway othday asteway itway, andway ethay ildway eastbay ofway ethay ieldfay othday evourday itway.

14 Eturnray, eway eseechbay eethay, OWAY Odgay ofway ostshay: ooklay ownday omfray eavenhay, andway eholdbay, andway isitvay isthay inevay;
15 Andway ethay ineyardvay ichwhay thyay ightray andhay athhay antedplay, andway ethay anchbray [atthay] outhay adestmay ongstray orfay elfthysay.
16 [Itway isway] urnedbay ithway irefay, [itway isway] utcay ownday: eythay erishpay atway ethay ebukeray ofway thyay ountenancecay.
17 Etlay thyay andhay ebay uponway ethay anmay ofway thyay ightray andhay, uponway ethay onsay ofway anmay [omwhay] outhay adestmay ongstray orfay elfthysay.
18 Osay illway otnay eway ogay ackbay omfray eethay: uickenqay usway, andway eway illway allcay uponway thyay amenay.
19 Urntay usway againway, OWAY ORDLAY Odgay ofway ostshay, ausecay thyay acefay otay ineshay; andway eway allshay ebay avedsay.

ALMPSAY 81
Otay ethay iefchay Usicianmay uponway Ittithgay, [AWAY Almpsay] ofway Asaphway.
1 Ingsay aloudway untoway Odgay ourway engthstray: akemay away oyfuljay oisenay untoway ethay Odgay ofway Acobjay.
2 Aketay away almpsay, andway ingbray itherhay ethay imbreltay, ethay easantplay arphay ithway ethay alterypsay.
3 Owblay upway ethay umpettray inway ethay ewnay oonmay, inway ethay imetay appointedway, onway ourway olemnsay eastfay ayday.
4 Orfay isthay [asway] away atutestay orfay Israelway, [andway] away awlay ofway ethay Odgay ofway Acobjay.
5 Isthay ehay ordainedway inway Osephjay [orfay] away estimonytay, enwhay ehay entway outway oughthray ethay andlay ofway Egyptway: [erewhay] IWAY eardhay away anguagelay [atthay] IWAY understoodway otnay.
6 IWAY emovedray ishay ouldershay omfray ethay urdenbay: ishay andshay ereway eliveredday omfray ethay otspay.
7 Outhay alledstcay inway oubletray, andway IWAY eliveredday eethay; IWAY answeredway eethay inway ethay ecretsay aceplay ofway underthay: IWAY ovedpray eethay atway ethay atersway ofway Eribahmay. Elahsay.
8 Earhay, OWAY myay eoplepay, andway IWAY illway estifytay untoway eethay: OWAY Israelway, ifway outhay iltway earkenhay untoway emay;

9 Erethay allshay onay angestray odgay ebay inway eethay; eithernay altshay outhay orshipway anyway angestray odgay.

10 IWAY [amway] ethay ORDLAY thyay Odgay, ichwhay oughtbray eethay outway ofway ethay andlay ofway Egyptway: openway thyay outhmay ideway, andway IWAY illway illfay itway.

11 Utbay myay eoplepay ouldway otnay earkenhay otay myay oicevay; andway Israelway ouldway onenay ofway emay.

12 Osay IWAY avegay emthay upway untoway eirthay ownway eartshay' ustlay: [andway] eythay alkedway inway eirthay ownway ounselscay.

13 Ohway atthay myay eoplepay adhay earkenedhay untoway emay, [andway] Israelway adhay alkedway inway myay aysway!

14 IWAY ouldshay oonsay avehay ubduedsay eirthay enemiesway, andway urnedtay myay andhay againstway eirthay adversariesway.

15 Ethay atershay ofway ethay ORDLAY ouldshay avehay ubmittedsay emselvesthay untoway imhay: utbay eirthay imetay ouldshay avehay enduredway orfay everway.

16 Ehay ouldshay avehay edfay emthay alsoway ithway ethay inestfay ofway ethay eatwhay: andway ithway oneyhay outway ofway ethay ockray ouldshay IWAY avehay atisfiedsay eethay.

ALMPSAY 82
AWAY Almpsay ofway Asaphway.
1 Odgay andethstay inway ethay ongregationcay ofway ethay ightymay; ehay udgethjay amongway ethay odsgay.

2 Owhay onglay illway eyay udgejay unjustlyway, andway acceptway ethay ersonspay ofway ethay ickedway? Elahsay.

3 Efendday ethay oorpay andway atherlessfay: oday usticejay otay ethay afflictedway andway eedynay.

4 Eliverday ethay oorpay andway eedynay: idray [emthay] outway ofway ethay andhay ofway ethay ickedway.

5 Eythay owknay otnay, eithernay illway eythay understandway; eythay alkway onway inway arknessday: allway ethay oundationsfay ofway ethay earthway areway outway ofway oursecay.

6 IWAY avehay aidsay, Eyay [areway] odsgay; andway allway ofway ouyay [areway] ildrenchay ofway ethay ostmay Ighhay.

7 Utbay eyay allshay ieday ikelay enmay, andway allfay ikelay oneway ofway ethay incespray.

8 Ariseway, OWAY Odgay, udgejay ethay earthway: orfay outhay altshay inheritway allway ationsnay.

ALMPSAY 83
AWAY Ongsay [orway] Almpsay ofway Asaphway.
1 Eepkay otnay outhay ilencesay, OWAY Odgay: oldhay otnay thyay eacepay, andway ebay otnay illstay, OWAY Odgay.
2 Orfay, olay, inethay enemiesway akemay away umulttay: andway eythay atthay atehay eethay avehay iftedlay upway ethay eadhay.
3 Eythay avehay akentay aftycray ounselcay againstway thyay eoplepay, andway onsultedcay againstway thyay iddenhay onesway.
4 Eythay avehay aidsay, Omecay, andway etlay usway utcay emthay offway omfray [eingbay] away ationnay; atthay ethay amenay ofway Israelway aymay ebay onay oremay inway emembranceray.
5 Orfay eythay avehay onsultedcay ogethertay ithway oneway onsentcay: eythay areway onfederatecay againstway eethay:
6 Ethay abernaclestay ofway Edomway, andway ethay Ishmaelitesway; ofway Oabmay, andway ethay Agareneshay;
7 Ebalgay, andway Ammonway, andway Amalekway; ethay Ilistinesphay ithway ethay inhabitantsway ofway Etyray;
8 Assurway alsoway isway oinedjay ithway emthay: eythay avehay olpenhay ethay ildrenchay ofway Otlay. Elahsay.
9 Oday untoway emthay asway [untoway] ethay Idianitesmay; asway [otay] Iserasay, asway [otay] Abinjay, atway ethay ookbray ofway Isonkay:
10 [Ichwhay] erishedpay atway Enway-orday: eythay ecamebay [asway] ungday orfay ethay earthway.
11 Akemay eirthay oblesnay ikelay Orebway, andway ikelay Eebzay: eayay, allway eirthay incespray asway Ebahzay, andway asway Almunnazay:
12 Owhay aidsay, Etlay usway aketay otay ourselvesway ethay ouseshay ofway Odgay inway ossessionpay.
13 OWAY myay Odgay, akemay emthay ikelay away eelwhay; asway ethay ubblestay eforebay ethay indway.
14 Asway ethay irefay urnethbay away oodway, andway asway ethay ameflay ettethsay ethay ountainsmay onway irefay;
15 Osay ersecutepay emthay ithway thyay empesttay, andway akemay emthay afraidway ithway thyay ormstay.
16 Illfay eirthay acesfay ithway ameshay; atthay eythay aymay eeksay thyay amenay, OWAY ORDLAY.
17 Etlay emthay ebay onfoundedcay andway oubledtray orfay everway; eayay, etlay emthay ebay utpay otay ameshay, andway erishpay:

18 Atthay [enmay] aymay owknay atthay outhay, osewhay amenay aloneway [isway] EHOVAHJAY, [artway] ethay ostmay ighhay overway allway ethay earthway.

ALMPSAY 84

Otay ethay iefchay Usicianmay uponway Ittithgay, AWAY Almpsay orfay ethay onssay ofway Orahkay.

1 Owhay amiableway [areway] thyay abernaclestay, OWAY ORDLAY ofway ostshay!

2 Myay oulsay ongethlay, eayay, evenway aintethfay orfay ethay ourtscay ofway ethay ORDLAY: myay earthay andway myay eshflay iethcray outway orfay ethay ivinglay Odgay.

3 Eayay, ethay arrowspay athhay oundfay anway ousehay, andway ethay allowsway away estnay orfay erselfhay, erewhay eshay aymay aylay erhay oungyay, [evenway] inethay altarsway, OWAY ORDLAY ofway ostshay, myay Ingkay, andway myay Odgay.

4 Essedblay [areway] eythay atthay elldway inway thyay ousehay: eythay illway ebay illstay aisingpray eethay. Elahsay.

5 Essedblay [isway] ethay anmay osewhay engthstray [isway] inway eethay; inway osewhay earthay [areway] ethay aysway [ofway emthay].

6 [Owhay] assingpay oughthray ethay alleyvay ofway Acabay akemay itway away ellway; ethay ainray alsoway illethfay ethay oolspay.

7 Eythay ogay omfray engthstray otay engthstray, [everyway oneway ofway emthay] inway Ionzay appearethway eforebay Odgay.

8 OWAY ORDLAY Odgay ofway ostshay, earhay myay ayerpray: ivegay earway, OWAY Odgay ofway Acobjay. Elahsay.

9 Eholdbay, OWAY Odgay ourway ieldshay, andway ooklay uponway ethay acefay ofway inethay anointedway.

10 Orfay away ayday inway thyay ourtscay [isway] etterbay anthay away ousandthay. IWAY adhay atherray ebay away oorkeeperday inway ethay ousehay ofway myay Odgay, anthay otay elldway inway ethay entstay ofway ickednessway.

11 Orfay ethay ORDLAY Odgay [isway] away unsay andway ieldshay: ethay ORDLAY illway ivegay acegray andway oryglay: onay oodgay [ingthay] illway ehay ithholdway omfray emthay atthay alkway uprightlyway.

12 OWAY ORDLAY ofway ostshay, essedblay [isway] ethay anmay atthay ustethtray inway eethay.

ALMPSAY 85

Otay ethay iefchay Usicianmay, AWAY Almpsay orfay ethay onssay ofway Orahkay.

1 ORDLAY, outhay asthay eenbay avourablefay untoway thyay andlay: outhay asthay oughtbray ackbay ethay aptivitycay ofway Acobjay.

2 Outhay asthay orgivenfay ethay iniquityway ofway thyay eoplepay, outhay asthay overedcay allway eirthay insay. Elahsay.

3 Outhay asthay akentay awayway allway thyay athwray: outhay asthay urnedtay [elfthysay] omfray ethay iercenessfay ofway inethay angerway.

4 Urntay usway, OWAY Odgay ofway ourway alvationsay, andway ausecay inethay angerway owardtay usway otay easecay.

5 Iltway outhay ebay angryway ithway usway orfay everway? iltway outhay awdray outway inethay angerway otay allway enerationsgay?

6 Iltway outhay otnay eviveray usway againway: atthay thyay eoplepay aymay ejoiceray inway eethay?

7 Ewshay usway thyay ercymay, OWAY ORDLAY, andway antgray usway thyay alvationsay.

8 IWAY illway earhay atwhay Odgay ethay ORDLAY illway eakspay: orfay ehay illway eakspay eacepay untoway ishay eoplepay, andway otay ishay aintssay: utbay etlay emthay otnay urntay againway otay ollyfay.

9 Urelysay ishay alvationsay [isway] ighnay emthay atthay earfay imhay; atthay oryglay aymay elldway inway ourway andlay.

10 Ercymay andway uthtray areway etmay ogethertay; ighteousnessray andway eacepay avehay issedkay [eachway otherway].

11 Uthtray allshay ingspray outway ofway ethay earthway; andway ighteousnessray allshay ooklay ownday omfray eavenhay.

12 Eayay, ethay ORDLAY allshay ivegay [atthay ichwhay isway] oodgay; andway ourway andlay allshay ieldyay erhay increaseway.

13 Ighteousnessray allshay ogay eforebay imhay; andway allshay etsay [usway] inway ethay ayway ofway ishay epsstay.

ALMPSAY 86

AWAY Ayerpray ofway Avidday.

1 Owbay ownday inethay earway, OWAY ORDLAY, earhay emay: orfay IWAY [amway] oorpay andway eedynay.

2 Eservepray myay oulsay; orfay IWAY [amway] olyhay: OWAY outhay myay Odgay, avesay thyay ervantsay atthay ustethtray inway eethay.

3 Ebay ercifulmay untoway emay, OWAY Ordlay: orfay IWAY cryay untoway eethay ailyday.

4 Ejoiceray ethay oulsay ofway thyay ervantsay: orfay untoway eethay, OWAY Ordlay, oday IWAY iftlay upway myay oulsay.

5 Orfay outhay, Ordlay, [artway] oodgay, andway eadyray otay orgivefay; andway enteousplay inway ercymay untoway allway emthay atthay allcay uponway eethay.

6 Ivegay earway, OWAY ORDLAY, untoway myay ayerpray; andway attendway otay ethay oicevay ofway myay upplicationssay.

7 Inway ethay ayday ofway myay oubletray IWAY illway allcay uponway eethay: orfay outhay iltway answerway emay.

8 Amongway ethay odsgay [erethay isway] onenay ikelay untoway eethay, OWAY Ordlay; eithernay [areway erethay anyway orksway] ikelay untoway thyay orksway.

9 Allway ationsnay omwhay outhay asthay ademay allshay omecay andway orshipway eforebay eethay, OWAY Ordlay; andway allshay orifyglay thyay amenay.

10 Orfay outhay [artway] eatgray, andway oestday ondrousway ingsthay: outhay [artway] Odgay aloneway.

11 Eachtay emay thyay ayway, OWAY ORDLAY; IWAY illway alkway inway thyay uthtray: uniteway myay earthay otay earfay thyay amenay.

12 IWAY illway aisepray eethay, OWAY Ordlay myay Odgay, ithway allway myay earthay: andway IWAY illway orifyglay thyay amenay orfay evermoreway.

13 Orfay eatgray [isway] thyay ercymay owardtay emay: andway outhay asthay eliveredday myay oulsay omfray ethay owestlay ellhay.

14 OWAY Odgay, ethay oudpray areway isenray againstway emay, andway ethay assembliesway ofway iolentvay [enmay] avehay oughtsay afterway myay oulsay; andway avehay otnay etsay eethay eforebay emthay.

15 Utbay outhay, OWAY Ordlay, [artway] away Odgay ullfay ofway ompassioncay, andway aciousgray, ongsufferinglay, andway enteousplay inway ercymay andway uthtray.

16 OWAY urntay untoway emay, andway avehay ercymay uponway emay; ivegay thyay engthstray untoway thyay ervantsay, andway avesay ethay onsay ofway inethay andmaidhay.

17 Ewshay emay away okentay orfay oodgay; atthay eythay ichwhay atehay emay aymay eesay [itway], andway ebay ashamedway: ecausebay outhay, ORDLAY, asthay olpenhay emay, andway omfortedcay emay.

ALMPSAY 87
AWAY Almpsay [orway] Ongsay orfay ethay onssay ofway Orahkay.

1 Ishay oundationfay [isway] inway ethay olyhay ountainsmay.
2 Ethay ORDLAY ovethlay ethay atesgay ofway Ionzay oremay anthay allway ethay ellingsdway ofway Acobjay.
3 Oriousglay ingsthay areway okenspay ofway eethay, OWAY itycay ofway Odgay. Elahsay.
4 IWAY illway akemay entionmay ofway Ahabray andway Abylonbay otay emthay atthay owknay emay: eholdbay Ilistiaphay, andway Etyray, ithway Ethiopiaway; isthay [anmay] asway ornbay erethay.
5 Andway ofway Ionzay itway allshay ebay aidsay, Isthay andway atthay anmay asway ornbay inway erhay: andway ethay ighesthay imselfhay allshay establishway erhay.
6 Ethay ORDLAY allshay ountcay, enwhay ehay itethwray upway ethay eoplepay, [atthay] isthay [anmay] asway ornbay erethay. Elahsay.
7 Asway ellway ethay ingerssay asway ethay ayersplay onway instrumentsway [allshay ebay erethay]: allway myay ingsspray [areway] inway eethay.

ALMPSAY 88

AWAY Ongsay [orway] Almpsay orfay ethay onssay ofway Orahkay, otay ethay iefchay Usicianmay uponway Ahalathmay Eannothlay, Aschilmay ofway Emanhay ethay Ezrahiteway.
1 OWAY ORDLAY Odgay ofway myay alvationsay, IWAY avehay iedcray ayday [andway] ightnay eforebay eethay:
2 Etlay myay ayerpray omecay eforebay eethay: inclineway inethay earway untoway myay cryay;
3 Orfay myay oulsay isway ullfay ofway oublestray: andway myay ifelay awethdray ighnay untoway ethay avegray.
4 IWAY amway ountedcay ithway emthay atthay ogay ownday intoway ethay itpay: IWAY amway asway away anmay [atthay athhay] onay engthstray:
5 Eefray amongway ethay eadday, ikelay ethay ainslay atthay ielay inway ethay avegray, omwhay outhay ememberestray onay oremay: andway eythay areway utcay offway omfray thyay andhay.
6 Outhay asthay aidlay emay inway ethay owestlay itpay, inway arknessday, inway ethay eepsday.
7 Thyay athwray iethlay ardhay uponway emay, andway outhay asthay afflictedway [emay] ithway allway thyay avesway. Elahsay.
8 Outhay asthay utpay awayway inemay acquaintanceway arfay omfray emay; outhay asthay ademay emay anway abominationway untoway

emthay: [IWAY amway] utshay upway, andway IWAY annotcay omecay orthfay.

9 Inemay eyeway ournethmay byay easonray ofway afflictionway: ORDLAY, IWAY avehay alledcay ailyday uponway eethay, IWAY avehay etchedstray outway myay andshay untoway eethay.

10 Iltway outhay ewshay ondersway otay ethay eadday? allshay ethay eadday ariseway [andway] aisepray eethay? Elahsay.

11 Allshay thyay ovingkindnesslay ebay eclaredday inway ethay avegray? [orway] thyay aithfulnessfay inway estructionday?

12 Allshay thyay ondersway ebay ownknay inway ethay arkday? andway thyay ighteousnessray inway ethay andlay ofway orgetfulnessfay?

13 Utbay untoway eethay avehay IWAY iedcray, OWAY ORDLAY; andway inway ethay orningmay allshay myay ayerpray eventpray eethay.

14 ORDLAY, whyay astestcay outhay offway myay oulsay? [whyay] idesthay outhay thyay acefay omfray emay?

15 IWAY [amway] afflictedway andway eadyray otay ieday omfray [myay] outhyay upway: [ilewhay] IWAY uffersay thyay errorstay IWAY amway istractedday.

16 Thyay iercefay athwray oethgay overway emay; thyay errorstay avehay utcay emay offway.

17 Eythay amecay oundray aboutway emay ailyday ikelay aterway; eythay ompassedcay emay aboutway ogethertay.

18 Overlay andway iendfray asthay outhay utpay arfay omfray emay, [andway] inemay acquaintanceway intoway arknessday.

ALMPSAY 89

Aschilmay ofway Ethanway ethay Ezrahiteway.

1 IWAY illway ingsay ofway ethay erciesmay ofway ethay ORDLAY orfay everway: ithway myay outhmay illway IWAY akemay ownknay thyay aithfulnessfay otay allway enerationsgay.

2 Orfay IWAY avehay aidsay, Ercymay allshay ebay uiltbay upway orfay everway: thyay aithfulnessfay altshay outhay establishway inway ethay eryvay eavenshay.

3 IWAY avehay ademay away ovenantcay ithway myay osenchay, IWAY avehay ornsway untoway Avidday myay ervantsay,

4 Thyay eedsay illway IWAY establishway orfay everway, andway uildbay upway thyay onethray otay allway enerationsgay. Elahsay.

5 Andway ethay eavenshay allshay aisepray thyay ondersway, OWAY ORDLAY: thyay aithfulnessfay alsoway inway ethay ongregationcay ofway ethay aintssay.

6 Orfay owhay inway ethay eavenhay ancay ebay omparedcay untoway ethay ORDLAY? [owhay] amongway ethay onssay ofway ethay ightymay ancay ebay ikenedlay untoway ethay ORDLAY?

7 Odgay isway eatlygray otay ebay earedfay inway ethay assemblyway ofway ethay aintssay, andway otay ebay adhay inway everenceray ofway allway [emthay atthay areway] aboutway imhay.

8 OWAY ORDLAY Odgay ofway ostshay, owhay [isway] away ongstray ORDLAY ikelay untoway eethay? orway otay thyay aithfulnessfay oundray aboutway eethay?

9 Outhay ulestray ethay agingray ofway ethay easay: enwhay ethay avesway ereofthay ariseway, outhay illeststay emthay.

10 Outhay asthay okenbray Ahabray inway iecespay, asway oneway atthay isway ainslay; outhay asthay atteredscay inethay enemiesway ithway thyay ongstray armway.

11 Ethay eavenshay [areway] inethay, ethay earthway alsoway [isway] inethay: [asway orfay] ethay orldway andway ethay ulnessfay ereofthay, outhay asthay oundedfay emthay.

12 Ethay orthnay andway ethay outhsay outhay asthay eatedcray emthay: Abortay andway Ermonhay allshay ejoiceray inway thyay amenay.

13 Outhay asthay away ightymay armway: ongstray isway thyay andhay, [andway] ighhay isway thyay ightray andhay.

14 Usticejay andway udgmentjay [areway] ethay abitationhay ofway thyay onethray: ercymay andway uthtray allshay ogay eforebay thyay acefay.

15 Essedblay [isway] ethay eoplepay atthay owknay ethay oyfuljay oundsay: eythay allshay alkway, OWAY ORDLAY, inway ethay ightlay ofway thyay ountenancecay.

16 Inway thyay amenay allshay eythay ejoiceray allway ethay ayday: andway inway thyay ighteousnessray allshay eythay ebay exaltedway.

17 Orfay outhay [artway] ethay oryglay ofway eirthay engthstray: andway inway thyay avourfay ourway ornhay allshay ebay exaltedway.

18 Orfay ethay ORDLAY [isway] ourway efenceday; andway ethay Olyhay Oneway ofway Israelway [isway] ourway ingkay.

19 Enthay outhay akestspay inway isionvay otay thyay olyhay oneway, andway aidstsay, IWAY avehay aidlay elphay uponway [oneway atthay isway] ightymay; IWAY avehay exaltedway [oneway] osenchay outway ofway ethay eoplepay.

20 IWAY avehay oundfay Avidday myay ervantsay; ithway myay olyhay oilway avehay IWAY anointedway imhay:

21 Ithway omwhay myay andhay allshay ebay establishedway: inemay armway alsoway allshay engthenstray imhay.

22 Ethay enemyway allshay otnay exactway uponway imhay; ornay ethay onsay ofway ickednessway afflictway imhay.

23 Andway IWAY illway eatbay ownday ishay oesfay eforebay ishay acefay, andway agueplay emthay atthay atehay imhay.

24 Utbay myay aithfulnessfay andway myay ercymay [allshay ebay] ithway imhay: andway inway myay amenay allshay ishay ornhay ebay exaltedway.

25 IWAY illway etsay ishay andhay alsoway inway ethay easay, andway ishay ightray andhay inway ethay iversray.

26 Ehay allshay cryay untoway emay, Outhay [artway] myay atherfay, myay Odgay, andway ethay ockray ofway myay alvationsay.

27 Alsoway IWAY illway akemay imhay [myay] irstbornfay, igherhay anthay ethay ingskay ofway ethay earthway.

28 Myay ercymay illway IWAY eepkay orfay imhay orfay evermoreway, andway myay ovenantcay allshay andstay astfay ithway imhay.

29 Ishay eedsay alsoway illway IWAY akemay [otay endureway] orfay everway, andway ishay onethray asway ethay aysday ofway eavenhay.

30 Ifway ishay ildrenchay orsakefay myay awlay, andway alkway otnay inway myay udgmentsjay;

31 Ifway eythay eakbray myay atutesstay, andway eepkay otnay myay ommandmentscay;

32 Enthay illway IWAY isitvay eirthay ansgressiontray ithway ethay odray, andway eirthay iniquityway ithway ipesstray.

33 Everthelessnay myay ovingkindnesslay illway IWAY otnay utterlyway aketay omfray imhay, ornay uffersay myay aithfulnessfay otay ailfay.

34 Myay ovenantcay illway IWAY otnay eakbray, ornay alterway ethay ingthay atthay isway onegay outway ofway myay ipslay.

35 Onceway avehay IWAY ornsway byay myay olinesshay atthay IWAY illway otnay ielay untoway Avidday.

36 Ishay eedsay allshay endureway orfay everway, andway ishay onethray asway ethay unsay eforebay emay.

37 Itway allshay ebay establishedway orfay everway asway ethay oonmay, andway [asway] away aithfulfay itnessway inway eavenhay. Elahsay.

38 Utbay outhay asthay astcay offway andway abhorredway, outhay asthay eenbay othwray ithway inethay anointedway.

39 Outhay asthay ademay oidvay ethay ovenantcay ofway thyay ervantsay: outhay asthay ofanedpray ishay owncray [byay astingcay itway] otay ethay oundgray.

40 Outhay asthay okenbray ownday allway ishay edgeshay; outhay asthay oughtbray ishay ongstray oldshay otay uinray.

41 Allway atthay asspay byay ethay ayway oilspay imhay: ehay isway away eproachray otay ishay eighboursnay.

42 Outhay asthay etsay upway ethay ightray andhay ofway ishay adversariesway; outhay asthay ademay allway ishay enemiesway otay ejoiceray.

43 Outhay asthay alsoway urnedtay ethay edgeway ofway ishay ordsway, andway asthay otnay ademay imhay otay andstay inway ethay attlebay.

44 Outhay asthay ademay ishay oryglay otay easecay, andway astcay ishay onethray ownday otay ethay oundgray.

45 Ethay aysday ofway ishay outhyay asthay outhay ortenedshay: outhay asthay overedcay imhay ithway ameshay. Elahsay.

46 Owhay onglay, ORDLAY? iltway outhay idehay elfthysay orfay everway? allshay thyay athwray urnbay ikelay irefay?

47 Ememberray owhay ortshay myay imetay isway: ereforewhay asthay outhay ademay allway enmay inway ainvay?

48 Atwhay anmay [isway ehay atthay] ivethlay, andway allshay otnay eesay eathday? allshay ehay eliverday ishay oulsay omfray ethay andhay ofway ethay avegray? Elahsay.

49 Ordlay, erewhay [areway] thyay ormerfay ovingkindnesseslay, [ichwhay] outhay arestsway untoway Avidday inway thyay uthtray?

50 Ememberray, Ordlay, ethay eproachray ofway thyay ervantssay; [owhay] IWAY oday earbay inway myay osombay [ethay eproachray ofway] allway ethay ightymay eoplepay;

51 Erewithwhay inethay enemiesway avehay eproachedray, OWAY ORDLAY; erewithwhay eythay avehay eproachedray ethay ootstepsfay ofway inethay anointedway.

52 Essedblay [ebay] ethay ORDLAY orfay evermoreway. Amenway, andway Amenway.

ALMPSAY 90

AWAY Ayerpray ofway Osesmay ethay anmay ofway Odgay.

1 Ordlay, outhay asthay eenbay ourway ellingdway aceplay inway allway enerationsgay.

2 Eforebay ethay ountainsmay ereway oughtbray orthfay, orway everway outhay adsthay ormedfay ethay earthway andway ethay orldway, evenway omfray everlastingway otay everlastingway, outhay [artway] Odgay.

3 Outhay urnesttay anmay otay estructionday; andway ayestsay, Eturnray, eyay ildrenchay ofway enmay.

4 Orfay away ousandthay earsyay inway thyay ightsay [areway utbay] asway esterdayyay enwhay itway isway astpay, andway [asway] away atchway inway ethay ightnay.

5 Outhay arriestcay emthay awayway asway ithway away oodflay; eythay areway [asway] away eepslay: inway ethay orningmay [eythay areway] ikelay assgray [ichwhay] owethgray upway.

6 Inway ethay orningmay itway ourishethflay, andway owethgray upway; inway ethay eveningway itway isway utcay ownday, andway itherethway.

7 Orfay eway areway onsumedcay byay inethay angerway, andway byay thyay athwray areway eway oubledtray.

8 Outhay asthay etsay ourway iniquitiesway eforebay eethay, ourway ecretsay [inssay] inway ethay ightlay ofway thyay ountenancecay.

9 Orfay allway ourway aysday areway assedpay awayway inway thyay athwray: eway endspay ourway earsyay asway away aletay [atthay isway oldtay].

10 Ethay aysday ofway ourway earsyay [areway] eescorethray earsyay andway entay; andway ifway byay easonray ofway engthstray [eythay ebay] ourscorefay earsyay, etyay [isway] eirthay engthstray abourlay andway orrowsay; orfay itway isway oonsay utcay offway, andway eway flyay awayway.

11 Owhay owethknay ethay owerpay ofway inethay angerway? evenway accordingway otay thyay earfay, [osay isway] thyay athwray.

12 Osay eachtay [usway] otay umbernay ourway aysday, atthay eway aymay applyway [ourway] eartshay untoway isdomway.

13 Eturnray, OWAY ORDLAY, owhay onglay? andway etlay itway epentray eethay oncerningcay thyay ervantssay.

14 OWAY atisfysay usway earlyway ithway thyay ercymay; atthay eway aymay ejoiceray andway ebay adglay allway ourway aysday.

15 Akemay usway adglay accordingway otay ethay aysday [ereinwhay] outhay asthay afflictedway usway, [andway] ethay earsyay [ereinwhay] eway avehay eensay evilway.

16 Etlay thyay orkway appearway untoway thyay ervantssay, andway thyay oryglay untoway eirthay ildrenchay.

17 Andway etlay ethay eautybay ofway ethay ORDLAY ourway Odgay ebay uponway usway: andway establishway outhay ethay orkway ofway ourway andshay uponway usway; eayay, ethay orkway ofway ourway andshay establishway outhay itway.

ALMPSAY 91

1 Ehay atthay ellethdway inway ethay ecretsay aceplay ofway ethay ostmay Ighhay allshay abideway underway ethay adowshay ofway ethay Almightyway.

2 IWAY illway aysay ofway ethay ORDLAY, [Ehay isway] myay efugeray andway myay ortressfay: myay Odgay; inway imhay illway IWAY usttray.

3 Urelysay ehay allshay eliverday eethay omfray ethay aresnay ofway ethay owlerfay, [andway] omfray ethay oisomenay estilencepay.

4 Ehay allshay overcay eethay ithway ishay eathersfay, andway underway ishay ingsway altshay outhay usttray: ishay uthtray [allshay ebay thyay] ieldshay andway ucklerbay.

5 Outhay altshay otnay ebay afraidway orfay ethay errortay byay ightnay; [ornay] orfay ethay arrowway [atthay] iethflay byay ayday;

6 [Ornay] orfay ethay estilencepay [atthay] alkethway inway arknessday; [ornay] orfay ethay estructionday [atthay] astethway atway oondaynay.

7 AWAY ousandthay allshay allfay atway thyay idesay, andway entay ousandthay atway thyay ightray andhay; [utbay] itway allshay otnay omecay ighnay eethay.

8 Onlyway ithway inethay eyesway altshay outhay eholdbay andway eesay ethay ewardray ofway ethay ickedway.

9 Ecausebay outhay asthay ademay ethay ORDLAY, [ichwhay isway] myay efugeray, [evenway] ethay ostmay Ighhay, thyay abitationhay;

10 Erethay allshay onay evilway efallbay eethay, eithernay allshay anyway agueplay omecay ighnay thyay ellingdway.

11 Orfay ehay allshay ivegay ishay angelsway argechay overway eethay, otay eepkay eethay inway allway thyay aysway.

12 Eythay allshay earbay eethay upway inway [eirthay] andshay, estlay outhay ashday thyay ootfay againstway away onestay.

13 Outhay altshay eadtray uponway ethay ionlay andway adderway: ethay oungyay ionlay andway ethay agondray altshay outhay ampletray underway eetfay.

14 Ecausebay ehay athhay etsay ishay ovelay uponway emay, ereforethay illway IWAY eliverday imhay: IWAY illway etsay imhay onway ighhay, ecausebay ehay athhay ownknay myay amenay.

15 Ehay allshay allcay uponway emay, andway IWAY illway answerway imhay: IWAY [illway ebay] ithway imhay inway oubletray; IWAY illway eliverday imhay, andway onourhay imhay.

16 Ithway onglay ifelay illway IWAY atisfysay imhay, andway ewshay imhay myay alvationsay.

ALMPSAY 92

AWAY Almpsay [orway] Ongsay orfay ethay abbathsay ayday.

1 [Itway isway away] oodgay [ingthay] otay ivegay anksthay untoway ethay ORDLAY, andway otay ingsay aisespray untoway thyay amenay, OWAY ostmay Ighhay:

2 Otay ewshay orthfay thyay ovingkindnesslay inway ethay orningmay, andway thyay aithfulnessfay everyway ightnay,

3 Uponway anway instrumentway ofway entay ingsstray, andway uponway ethay alterypsay; uponway ethay arphay ithway away olemnsay oundsay.

4 Orfay outhay, ORDLAY, asthay ademay emay adglay oughthray thyay orkway: IWAY illway iumphtray inway ethay orksway ofway thyay andshay.

5 OWAY ORDLAY, owhay eatgray areway thyay orksway! [andway] thyay oughtsthay areway eryvay eepday.

6 AWAY utishbray anmay owethknay otnay; eithernay othday away oolfay understandway isthay.

7 Enwhay ethay ickedway ingspray asway ethay assgray, andway enwhay allway ethay orkersway ofway iniquityway oday ourishflay; [itway isway] atthay eythay allshay ebay estroyedday orfay everway:

8 Utbay outhay, ORDLAY, [artway ostmay] ighhay orfay evermoreway.

9 Orfay, olay, inethay enemiesway, OWAY ORDLAY, orfay, olay, inethay enemiesway allshay erishpay; allway ethay orkersway ofway iniquityway allshay ebay atteredscay.

10 Utbay myay ornhay altshay outhay exaltway ikelay [ethay ornhay ofway] anway unicornway: IWAY allshay ebay anointedway ithway eshfray oilway.

11 Inemay eyeway alsoway allshay eesay [myay esireday] onway inemay enemiesway, [andway] inemay earsway allshay earhay [myay esireday] ofway ethay ickedway atthay iseray upway againstway emay.

12 Ethay ighteousray allshay ourishflay ikelay ethay almpay eetray: ehay allshay owgray ikelay away edarcay inway Ebanonlay.

13 Osethay atthay ebay antedplay inway ethay ousehay ofway ethay ORDLAY allshay ourishflay inway ethay ourtscay ofway ourway Odgay.

14 Eythay allshay illstay ingbray orthfay uitfray inway oldway ageway; eythay allshay ebay atfay andway ourishingflay;

15 Otay ewshay atthay ethay ORDLAY [isway] uprightway: [ehay isway] myay ockray, andway [erethay isway] onay unrighteousnessway inway imhay.

ALMPSAY 93
1 Ethay ORDLAY eignethray, ehay isway othedclay ithway ajestymay;
ethay ORDLAY isway othedclay ithway engthstray, [erewithwhay] ehay
athhay irdedgay imselfhay: ethay orldway alsoway isway ablishedstay,
atthay itway annotcay ebay ovedmay.
2 Thyay onethray [isway] establishedway ofway oldway: outhay [artway]
omfray everlastingway.
3 Ethay oodsflay avehay iftedlay upway, OWAY ORDLAY, ethay
oodsflay avehay iftedlay upway eirthay oicevay; ethay oodsflay iftlay
upway eirthay avesway.
4 Ethay ORDLAY onway ighhay [isway] ightiermay anthay ethay oisenay
ofway anymay atersway, [eayay, anthay] ethay ightymay avesway ofway
ethay easay.
5 Thyay estimoniestay areway eryvay uresay: olinesshay ecomethbay
inethay ousehay, OWAY ORDLAY, orfay everway.

ALMPSAY 94
1 OWAY ORDLAY Odgay, otay omwhay engeancevay elongethbay;
OWAY Odgay, otay omwhay engeancevay elongethbay, ewshay
elfthysay.
2 Iftlay upway elfthysay, outhay udgejay ofway ethay earthway: enderray
away ewardray otay ethay oudpray.
3 ORDLAY, owhay onglay allshay ethay ickedway, owhay onglay allshay
ethay ickedway iumphtray?
4 [Owhay onglay] allshay eythay utterway [andway] eakspay ardhay
ingsthay? [andway] allway ethay orkersway ofway iniquityway oastbay
emselvesthay?
5 Eythay eakbray inway iecespay thyay eoplepay, OWAY ORDLAY,
andway afflictway inethay eritagehay.
6 Eythay ayslay ethay idowway andway ethay angerstray, andway
urdermay ethay atherlessfay.
7 Etyay eythay aysay, Ethay ORDLAY allshay otnay eesay, eithernay
allshay ethay Odgay ofway Acobjay egardray [itway].
8 Understandway, eyay utishbray amongway ethay eoplepay: andway
[eyay] oolsfay, enwhay illway eyay ebay iseway?
9 Ehay atthay antedplay ethay earway, allshay ehay otnay earhay? ehay
atthay ormedfay ethay eyeway, allshay ehay otnay eesay?
10 Ehay atthay astisethchay ethay eathenhay, allshay otnay ehay
orrectcay? ehay atthay eachethtay anmay owledgeknay, [allshay otnay
ehay owknay]?

11 Ethay ORDLAY owethknay ethay oughtsthay ofway anmay, atthay eythay [areway] anityvay.

12 Essedblay [isway] ethay anmay omwhay outhay astenestchay, OWAY ORDLAY, andway eachesttay imhay outway ofway thyay awlay;

13 Atthay outhay ayestmay ivegay imhay estray omfray ethay aysday ofway adversityway, untilway ethay itpay ebay iggedday orfay ethay ickedway.

14 Orfay ethay ORDLAY illway otnay astcay offway ishay eoplepay, eithernay illway ehay orsakefay ishay inheritanceway.

15 Utbay udgmentjay allshay eturnray untoway ighteousnessray: andway allway ethay uprightway inway earthay allshay ollowfay itway.

16 Owhay illway iseray upway orfay emay againstway ethay evildoersway? [orway] owhay illway andstay upway orfay emay againstway ethay orkersway ofway iniquityway?

17 Unlessway ethay ORDLAY [adhay eenbay] myay elphay, myay oulsay adhay almostway eltdway inway ilencesay.

18 Enwhay IWAY aidsay, Myay ootfay ippethslay; thyay ercymay, OWAY ORDLAY, eldhay emay upway.

19 Inway ethay ultitudemay ofway myay oughtsthay ithinway emay thyay omfortscay elightday myay oulsay.

20 Allshay ethay onethray ofway iniquityway avehay ellowshipfay ithway eethay, ichwhay amethfray ischiefmay byay away awlay?

21 Eythay athergay emselvesthay ogethertay againstway ethay oulsay ofway ethay ighteousray, andway ondemncay ethay innocentway oodblay.

22 Utbay ethay ORDLAY isway myay efenceday; andway myay Odgay [isway] ethay ockray ofway myay efugeray.

23 Andway ehay allshay ingbray uponway emthay eirthay ownway iniquityway, andway allshay utcay emthay offway inway eirthay ownway ickednessway; [eayay], ethay ORDLAY ourway Odgay allshay utcay emthay offway.

ALMPSAY 95

1 OWAY omecay, etlay usway ingsay untoway ethay ORDLAY: etlay usway akemay away oyfuljay oisenay otay ethay ockray ofway ourway alvationsay.

2 Etlay usway omecay eforebay ishay esencepray ithway anksgivingthay, andway akemay away oyfuljay oisenay untoway imhay ithway almspsay.

3 Orfay ethay ORDLAY [isway] away eatgray Odgay, andway away eatgray Ingkay aboveway allway odsgay.

4 Inway ishay andhay [areway] ethay eepday acesplay ofway ethay earthway: ethay engthstray ofway ethay illshay [isway] ishay alsoway.

5 Ethay easay [isway] ishay, andway ehay ademay itway: andway ishay andshay ormedfay ethay dryay [andlay].

6 OWAY omecay, etlay usway orshipway andway owbay ownday: etlay usway eelknay eforebay ethay ORDLAY ourway akermay.

7 Orfay ehay [isway] ourway Odgay; andway eway [areway] ethay eoplepay ofway ishay asturepay, andway ethay eepshay ofway ishay andhay. Otay ayday ifway eyay illway earhay ishay oicevay,

8 Ardenhay otnay ouryay earthay, asway inway ethay ovocationpray, [andway] asway [inway] ethay ayday ofway emptationtay inway ethay ildernessway:

9 Enwhay ouryay athersfay emptedtay emay, ovedpray emay, andway awsay myay orkway.

10 Ortyfay earsyay onglay asway IWAY ievedgray ithway [isthay] enerationgay, andway aidsay, Itway [isway] away eoplepay atthay oday errway inway eirthay earthay, andway eythay avehay otnay ownknay myay aysway:

11 Untoway omwhay IWAY aresway inway myay athwray atthay eythay ouldshay otnay enterway intoway myay estray.

ALMPSAY 96

1 OWAY ingsay untoway ethay ORDLAY away ewnay ongsay: ingsay untoway ethay ORDLAY, allway ethay earthway.

2 Ingsay untoway ethay ORDLAY, essblay ishay amenay; ewshay orthfay ishay alvationsay omfray ayday otay ayday.

3 Eclareday ishay oryglay amongway ethay eathenhay, ishay ondersway amongway allway eoplepay.

4 Orfay ethay ORDLAY [isway] eatgray, andway eatlygray otay ebay aisedpray: ehay [isway] otay ebay earedfay aboveway allway odsgay.

5 Orfay allway ethay odsgay ofway ethay ationsnay [areway] idolsway: utbay ethay ORDLAY ademay ethay eavenshay.

6 Onourhay andway ajestymay [areway] eforebay imhay: engthstray andway eautybay [areway] inway ishay anctuarysay.

7 Ivegay untoway ethay ORDLAY, OWAY eyay indredskay ofway ethay eoplepay, ivegay untoway ethay ORDLAY oryglay andway engthstray.

8 Ivegay untoway ethay ORDLAY ethay oryglay [ueday untoway] ishay amenay: ingbray anway offeringway, andway omecay intoway ishay ourtscay.

9 OWAY orshipway ethay ORDLAY inway ethay eautybay ofway olinesshay: earfay eforebay imhay, allway ethay earthway.

10 Aysay amongway ethay eathenhay [atthay] ethay ORDLAY eignethray: ethay orldway alsoway allshay ebay establishedway atthay itway allshay otnay ebay ovedmay: ehay allshay udgejay ethay eoplepay ighteouslyray.

11 Etlay ethay eavenshay ejoiceray, andway etlay ethay earthway ebay adglay; etlay ethay easay oarray, andway ethay ulnessfay ereofthay.

12 Etlay ethay ieldfay ebay oyfuljay, andway allway atthay [isway] ereinthay: enthay allshay allway ethay eestray ofway ethay oodway ejoiceray

13 Eforebay ethay ORDLAY: orfay ehay omethcay, orfay ehay omethcay otay udgejay ethay earthway: ehay allshay udgejay ethay orldway ithway ighteousnessray, andway ethay eoplepay ithway ishay uthtray.

ALMPSAY 97

1 Ethay ORDLAY eignethray; etlay ethay earthway ejoiceray; etlay ethay ultitudemay ofway islesway ebay adglay [ereofthay].

2 Oudsclay andway arknessday [areway] oundray aboutway imhay: ighteousnessray andway udgmentjay [areway] ethay abitationhay ofway ishay onethray.

3 AWAY irefay oethgay eforebay imhay, andway urnethbay upway ishay enemiesway oundray aboutway.

4 Ishay ightningslay enlightenedway ethay orldway: ethay earthway awsay, andway embledtray.

5 Ethay illshay eltedmay ikelay axway atway ethay esencepray ofway ethay ORDLAY, atway ethay esencepray ofway ethay Ordlay ofway ethay olewhay earthway.

6 Ethay eavenshay eclareday ishay ighteousnessray, andway allway ethay eoplepay eesay ishay oryglay.

7 Onfoundedcay ebay allway eythay atthay ervesay avengray imagesway, atthay oastbay emselvesthay ofway idolsway: orshipway imhay, allway [eyay] odsgay.

8 Ionzay eardhay, andway asway adglay; andway ethay aughtersday ofway Udahjay ejoicedray ecausebay ofway thyay udgmentsjay, OWAY ORDLAY.

9 Orfay outhay, ORDLAY, [artway] ighhay aboveway allway ethay earthway: outhay artway exaltedway arfay aboveway allway odsgay.

10 Eyay atthay ovelay ethay ORDLAY, atehay evilway: ehay
eservethpray ethay oulssay ofway ishay aintssay; ehay eliverethday emthay
outway ofway ethay andhay ofway ethay ickedway.

11 Ightlay isway ownsay orfay ethay ighteousray, andway adnessglay orfay
ethay uprightway inway earthay.

12 Ejoiceray inway ethay ORDLAY, eyay ighteousray; andway ivegay
anksthay atway ethay emembranceray ofway ishay olinesshay.

ALMPSAY 98
AWAY Almpsay.

1 OWAY ingsay untoway ethay ORDLAY away ewnay ongsay; orfay
ehay athhay oneday arvellousmay ingsthay: ishay ightray andhay, andway
ishay olyhay armway, athhay ottengay imhay ethay ictoryvay.

2 Ethay ORDLAY athhay ademay ownknay ishay alvationsay: ishay
ighteousnessray athhay ehay openlyway ewedshay inway ethay ightsay
ofway ethay eathenhay.

3 Ehay athhay ememberedray ishay ercymay andway ishay uthtray
owardtay ethay ousehay ofway Israelway: allway ethay endsway ofway
ethay earthway avehay eensay ethay alvationsay ofway ourway Odgay.

4 Akemay away oyfuljay oisenay untoway ethay ORDLAY, allway ethay
earthway: akemay away oudlay oisenay, andway ejoiceray, andway ingsay
aisepray.

5 Ingsay untoway ethay ORDLAY ithway ethay arphay; ithway ethay
arphay, andway ethay oicevay ofway away almpsay.

6 Ithway umpetstray andway oundsay ofway ornetcay akemay away
oyfuljay oisenay eforebay ethay ORDLAY, ethay Ingkay.

7 Etlay ethay easay oarray, andway ethay ulnessfay ereofthay; ethay
orldway, andway eythay atthay elldway ereinthay.

8 Etlay ethay oodsflay apclay [eirthay] andshay: etlay ethay illshay ebay
oyfuljay ogethertay

9 Eforebay ethay ORDLAY; orfay ehay omethcay otay udgejay ethay
earthway: ithway ighteousnessray allshay ehay udgejay ethay orldway,
andway ethay eoplepay ithway equityway.

ALMPSAY 99
1 Ethay ORDLAY eignethray; etlay ethay eoplepay embletray: ehay
ittethsay [etweenbay] ethay erubimschay; etlay ethay earthway ebay
ovedmay.

2 Ethay ORDLAY [isway] eatgray inway Ionzay; andway ehay [isway]
ighhay aboveway allway ethay eoplepay.

3 Etlay emthay aisepray thyay eatgray andway erribletay amenay; [orfay] itway [isway] olyhay.

4 Ethay ingkay'say engthstray alsoway ovethlay udgmentjay; outhay ostday establishway equityway, outhay executestway udgmentjay andway ighteousnessray inway Acobjay.

5 Exaltway eyay ethay ORDLAY ourway Odgay, andway orshipway atway ishay ootstoolfay; [orfay] ehay [isway] olyhay.

6 Osesmay andway Aaronway amongway ishay iestspray, andway Amuelsay amongway emthay atthay allcay uponway ishay amenay; eythay alledcay uponway ethay ORDLAY, andway ehay answeredway emthay.

7 Ehay akespay untoway emthay inway ethay oudyclay illarpay: eythay eptkay ishay estimoniestay, andway ethay ordinanceway [atthay] ehay avegay emthay.

8 Outhay answeredstway emthay, OWAY ORDLAY ourway Odgay: outhay astway away Odgay atthay orgavestfay emthay, oughthay outhay ookesttay engeancevay ofway eirthay inventionsway.

9 Exaltway ethay ORDLAY ourway Odgay, andway orshipway atway ishay olyhay illhay; orfay ethay ORDLAY ourway Odgay [isway] olyhay.

ALMPSAY 100
AWAY Almpsay ofway aisepray.

1 Akemay away oyfuljay oisenay untoway ethay ORDLAY, allway eyay andslay.

2 Ervesay ethay ORDLAY ithway adnessglay: omecay eforebay ishay esencepray ithway ingingsay.

3 Owknay eyay atthay ethay ORDLAY ehay [isway] Odgay: [itway isway] ehay [atthay] athhay ademay usway, andway otnay eway ourselvesway; [eway areway] ishay eoplepay, andway ethay eepshay ofway ishay asturepay.

4 Enterway intoway ishay atesgay ithway anksgivingthay, [andway] intoway ishay ourtscay ithway aisepray: ebay ankfulthay untoway imhay, [andway] essblay ishay amenay.

5 Orfay ethay ORDLAY [isway] oodgay; ishay ercymay [isway] everlastingway; andway ishay uthtray [endurethway] otay allway enerationsgay.

ALMPSAY 101
AWAY Almpsay ofway Avidday.

1 IWAY illway ingsay ofway ercymay andway udgmentjay: untoway eethay, OWAY ORDLAY, illway IWAY ingsay.

2 IWAY illway ehavebay elfmysay iselyway inway away erfectpay ayway.
OWAY enwhay iltway outhay omecay untoway emay? IWAY illway
alkway ithinway myay ousehay ithway away erfectpay earthay.

3 IWAY illway etsay onay ickedway ingthay eforebay inemay eyesway:
IWAY atehay ethay orkway ofway emthay atthay urntay asideway; [itway]
allshay otnay eaveclay otay emay.

4 AWAY owardfray earthay allshay epartday omfray emay: IWAY illway
otnay owknay away ickedway [ersonpay].

5 Osowhay ivilypray anderethslay ishay eighbournay, imhay illway IWAY
utcay offway: imhay atthay athhay anway ighhay ooklay andway away
oudpray earthay illway otnay IWAY uffersay.

6 Inemay eyesway [allshay ebay] uponway ethay aithfulfay ofway ethay
andlay, atthay eythay aymay elldway ithway emay: ehay atthay alkethway
inway away erfectpay ayway, ehay allshay ervesay emay.

7 Ehay atthay orkethway eceitday allshay otnay elldway ithinway myay
ousehay: ehay atthay ellethtay ieslay allshay otnay arrytay inway myay
ightsay.

8 IWAY illway earlyway estroyday allway ethay ickedway ofway ethay
andlay; atthay IWAY aymay utcay offway allway ickedway oersday
omfray ethay itycay ofway ethay ORDLAY.

ALMPSAY 102
AWAY Ayerpray ofway ethay afflictedway, enwhay ehay isway
overwhelmedway, andway ourethpay outway ishay omplaintcay eforebay
ethay ORDLAY.

1 Earhay myay ayerpray, OWAY ORDLAY, andway etlay myay cryay
omecay untoway eethay.

2 Idehay otnay thyay acefay omfray emay inway ethay ayday [enwhay]
IWAY amway inway oubletray; inclineway inethay earway untoway
emay: inway ethay ayday [enwhay] IWAY allcay answerway emay
eedilyspay.

3 Orfay myay aysday areway onsumedcay ikelay okesmay, andway myay
onesbay areway urnedbay asway anway earthhay.

4 Myay earthay isway ittensmay, andway itheredway ikelay assgray; osay
atthay IWAY orgetfay otay eatway myay eadbray.

5 Byay easonray ofway ethay oicevay ofway myay oaninggray myay
onesbay eaveclay otay myay inskay.

6 IWAY amway ikelay away elicanpay ofway ethay ildernessway: IWAY
amway ikelay anway owlway ofway ethay esertday.

7 IWAY atchway, andway amway asway away arrowspay aloneway uponway ethay ousehay optay.

8 Inemay enemiesway eproachray emay allway ethay ayday; [andway] eythay atthay areway admay againstway emay areway ornsway againstway emay.

9 Orfay IWAY avehay eatenway ashesway ikelay eadbray, andway ingledmay myay inkdray ithway eepingway,

10 Ecausebay ofway inethay indignationway andway thyay athwray: orfay outhay asthay iftedlay emay upway, andway astcay emay ownday.

11 Myay aysday [areway] ikelay away adowshay atthay eclinethday; andway IWAY amway itheredway ikelay assgray.

12 Utbay outhay, OWAY ORDLAY, altshay endureway orfay everway; andway thyay emembranceray untoway allway enerationsgay.

13 Outhay altshay ariseway, [andway] avehay ercymay uponway Ionzay: orfay ethay imetay otay avourfay erhay, eayay, ethay etsay imetay, isway omecay.

14 Orfay thyay ervantssay aketay easureplay inway erhay onesstay, andway avourfay ethay ustday ereofthay.

15 Osay ethay eathenhay allshay earfay ethay amenay ofway ethay ORDLAY, andway allway ethay ingskay ofway ethay earthway thyay oryglay.

16 Enwhay ethay ORDLAY allshay uildbay upway Ionzay, ehay allshay appearway inway ishay oryglay.

17 Ehay illway egardray ethay ayerpray ofway ethay estituteday, andway otnay espiseday eirthay ayerpray.

18 Isthay allshay ebay ittenwray orfay ethay enerationgay otay omecay: andway ethay eoplepay ichwhay allshay ebay eatedcray allshay aisepray ethay ORDLAY.

19 Orfay ehay athhay ookedlay ownday omfray ethay eighthay ofway ishay anctuarysay; omfray eavenhay idday ethay ORDLAY eholdbay ethay earthway;

20 Otay earhay ethay oaninggray ofway ethay isonerpray; otay ooselay osethay atthay areway appointedway otay eathday;

21 Otay eclareday ethay amenay ofway ethay ORDLAY inway Ionzay, andway ishay aisepray inway Erusalemjay;

22 Enwhay ethay eoplepay areway atheredgay ogethertay, andway ethay ingdomskay, otay ervesay ethay ORDLAY.

23 Ehay eakenedway myay engthstray inway ethay ayway; ehay ortenedshay myay aysday.

24 IWAY aidsay, OWAY myay Odgay, aketay emay otnay awayway inway ethay idstmay ofway myay aysday: thyay earsyay [areway] oughoutthray allway enerationsgay.

25 Ofway oldway asthay outhay aidlay ethay oundationfay ofway ethay earthway: andway ethay eavenshay [areway] ethay orkway ofway thyay andshay.

26 Eythay allshay erishpay, utbay outhay altshay endureway: eayay, allway ofway emthay allshay axway oldway ikelay away armentgay; asway away esturevay altshay outhay angechay emthay, andway eythay allshay ebay angedchay:

27 Utbay outhay [artway] ethay amesay, andway thyay earsyay allshay avehay onay endway.

28 Ethay ildrenchay ofway thyay ervantssay allshay ontinuecay, andway eirthay eedsay allshay ebay establishedway eforebay eethay.

ALMPSAY 103
[AWAY Almpsay] ofway Avidday.

1 Essblay ethay ORDLAY, OWAY myay oulsay: andway allway atthay isway ithinway emay, [essblay] ishay olyhay amenay.

2 Essblay ethay ORDLAY, OWAY myay oulsay, andway orgetfay otnay allway ishay enefitsbay:

3 Owhay orgivethfay allway inethay iniquitiesway; owhay ealethhay allway thyay iseasesday;

4 Owhay edeemethray thyay ifelay omfray estructionday; owhay ownethcray eethay ithway ovingkindnesslay andway endertay erciesmay;

5 Owhay atisfiethsay thyay outhmay ithway oodgay [ingsthay; osay atthay] thyay outhyay isway enewedray ikelay ethay eagleway'say.

6 Ethay ORDLAY executethway ighteousnessray andway udgmentjay orfay allway atthay areway oppressedway.

7 Ehay ademay ownknay ishay aysway untoway Osesmay, ishay actsway untoway ethay ildrenchay ofway Israelway.

8 Ethay ORDLAY [isway] ercifulmay andway aciousgray, owslay otay angerway, andway enteousplay inway ercymay.

9 Ehay illway otnay alwaysway idechay: eithernay illway ehay eepkay [ishay angerway] orfay everway.

10 Ehay athhay otnay ealtday ithway usway afterway ourway inssay; ornay ewardedray usway accordingway otay ourway iniquitiesway.

11 Orfay asway ethay eavenhay isway ighhay aboveway ethay earthway, [osay] eatgray isway ishay ercymay owardtay emthay atthay earfay imhay.

12 Asway arfay asway ethay eastway isway omfray ethay estway, [osay] arfay athhay ehay emovedray ourway ansgressionstray omfray usway.

13 Ikelay asway away atherfay itiethpay [ishay] ildrenchay, [osay] ethay ORDLAY itiethpay emthay atthay earfay imhay.

14 Orfay ehay owethknay ourway amefray; ehay ememberethray atthay eway [areway] ustday.

15 [Asway orfay] anmay, ishay aysday [areway] asway assgray: asway away owerflay ofway ethay ieldfay, osay ehay ourishethflay.

16 Orfay ethay indway assethpay overway itway, andway itway isway onegay; andway ethay aceplay ereofthay allshay owknay itway onay oremay.

17 Utbay ethay ercymay ofway ethay ORDLAY [isway] omfray everlastingway otay everlastingway uponway emthay atthay earfay imhay, andway ishay ighteousnessray untoway ildrenchay'say ildrenchay;

18 Otay uchsay asway eepkay ishay ovenantcay, andway otay osethay atthay ememberray ishay ommandmentscay otay oday emthay.

19 Ethay ORDLAY athhay eparedpray ishay onethray inway ethay eavenshay; andway ishay ingdomkay ulethray overway allway.

20 Essblay ethay ORDLAY, eyay ishay angelsway, atthay excelway inway engthstray, atthay oday ishay ommandmentscay, earkeninghay untoway ethay oicevay ofway ishay ordway.

21 Essblay eyay ethay ORDLAY, allway [eyay] ishay ostshay; [eyay] inistersmay ofway ishay, atthay oday ishay easureplay.

22 Essblay ethay ORDLAY, allway ishay orksway inway allway acesplay ofway ishay ominionday: essblay ethay ORDLAY, OWAY myay oulsay.

ALMPSAY 104

1 Essblay ethay ORDLAY, OWAY myay oulsay. OWAY ORDLAY myay Odgay, outhay artway eryvay eatgray; outhay artway othedclay ithway onourhay andway ajestymay.

2 Owhay overestcay [elfthysay] ithway ightlay asway [ithway] away armentgay: owhay etcheststray outway ethay eavenshay ikelay away urtaincay:

3 Owhay ayethlay ethay eamsbay ofway ishay amberschay inway ethay atersway: owhay akethmay ethay oudsclay ishay ariotchay: owhay alkethway uponway ethay ingsway ofway ethay indway:

4 Owhay akethmay ishay angelsway iritsspay; ishay inistersmay away amingflay irefay:

5 [Owhay] aidlay ethay oundationsfay ofway ethay earthway, [atthay] itway ouldshay otnay ebay emovedray orfay everway.

6 Outhay overedstcay itway ithway ethay eepday asway [ithway] away armentgay: ethay atersway oodstay aboveway ethay ountainsmay.

7 Atway thyay ebukeray eythay edflay; atway ethay oicevay ofway thyay underthay eythay astedhay awayway.

8 Eythay ogay upway byay ethay ountainsmay; eythay ogay ownday byay ethay alleysvay untoway ethay aceplay ichwhay outhay asthay oundedfay orfay emthay.

9 Outhay asthay etsay away oundbay atthay eythay aymay otnay asspay overway; atthay eythay urntay otnay againway otay overcay ethay earthway.

10 Ehay endethsay ethay ingsspray intoway ethay alleysvay, [ichwhay] unray amongway ethay illshay.

11 Eythay ivegay inkdray otay everyway eastbay ofway ethay ieldfay: ethay ildway assesway uenchqay eirthay irstthay.

12 Byay emthay allshay ethay owlsfay ofway ethay eavenhay avehay eirthay abitationhay, [ichwhay] ingsay amongway ethay anchesbray.

13 Ehay aterethway ethay illshay omfray ishay amberschay: ethay earthway isway atisfiedsay ithway ethay uitfray ofway thyay orksway.

14 Ehay ausethcay ethay assgray otay owgray orfay ethay attlecay, andway erbhay orfay ethay ervicesay ofway anmay: atthay ehay aymay ingbray orthfay oodfay outway ofway ethay earthway;

15 Andway ineway [atthay] akethmay adglay ethay earthay ofway anmay, [andway] oilway otay akemay [ishay] acefay otay ineshay, andway eadbray [ichwhay] engthenethstray anmay'say earthay.

16 Ethay eestray ofway ethay ORDLAY areway ullfay [ofway apsay]; ethay edarscay ofway Ebanonlay, ichwhay ehay athhay antedplay;

17 Erewhay ethay irdsbay akemay eirthay estsnay: [asway orfay] ethay orkstay, ethay irfay eestray [areway] erhay ousehay.

18 Ethay ighhay illshay [areway] away efugeray orfay ethay ildway oatsgay; [andway] ethay ocksray orfay ethay oniescay.

19 Ehay appointedway ethay oonmay orfay easonssay: ethay unsay owethknay ishay oinggay ownday.

20 Outhay akestmay arknessday, andway itway isway ightnay: ereinwhay allway ethay eastsbay ofway ethay orestfay oday eepcray [orthfay].

21 Ethay oungyay ionslay oarray afterway eirthay eypray, andway eeksay eirthay eatmay omfray Odgay.

22 Ethay unsay arisethway, eythay athergay emselvesthay ogethertay, andway aylay emthay ownday inway eirthay ensday.

23 Anmay oethgay orthfay untoway ishay orkway andway otay ishay abourlay untilway ethay eveningway.

24 OWAY ORDLAY, owhay anifoldmay areway thyay orksway! inway isdomway asthay outhay ademay emthay allway: ethay earthway isway ullfay ofway thyay ichesray.

25 [Osay isway] isthay eatgray andway ideway easay, ereinwhay [areway] ingsthay eepingcray innumerableway, othbay allsmay andway eatgray eastsbay.

26 Erethay ogay ethay ipsshay: [erethay isway] atthay eviathanlay, [omwhay] outhay asthay ademay otay ayplay ereinthay.

27 Esethay aitway allway uponway eethay; atthay outhay ayestmay ivegay [emthay] eirthay eatmay inway ueday easonsay.

28 [Atthay] outhay ivestgay emthay eythay athergay: outhay openestway inethay andhay, eythay areway illedfay ithway oodgay.

29 Outhay idesthay thyay acefay, eythay areway oubledtray: outhay akesttay awayway eirthay eathbray, eythay ieday, andway eturnray otay eirthay ustday.

30 Outhay endestsay orthfay thyay iritspay, eythay areway eatedcray: andway outhay enewestray ethay acefay ofway ethay earthway.

31 Ethay oryglay ofway ethay ORDLAY allshay endureway orfay everway: ethay ORDLAY allshay ejoiceray inway ishay orksway.

32 Ehay ookethlay onway ethay earthway, andway itway emblethtray: ehay ouchethtay ethay illshay, andway eythay okesmay.

33 IWAY illway ingsay untoway ethay ORDLAY asway onglay asway IWAY ivelay: IWAY illway ingsay aisepray otay myay Odgay ilewhay IWAY avehay myay eingbay.

34 Myay editationmay ofway imhay allshay ebay eetsway: IWAY illway ebay adglay inway ethay ORDLAY.

35 Etlay ethay innerssay ebay onsumedcay outway ofway ethay earthway, andway etlay ethay ickedway ebay onay oremay. Essblay outhay ethay ORDLAY, OWAY myay oulsay. Aisepray eyay ethay ORDLAY.

ALMPSAY 105

1 OWAY ivegay anksthay untoway ethay ORDLAY; allcay uponway ishay amenay: akemay ownknay ishay eedsday amongway ethay eoplepay.

2 Ingsay untoway imhay, ingsay almspsay untoway imhay: alktay eyay ofway allway ishay ondrousway orksway.

3 Oryglay eyay inway ishay olyhay amenay: etlay ethay earthay ofway emthay ejoiceray atthay eeksay ethay ORDLAY.

4 Eeksay ethay ORDLAY, andway ishay engthstray: eeksay ishay acefay evermoreway.

5 Ememberray ishay arvellousmay orksway atthay ehay athhay oneday; ishay ondersway, andway ethay udgmentsjay ofway ishay outhmay;
6 OWAY eyay eedsay ofway Abrahamway ishay ervantsay, eyay ildrenchay ofway Acobjay ishay osenchay.
7 Ehay [isway] ethay ORDLAY ourway Odgay: ishay udgmentsjay [areway] inway allway ethay earthway.
8 Ehay athhay ememberedray ishay ovenantcay orfay everway, ethay ordway [ichwhay] ehay ommandedcay otay away ousandthay enerationsgay.
9 Ichwhay [ovenantcay] ehay ademay ithway Abrahamway, andway ishay oathway untoway Isaacway;
10 Andway onfirmedcay ethay amesay untoway Acobjay orfay away awlay, [andway] otay Israelway [orfay] anway everlastingway ovenantcay:
11 Ayingsay, Untoway eethay illway IWAY ivegay ethay andlay ofway Anaancay, ethay otlay ofway ouryay inheritanceway:
12 Enwhay eythay ereway [utbay] away ewfay enmay inway umbernay; eayay, eryvay ewfay, andway angersstray inway itway.
13 Enwhay eythay entway omfray oneway ationnay otay anotherway, omfray [oneway] ingdomkay otay anotherway eoplepay;
14 Ehay ufferedsay onay anmay otay oday emthay ongwray: eayay, ehay eprovedray ingskay orfay eirthay akessay;
15 [Ayingsay], Ouchtay otnay inemay anointedway, andway oday myay ophetspray onay armhay.
16 Oreovermay ehay alledcay orfay away aminefay uponway ethay andlay: ehay akebray ethay olewhay affstay ofway eadbray.
17 Ehay entsay away anmay eforebay emthay, [evenway] Osephjay, [owhay] asway oldsay orfay away ervantsay:
18 Osewhay eetfay eythay urthay ithway ettersfay: ehay asway aidlay inway ironway:
19 Untilway ethay imetay atthay ishay ordway amecay: ethay ordway ofway ethay ORDLAY iedtray imhay.
20 Ethay ingkay entsay andway oosedlay imhay; [evenway] ethay ulerray ofway ethay eoplepay, andway etlay imhay ogay eefray.
21 Ehay ademay imhay ordlay ofway ishay ousehay, andway ulerray ofway allway ishay ubstancesay:
22 Otay indbay ishay incespray atway ishay easureplay; andway eachtay ishay enatorssay isdomway.
23 Israelway alsoway amecay intoway Egyptway; andway Acobjay ojournedsay inway ethay andlay ofway Amhay.

24 Andway ehay increasedway ishay eoplepay eatlygray; andway ademay emthay ongerstray anthay eirthay enemiesway.

25 Ehay urnedtay eirthay earthay otay atehay ishay eoplepay, otay ealday ubtillysay ithway ishay ervantssay.

26 Ehay entsay Osesmay ishay ervantsay; [andway] Aaronway omwhay ehay adhay osenchay.

27 Eythay ewedshay ishay ignssay amongway emthay, andway ondersway inway ethay andlay ofway Amhay.

28 Ehay entsay arknessday, andway ademay itway arkday; andway eythay ebelledray otnay againstway ishay ordway.

29 Ehay urnedtay eirthay atersway intoway oodblay, andway ewslay eirthay ishfay.

30 Eirthay andlay oughtbray orthfay ogsfray inway abundanceway, inway ethay amberschay ofway eirthay ingskay.

31 Ehay akespay, andway erethay amecay iversday ortssay ofway iesflay, [andway] icelay inway allway eirthay oastscay.

32 Ehay avegay emthay ailhay orfay ainray, [andway] amingflay irefay inway eirthay andlay.

33 Ehay otesmay eirthay inesvay alsoway andway eirthay igfay eestray; andway akebray ethay eestray ofway eirthay oastscay.

34 Ehay akespay, andway ethay ocustslay amecay, andway aterpillerscay, andway atthay ithoutway umbernay,

35 Andway idday eatway upway allway ethay erbshay inway eirthay andlay, andway evouredday ethay uitfray ofway eirthay oundgray.

36 Ehay otesmay alsoway allway ethay irstbornfay inway eirthay andlay, ethay iefchay ofway allway eirthay engthstray.

37 Ehay oughtbray emthay orthfay alsoway ithway ilversay andway oldgay: andway [erethay asway] otnay oneway eeblefay [ersonpay] amongway eirthay ibestray.

38 Egyptway asway adglay enwhay eythay epartedday: orfay ethay earfay ofway emthay ellfay uponway emthay.

39 Ehay eadspray away oudclay orfay away overingcay; andway irefay otay ivegay ightlay inway ethay ightnay.

40 [Ethay eoplepay] askedway, andway ehay oughtbray uailsqay, andway atisfiedsay emthay ithway ethay eadbray ofway eavenhay.

41 Ehay openedway ethay ockray, andway ethay atersway ushedgay outway; eythay anray inway ethay dryay acesplay [ikelay] away iverray.

42 Orfay ehay ememberedray ishay olyhay omisepray, [andway] Abrahamway ishay ervantsay.

43 Andway ehay oughtbray orthfay ishay eoplepay ithway oyjay,
[andway] ishay osenchay ithway adnessglay:
44 Andway avegay emthay ethay andslay ofway ethay eathenhay: andway
eythay inheritedway ethay abourlay ofway ethay eoplepay;
45 Atthay eythay ightmay observeway ishay atutesstay, andway eepkay
ishay awslay. Aisepray eyay ethay ORDLAY.

ALMPSAY 106

1 Aisepray eyay ethay ORDLAY. OWAY ivegay anksthay untoway ethay
ORDLAY; orfay [ehay isway] oodgay: orfay ishay ercymay
[endurethway] orfay everway.
2 Owhay ancay utterway ethay ightymay actsway ofway ethay ORDLAY?
[owhay] ancay ewshay orthfay allway ishay aisepray?
3 Essedblay [areway] eythay atthay eepkay udgmentjay, [andway] ehay
atthay oethday ighteousnessray atway allway imestay.
4 Ememberray emay, OWAY ORDLAY, ithway ethay avourfay [atthay
outhay earestbay untoway] thyay eoplepay: OWAY isitvay emay ithway
thyay alvationsay;
5 Atthay IWAY aymay eesay ethay oodgay ofway thyay osenchay, atthay
IWAY aymay ejoiceray inway ethay adnessglay ofway thyay ationnay,
atthay IWAY aymay oryglay ithway inethay inheritanceway.
6 Eway avehay innedsay ithway ourway athersfay, eway avehay
ommittedcay iniquityway, eway avehay oneday ickedlyway.
7 Ourway athersfay understoodway otnay thyay ondersway inway
Egyptway; eythay ememberedray otnay ethay ultitudemay ofway thyay
erciesmay; utbay ovokedpray [imhay] atway ethay easay, [evenway] atway
ethay Edray easay.
8 Everthelessnay ehay avedsay emthay orfay ishay amenay'say akesay,
atthay ehay ightmay akemay ishay ightymay owerpay otay ebay ownknay.
9 Ehay ebukedray ethay Edray easay alsoway, andway itway asway
ieddray upway: osay ehay edlay emthay oughthray ethay epthsday, asway
oughthray ethay ildernessway.
10 Andway ehay avedsay emthay omfray ethay andhay ofway imhay
atthay atedhay [emthay], andway edeemedray emthay omfray ethay
andhay ofway ethay enemyway.
11 Andway ethay atersway overedcay eirthay enemiesway: erethay asway
otnay oneway ofway emthay eftlay.
12 Enthay elievedbay eythay ishay ordsway; eythay angsay ishay aisepray.
13 Eythay oonsay orgatfay ishay orksway; eythay aitedway otnay orfay
ishay ounselcay:

14 Utbay ustedlay exceedinglyway inway ethay ildernessway, andway emptedtay Odgay inway ethay esertday.

15 Andway ehay avegay emthay eirthay equestray; utbay entsay eannesslay intoway eirthay oulsay.

16 Eythay enviedway Osesmay alsoway inway ethay ampcay, [andway] Aaronway ethay aintsay ofway ethay ORDLAY.

17 Ethay earthway openedway andway allowedsway upway Athanday, andway overedcay ethay ompanycay ofway Abiramway.

18 Andway away irefay asway indledkay inway eirthay ompanycay; ethay ameflay urnedbay upway ethay ickedway.

19 Eythay ademay away alfcay inway Orebhay, andway orshippedway ethay oltenmay imageway.

20 Usthay eythay angedchay eirthay oryglay intoway ethay imilitudesay ofway anway oxway atthay eatethway assgray.

21 Eythay orgatfay Odgay eirthay avioursay, ichwhay adhay oneday eatgray ingsthay inway Egyptway;

22 Ondrousway orksway inway ethay andlay ofway Amhay, [andway] erribletay ingsthay byay ethay Edray easay.

23 Ereforethay ehay aidsay atthay ehay ouldway estroyday emthay, adhay otnay Osesmay ishay osenchay oodstay eforebay imhay inway ethay eachbray, otay urntay awayway ishay athwray, estlay ehay ouldshay estroyday [emthay].

24 Eayay, eythay espisedday ethay easantplay andlay, eythay elievedbay otnay ishay ordway:

25 Utbay urmuredmay inway eirthay entstay, [andway] earkenedhay otnay untoway ethay oicevay ofway ethay ORDLAY.

26 Ereforethay ehay iftedlay upway ishay andhay againstway emthay, otay overthrowway emthay inway ethay ildernessway:

27 Otay overthrowway eirthay eedsay alsoway amongway ethay ationsnay, andway otay atterscay emthay inway ethay andslay.

28 Eythay oinedjay emselvesthay alsoway untoway Aalbay-eorpay, andway ateway ethay acrificessay ofway ethay eadday.

29 Usthay eythay ovokedpray [imhay] otay angerway ithway eirthay inventionsway: andway ethay agueplay akebray inway uponway emthay.

30 Enthay oodstay upway Inehasphay, andway executedway udgmentjay: andway [osay] ethay agueplay asway ayedstay.

31 Andway atthay asway ountedcay untoway imhay orfay ighteousnessray untoway allway enerationsgay orfay evermoreway.

32 Eythay angeredway [imhay] alsoway atway ethay atersway ofway ifestray, osay atthay itway entway illway ithway Osesmay orfay eirthay akessay:

33 Ecausebay eythay ovokedpray ishay iritspay, osay atthay ehay akespay unadvisedlyway ithway ishay ipslay.

34 Eythay idday otnay estroyday ethay ationsnay, oncerningcay omwhay ethay ORDLAY ommandedcay emthay:

35 Utbay ereway ingledmay amongway ethay eathenhay, andway earnedlay eirthay orksway.

36 Andway eythay ervedsay eirthay idolsway: ichwhay ereway away aresnay untoway emthay.

37 Eayay, eythay acrificedsay eirthay onssay andway eirthay aughtersday untoway evilsday,

38 Andway edshay innocentway oodblay, [evenway] ethay oodblay ofway eirthay onssay andway ofway eirthay aughtersday, omwhay eythay acrificedsay untoway ethay idolsway ofway Anaancay: andway ethay andlay asway ollutedpay ithway oodblay.

39 Usthay ereway eythay efiledday ithway eirthay ownway orksway, andway entway away oringwhay ithway eirthay ownway inventionsway.

40 Ereforethay asway ethay athwray ofway ethay ORDLAY indledkay againstway ishay eoplepay, insomuchway atthay ehay abhorredway ishay ownway inheritanceway.

41 Andway ehay avegay emthay intoway ethay andhay ofway ethay eathenhay; andway eythay atthay atedhay emthay uledray overway emthay.

42 Eirthay enemiesway alsoway oppressedway emthay, andway eythay ereway oughtbray intoway ubjectionsay underway eirthay andhay.

43 Anymay imestay idday ehay eliverday emthay; utbay eythay ovokedpray [imhay] ithway eirthay ounselcay, andway ereway oughtbray owlay orfay eirthay iniquityway.

44 Everthelessnay ehay egardedray eirthay afflictionway, enwhay ehay eardhay eirthay cryay:

45 Andway ehay emberedray orfay emthay ishay ovenantcay, andway epentedray accordingway otay ethay ultitudemay ofway ishay erciesmay.

46 Ehay ademay emthay alsoway otay ebay itiedpay ofway allway osethay atthay arriedcay emthay aptivescay.

47 Avesay usway, OWAY ORDLAY ourway Odgay, andway athergay usway omfray amongway ethay eathenhay, otay ivegay anksthay untoway thyay olyhay amenay, [andway] otay iumphtray inway thyay aisepray.

48 Essedblay [ebay] ethay ORDLAY Odgay ofway Israelway omfray everlastingway otay everlastingway: andway etlay allway ethay eoplepay aysay, Amenway. Aisepray eyay ethay ORDLAY.

ALMPSAY 107

1 OWAY ivegay anksthay untoway ethay ORDLAY, orfay [ehay isway] oodgay: orfay ishay ercymay [endurethway] orfay everway.

2 Etlay ethay edeemedray ofway ethay ORDLAY aysay [osay], omwhay ehay athhay edeemedray omfray ethay andhay ofway ethay enemyway;

3 Andway atheredgay emthay outway ofway ethay andslay, omfray ethay eastway, andway omfray ethay estway, omfray ethay orthnay, andway omfray ethay outhsay.

4 Eythay anderedway inway ethay ildernessway inway away olitarysay ayway; eythay oundfay onay itycay otay elldway inway.

5 Ungryhay andway irstythay, eirthay oulsay aintedfay inway emthay.

6 Enthay eythay iedcray untoway ethay ORDLAY inway eirthay oubletray, [andway] ehay eliveredday emthay outway ofway eirthay istressesday.

7 Andway ehay edlay emthay orthfay byay ethay ightray ayway, atthay eythay ightmay ogay otay away itycay ofway abitationhay.

8 Ohway atthay [enmay] ouldway aisepray ethay ORDLAY [orfay] ishay oodnessgay, andway [orfay] ishay onderfulway orksway otay ethay ildrenchay ofway enmay!

9 Orfay ehay atisfiethsay ethay onginglay oulsay, andway illethfay ethay ungryhay oulsay ithway oodnessgay.

10 Uchsay asway itsay inway arknessday andway inway ethay adowshay ofway eathday, [eingbay] oundbay inway afflictionway andway ironway;

11 Ecausebay eythay ebelledray againstway ethay ordsway ofway Odgay, andway ontemnedcay ethay ounselcay ofway ethay ostmay Ighhay:

12 Ereforethay ehay oughtbray ownday eirthay earthay ithway abourlay; eythay ellfay ownday, andway [erethay asway] onenay otay elphay.

13 Enthay eythay iedcray untoway ethay ORDLAY inway eirthay oubletray, [andway] ehay avedsay emthay outway ofway eirthay istressesday.

14 Ehay oughtbray emthay outway ofway arknessday andway ethay adowshay ofway eathday, andway akebray eirthay andsbay inway undersay.

15 Ohway atthay [enmay] ouldway aisepray ethay ORDLAY [orfay] ishay oodnessgay, andway [orfay] ishay onderfulway orksway otay ethay ildrenchay ofway enmay!

16 Orfay ehay athhay okenbray ethay atesgay ofway assbray, andway utcay ethay arsbay ofway ironway inway undersay.

17 Oolsfay ecausebay ofway eirthay ansgressiontray, andway ecausebay ofway eirthay iniquitiesway, areway afflictedway.

18 Eirthay oulsay abhorrethway allway annermay ofway eatmay; andway eythay awdray earnay untoway ethay atesgay ofway eathday.

19 Enthay eythay cryay untoway ethay ORDLAY inway eirthay oubletray, [andway] ehay avethsay emthay outway ofway eirthay istressesday.

20 Ehay entsay ishay ordway, andway ealedhay emthay, andway eliveredday [emthay] omfray eirthay estructionsday.

21 Ohway atthay [enmay] ouldway aisepray ethay ORDLAY [orfay] ishay oodnessgay, andway [orfay] ishay onderfulway orksway otay ethay ildrenchay ofway enmay!

22 Andway etlay emthay acrificesay ethay acrificessay ofway anksgivingthay, andway eclareday ishay orksway ithway ejoicingray.

23 Eythay atthay ogay owndah otay ethay easay inway ipsshay, atthay oday usinessbay inway eatgray atersway;

24 Esethay eesay ethay orksway ofway ethay ORDLAY, andway ishay ondersway inway ethay eepday.

25 Orfay ehay ommandethcay, andway aisethray ethay ormystay indway, ichwhay iftethlay upway ethay avesway ereofthay.

26 Eythay ountmay upway otay ethay eavenhay, eythay ogay owndah againway otay ethay epthsday: eirthay oulsay isway eltedmay ecausebay ofway oubletray.

27 Eythay eelray otay andway ofray, andway aggerstay ikelay away unkendray anmay, andway areway atway eirthay itsway' endway.

28 Enthay eythay cryay untoway ethay ORDLAY inway eirthay oubletray, andway ehay ingethbray emthay outway ofway eirthay istressesday.

29 Ehay akethmay ethay ormstay away almcay, osay atthay ethay avesway ereofthay areway illstay.

30 Enthay areway eythay adglay ecausebay eythay ebay uietqay; osay ehay ingethbray emthay untoway eirthay esiredday avenhay.

31 Ohway atthay [enmay] ouldway aisepray ethay ORDLAY [orfay] ishay oodnessgay, andway [orfay] ishay onderfulway orksway otay ethay ildrenchay ofway enmay!

32 Etlay emthay exaltway imhay alsoway inway ethay ongregationcay ofway ethay eoplepay, andway aisepray imhay inway ethay assemblyway ofway ethay eldersway.

33 Ehay urnethtay iversray intoway away ildernessway, andway ethay aterspringsway intoway dryay oundgray;

34 AWAY uitfulfray andlay intoway arrennessbay, orfay ethay ickednessway ofway emthay atthay elldway ereinthay.

35 Ehay urnethtay ethay ildernessway intoway away andingstay aterway, andway dryay oundgray intoway aterspringsway.

36 Andway erethay ehay akethmay ethay ungryhay otay elldway, atthay eythay aymay eparepray away itycay orfay abitationhay;

37 Andway owsay ethay ieldsfay, andway antplay ineyardsvay, ichwhay aymay ieldyay uitsfray ofway increaseway.

38 Ehay essethblay emthay alsoway, osay atthay eythay areway ultipliedmay eatlygray; andway ufferethsay otnay eirthay attlecay otay ecreaseday.

39 Againway, eythay areway inishedmay andway oughtbray owlay oughthray oppressionway, afflictionway, andway orrowsay.

40 Ehay ourethpay ontemptcay uponway incespray, andway ausethcay emthay otay anderway inway ethay ildernessway, [erewhay erethay isway] onay ayway.

41 Etyay ettethsay ehay ethay oorpay onway ighhay omfray afflictionway, andway akethmay [imhay] amiliesfay ikelay away ockflay.

42 Ethay ighteousray allshay eesay [itway], andway ejoiceray: andway allway iniquityway allshay opstay erhay outhmay.

43 Osowhay [isway] iseway, andway illway observeway esethay [ingsthay], evenway eythay allshay understandway ethay ovingkindnesslay ofway ethay ORDLAY.

ALMPSAY 108
AWAY Ongsay [orway] Almpsay ofway Avidday.

1 OWAY Odgay, myay earthay isway ixedfay; IWAY illway ingsay andway ivegay aisepray, evenway ithway myay oryglay.

2 Awakeway, alterypsay andway arphay: IWAY [elfmysay] illway awakeway earlyway.

3 IWAY illway aisepray eethay, OWAY ORDLAY, amongway ethay eoplepay: andway IWAY illway ingsay aisespray untoway eethay amongway ethay ationsnay.

4 Orfay thyay ercymay [isway] eatgray aboveway ethay eavenshay: andway thyay uthtray [eachethray] untoway ethay oudsclay.

5 Ebay outhay exaltedway, OWAY Odgay, aboveway ethay eavenshay: andway thyay oryglay aboveway allway ethay earthway;

6 Atthay thyay elovedbay aymay ebay eliveredday: avesay [ithway] thyay ightray andhay, andway answerway emay.

7 Odgay athhay okenspay inway ishay olinesshay; IWAY illway ejoiceray, IWAY illway ivideday Echemshay, andway etemay outway ethay alleyvay ofway Uccothsay.

8 Ileadgay [isway] inemay; Anassehmay [isway] inemay; Ephraimway alsoway [isway] ethay engthstray ofway inemay eadhay; Udahjay [isway] myay awgiverlay;

9 Oabmay [isway] myay ashpotway; overway Edomway illway IWAY astcay outway myay oeshay; overway Ilistiaphay illway IWAY iumphtray.

10 Owhay illway ingbray emay intoway ethay ongstray itycay? owhay illway eadlay emay intoway Edomway?

11 [Iltway] otnay [outhay], OWAY Odgay, [owhay] asthay astcay usway offway? andway iltway otnay outhay, OWAY Odgay, ogay orthfay ithway ourway ostshay?

12 Ivegay usway elphay omfray oubletray: orfay ainvay [isway] ethay elphay ofway anmay.

13 Oughthray Odgay eway allshay oday aliantlyvay: orfay ehay [itway isway atthay] allshay eadtray ownday ourway enemiesway.

ALMPSAY 109

Otay ethay iefchay Usicianmay, AWAY Almpsay ofway Avidday.

1 Oldhay otnay thyay eacepay, OWAY Odgay ofway myay aisepray;

2 Orfay ethay outhmay ofway ethay ickedway andway ethay outhmay ofway ethay eceitfulday areway openedway againstway emay: eythay avehay okenspay againstway emay ithway away inglyay onguetay.

3 Eythay ompassedcay emay aboutway alsoway ithway ordsway ofway atredhay; andway oughtfay againstway emay ithoutway away ausecay.

4 Orfay myay ovelay eythay areway myay adversariesway: utbay IWAY [ivegay elfmysay untoway] ayerpray.

5 Andway eythay avehay ewardedray emay evilway orfay oodgay, andway atredhay orfay myay ovelay.

6 Etsay outhay away ickedway anmay overway imhay: andway etlay Atansay andstay atway ishay ightray andhay.

7 Enwhay ehay allshay ebay udgedjay, etlay imhay ebay ondemnedcay: andway etlay ishay ayerpray ecomebay insay.

8 Etlay ishay aysday ebay ewfay; [andway] etlay anotherway aketay ishay officeway.

9 Etlay ishay ildrenchay ebay atherlessfay, andway ishay ifeway away idowway.

10 Etlay ishay ildrenchay ebay ontinuallycay agabondsvay, andway egbay: etlay emthay eeksay [eirthay eadbray] alsoway outway ofway eirthay esolateday acesplay.

11 Etlay ethay extortionerway atchcay allway atthay ehay athhay; andway etlay ethay angersstray oilspay ishay abourlay.

12 Etlay erethay ebay onenay otay extendway ercymay untoway imhay: eithernay etlay erethay ebay anyway otay avourfay ishay atherlessfay ildrenchay.

13 Etlay ishay osteritypay ebay utcay offway; [andway] inway ethay enerationgay ollowingfay etlay eirthay amenay ebay ottedblay outway.

14 Etlay ethay iniquityway ofway ishay athersfay ebay ememberedray ithway ethay ORDLAY; andway etlay otnay ethay insay ofway ishay othermay ebay ottedblay outway.

15 Etlay emthay ebay eforebay ethay ORDLAY ontinuallycay, atthay ehay aymay utcay offway ethay emorymay ofway emthay omfray ethay earthway.

16 Ecausebay atthay ehay ememberedray otnay otay ewshay ercymay, utbay ersecutedpay ethay oorpay andway eedynay anmay, atthay ehay ightmay evenway ayslay ethay okenbray inway earthay.

17 Asway ehay ovedlay ursingcay, osay etlay itway omecay untoway imhay: asway ehay elightedday otnay inway essingblay, osay etlay itway ebay arfay omfray imhay.

18 Asway ehay othedclay imselfhay ithway ursingcay ikelay asway ithway ishay armentgay, osay etlay itway omecay intoway ishay owelsbay ikelay aterway, andway ikelay oilway intoway ishay onesbay.

19 Etlay itway ebay untoway imhay asway ethay armentgay [ichwhay] overethcay imhay, andway orfay away irdlegay erewithwhay ehay isway irdedgay ontinuallycay.

20 [Etlay] isthay [ebay] ethay ewardray ofway inemay adversaresway omfray ethay ORDLAY, andway ofway emthay atthay eakspay evilway againstway myay oulsay.

21 Utbay oday outhay orfay emay, OWAY ODGAY ethay Ordlay, orfay thyay amenay'say akesay: ecausebay thyay ercymay [isway] oodgay, eliverday outhay emay.

22 Orfay IWAY [amway] oorpay andway eedynay, andway myay earthay isway oundedway ithinway emay.

23 IWAY amway onegay ikelay ethay adowshay enwhay itway eclinethday: IWAY amway ossedtay upway andway ownday asway ethay ocustlay.

24 Myay eesknay areway eakway oughthray astingfay; andway myay eshflay ailethfay ofway atnessfay.

25 IWAY ecamebay alsoway away eproachray untoway emthay: [enwhay] eythay ookedlay uponway emay eythay akedshay eirthay eadshay.

26 Elphay emay, OWAY ORDLAY myay Odgay: OWAY avesay emay accordingway otay thyay ercymay:

27 Atthay eythay aymay owknay atthay isthay [isway] thyay andhay; [atthay] outhay, ORDLAY, asthay oneday itway.

28 Etlay emthay ursecay, utbay essblay outhay: enwhay eythay ariseway, etlay emthay ebay ashamedway; utbay etlay thyay ervantsay ejoiceray.

29 Etlay inemay adversariesway ebay othedclay ithway ameshay, andway etlay emthay overcay emselvesthay ithway eirthay ownway onfusioncay, asway ithway away antlemay.

30 IWAY illway eatlygray aisepray ethay ORDLAY ithway myay outhmay; eayay, IWAY illway aisepray imhay amongway ethay ultitudemay.

31 Orfay ehay allshay andstay atway ethay ightray andhay ofway ethay oorpay, otay avesay [imhay] omfray osethay atthay ondemncay ishay oulsay.

ALMPSAY 110
AWAY Almpsay ofway Avidday.

1 Ethay ORDLAY aidsay untoway myay Ordlay, Itsay outhay atway myay ightray andhay, untilway IWAY akemay inethay enemiesway thyay ootstoolfay.

2 Ethay ORDLAY allshay endsay ethay odray ofway thyay engthstray outway ofway Ionzay: uleray outhay inway ethay idstmay ofway inethay enemiesway.

3 Thyay eoplepay [allshay ebay] illingway inway ethay ayday ofway thyay owerpay, inway ethay eautiesbay ofway olinesshay omfray ethay ombway ofway ethay orningmay: outhay asthay ethay ewday ofway thyay outhyay.

4 Ethay ORDLAY athhay ornsway, andway illway otnay epentray, Outhay [artway] away iestpray orfay everway afterway ethay orderway ofway Elchizedekmay.

5 Ethay Ordlay atway thyay ightray andhay allshay ikestray oughthray ingskay inway ethay ayday ofway ishay athwray.

6 Ehay allshay udgejay amongway ethay eathenhay, ehay allshay illfay [ethay acesplay] ithway ethay eadday odiesbay; ehay allshay oundway ethay eadshay overway anymay ountriescay.

7 Ehay allshay inkdray ofway ethay ookbray inway ethay ayway: ereforethay allshay ehay iftlay upway ethay eadhay.

ALMPSAY 111

1 Aisepray eyay ethay ORDLAY. IWAY illway aisepray ethay ORDLAY ithway [myay] olewhay earthay, inway ethay assemblyway ofway ethay uprightway, andway [inway] ethay ongregationcay.
2 Ethay orksway ofway ethay ORDLAY [areway] eatgray, oughtsay outway ofway allway emthay atthay avehay easureplay ereinthay.
3 Ishay orkway [isway] onourablehay andway oriousglay: andway ishay ighteousnessray endurethway orfay everway.
4 Ehay athhay ademay ishay onderfulway orksway otay ebay ememberedray: ethay ORDLAY [isway] aciousgray andway ullfay ofway ompassioncay.
5 Ehay athhay ivengay eatmay untoway emthay atthay earfay imhay: ehay illway everway ebay indfulmay ofway ishay ovenantcay.
6 Ehay athhay ewedshay ishay eoplepay ethay owerpay ofway ishay orksway, atthay ehay aymay ivegay emthay ethay eritagehay ofway ethay eathenhay.
7 Ethay orksway ofway ishay andshay [areway] erityvay andway udgmentjay; allway ishay ommandmentscay [areway] uresay.
8 Eythay andstay astfay orfay everway andway everway, [andway areway] oneday inway uthtray andway uprightnessway.
9 Ehay entsay edemptionray untoway ishay eoplepay: ehay athhay ommandedcay ishay ovenantcay orfay everway: olyhay andway everendray [isway] ishay amenay.
10 Ethay earfay ofway ethay ORDLAY [isway] ethay eginningbay ofway isdomway: away oodgay understandingway avehay allway eythay atthay oday [ishay ommandmentscay]: ishay aisepray endurethway orfay everway.

ALMPSAY 112

1 Aisepray eyay ethay ORDLAY. Essedblay [isway] ethay anmay [atthay] earethfay ethay ORDLAY, [atthay] elightethday eatlygray inway ishay ommandmentscay.
2 Ishay eedsay allshay ebay ightymay uponway earthway: ethay enerationgay ofway ethay uprightway allshay ebay essedblay.
3 Ealthway andway ichesray [allshay ebay] inway ishay ousehay: andway ishay ighteousnessray endurethway orfay everway.

4 Untoway ethay uprightway erethay arisethway ightlay inway ethay arknessday: [ehay isway] aciousgray, andway ullfay ofway ompassioncay, andway ighteousray.

5 AWAY oodgay anmay ewethshay avourfay, andway endethlay: ehay illway uidegay ishay affairsway ithway iscretionday.

6 Urelysay ehay allshay otnay ebay ovedmay orfay everway: ethay ighteousray allshay ebay inway everlastingway emembranceray.

7 Ehay allshay otnay ebay afraidway ofway evilway idingstay: ishay earthay isway ixedfay, ustingtray inway ethay ORDLAY.

8 Ishay earthay [isway] establishedway, ehay allshay otnay ebay afraidway, untilway ehay eesay [ishay esireday] uponway ishay enemiesway.

9 Ehay athhay ispersedday, ehay athhay ivengay otay ethay oorpay; ishay ighteousnessray endurethway orfay everway; ishay ornhay allshay ebay exaltedway ithway onourhay.

10 Ethay ickedway allshay eesay [itway], andway ebay ievedgray; ehay allshay ashgnay ithway ishay eethtay, andway eltmay awayway: ethay esireday ofway ethay ickedway allshay erishpay.

ALMPSAY 113

1 Aisepray eyay ethay ORDLAY. Aisepray, OWAY eyay ervantssay ofway ethay ORDLAY, aisepray ethay amenay ofway ethay ORDLAY.

2 Essedblay ebay ethay amenay ofway ethay ORDLAY omfray isthay imetay orthfay andway orfay evermoreway.

3 Omfray ethay isingray ofway ethay unsay untoway ethay oinggay ownday ofway ethay amesay ethay ORDLAY'SAY amenay [isway] otay ebay aisedpray.

4 Ethay ORDLAY [isway] ighhay aboveway allway ationsnay, [andway] ishay oryglay aboveway ethay eavenshay.

5 Owhay [isway] ikelay untoway ethay ORDLAY ourway Odgay, owhay ellethdway onway ighhay,

6 Owhay umblethhay [imselfhay] otay eholdbay [ethay ingsthay atthay areway] inway eavenhay, andway inway ethay earthway!

7 Ehay aisethray upway ethay oorpay outway ofway ethay ustday, [andway] iftethlay ethay eedynay outway ofway ethay unghilllday;

8 Atthay ehay aymay etsay [imhay] ithway incespray, [evenway] ithway ethay incespray ofway ishay eoplepay.

9 Ehay akethmay ethay arrenbay omanway otay eepkay ousehay, [andway otay ebay] away oyfuljay othermay ofway ildrenchay. Aisepray eyay ethay ORDLAY.

ALMPSAY 114

1 Enwhay Israelway entway outway ofway Egyptway, ethay ousehay ofway Acobjay omfray away eoplepay ofway angestray anguagelay;

2 Udahjay asway ishay anctuarysay, [andway] Israelway ishay ominionday.

3 Ethay easay awsay [itway], andway edflay: Ordanjay asway ivendray ackbay.

4 Ethay ountainsmay ippedskay ikelay amsray, [andway] ethay ittlelay illshay ikelay ambslay.

5 Atwhay [ailedway] eethay, OWAY outhay easay, atthay outhay eddestflay? outhay Ordanjay, [atthay] outhay astway ivendray ackbay?

6 Eyay ountainsmay, [atthay] eyay ippedskay ikelay amsray; [andway] eyay ittlelay illshay, ikelay ambslay?

7 Embletray, outhay earthway, atway ethay esencepray ofway ethay Ordlay, atway ethay esencepray ofway ethay Odgay ofway Acobjay;

8 Ichwhay urnedtay ethay ockray [intoway] away andingstay aterway, ethay intflay intoway away ountainfay ofway atersway.

ALMPSAY 115

1 Otnay untoway usway, OWAY ORDLAY, otnay untoway usway, utbay untoway thyay amenay ivegay oryglay, orfay thyay ercymay, [andway] orfay thyay uthtray'say akesay.

2 Ereforewhay ouldshay ethay eathenhay aysay, Erewhay [isway] ownay eirthay Odgay?

3 Utbay ourway Odgay [isway] inway ethay eavenshay: ehay athhay oneday atsoeverwhay ehay athhay easedplay.

4 Eirthay idolsway [areway] ilversay andway oldgay, ethay orkway ofway enmay'say andshay.

5 Eythay avehay outhsmay, utbay eythay eakspay otnay: eyesway avehay eythay, utbay eythay eesay otnay:

6 Eythay avehay earsway, utbay eythay earhay otnay: osesnay avehay eythay, utbay eythay ellsmay otnay:

7 Eythay avehay andshay, utbay eythay andlehay otnay: eetfay avehay eythay, utbay eythay alkway otnay: eithernay eakspay eythay oughthray eirthay oatthray.

8 Eythay atthay akemay emthay areway ikelay untoway emthay; [osay isway] everyway oneway atthay ustethtray inway emthay.

9 OWAY Israelway, usttray outhay inway ethay ORDLAY: ehay [isway] eirthay elphay andway eirthay ieldshay.

10 OWAY ousehay ofway Aaronway, usttray inway ethay ORDLAY: ehay [isway] eirthay elphay andway eirthay ieldshay.
11 Eyay atthay earfay ethay ORDLAY, usttray inway ethay ORDLAY: ehay [isway] eirthay elphay andway eirthay ieldshay.
12 Ethay ORDLAY athhay eenbay indfulmay ofway usway: ehay illway essblay [usway]; ehay illway essblay ethay ousehay ofway Israelway; ehay illway essblay ethay ousehay ofway Aaronway.
13 Ehay illway essblay emthay atthay earfay ethay ORDLAY, [othbay] allsmay andway eatgray.
14 Ethay ORDLAY allshay increaseway ouyay oremay andway oremay, ouyay andway ouryay ildrenchay.
15 Eyay [areway] essedblay ofway ethay ORDLAY ichwhay ademay eavenhay andway earthway.
16 Ethay eavenhay, [evenway] ethay eavenshay, [areway] ethay ORDLAY'SAY: utbay ethay earthway athhay ehay ivengay otay ethay ildrenchay ofway enmay.
17 Ethay eadday aisepray otnay ethay ORDLAY, eithernay anyway atthay ogay ownday intoway ilencesay.
18 Utbay eway illway essblay ethay ORDLAY omfray isthay imetay orthfay andway orfay evermoreway. Aisepray ethay ORDLAY.

ALMPSAY 116

1 IWAY ovelay ethay ORDLAY, ecausebay ehay athhay eardhay myay oicevay [andway] myay upplicationssay.
2 Ecausebay ehay athhay inclinedway ishay earway untoway emay, ereforethay illway IWAY allcay uponway [imhay] asway onglay asway IWAY ivelay.
3 Ethay orrowssay ofway eathday ompassedcay emay, andway ethay ainspay ofway ellhay atgay oldhay uponway emay: IWAY oundfay oubletray andway orrowsay.
4 Enthay alledcay IWAY uponway ethay amenay ofway ethay ORDLAY; OWAY ORDLAY, IWAY eseechbay eethay, eliverday myay oulsay.
5 Aciousgray [isway] ethay ORDLAY, andway ighteousray; eayay, ourway Odgay [isway] ercifulmay.
6 Ethay ORDLAY eservethpray ethay implesay: IWAY asway oughtbray owlay, andway ehay elpedhay emay.
7 Eturnray untoway thyay estray, OWAY myay oulsay; orfay ethay ORDLAY athhay ealtday ountifullybay ithway eethay.
8 Orfay outhay asthay eliveredday myay oulsay omfray eathday, inemay eyesway omfray earstay, [andway] myay eetfay omfray allingfay.

9 IWAY illway alkway eforebay ethay ORDLAY inway ethay andlay ofway ethay ivinglay.

10 IWAY elievedbay, ereforethay avehay IWAY okenspay: IWAY asway eatlygray afflictedway:

11 IWAY aidsay inway myay astehay, Allway enmay [areway] iarslay.

12 Atwhay allshay IWAY enderray untoway ethay ORDLAY [orfay] allway ishay enefitsbay owardtay emay?

13 IWAY illway aketay ethay upcay ofway alvationsay, andway allcay uponway ethay amenay ofway ethay ORDLAY.

14 IWAY illway aypay myay owsvay untoway ethay ORDLAY ownay inway ethay esencepray ofway allway ishay eoplepay.

15 Eciouspray inway ethay ightsay ofway ethay ORDLAY [isway] ethay eathday ofway ishay aintssay.

16 OWAY ORDLAY, ulytray IWAY [amway] thyay ervantsay; IWAY [amway] thyay ervantsay, [andway] ethay onsay ofway inethay andmaidhay: outhay asthay oosedlay myay ondsbay.

17 IWAY illway offerway otay eethay ethay acrificesay ofway anksgivingthay, andway illway allcay uponway ethay amenay ofway ethay ORDLAY.

18 IWAY illway aypay myay owsvay untoway ethay ORDLAY ownay inway ethay esencepray ofway allway ishay eoplepay,

19 Inway ethay ourtscay ofway ethay ORDLAY'SAY ousehay, inway ethay idstmay ofway eethay, OWAY Erusalemjay. Aisepray eyay ethay ORDLAY.

ALMPSAY 117

1 OWAY aisepray ethay ORDLAY, allway eyay ationsnay: aisepray imhay, allway eyay eoplepay.

2 Orfay ishay ercifulmay indnesskay isway eatgray owardtay usway: andway ethay uthtray ofway ethay ORDLAY [endurethway] orfay everway. Aisepray eyay ethay ORDLAY.

ALMPSAY 118

1 OWAY ivegay anksthay untoway ethay ORDLAY; orfay [ehay isway] oodgay: ecausebay ishay ercymay [endurethway] orfay everway.

2 Etlay Israelway ownay aysay, atthay ishay ercymay [endurethway] orfay everway.

3 Etlay ethay ousehay ofway Aaronway ownay aysay, atthay ishay ercymay [endurethway] orfay everway.

4 Etlay emthay ownay atthay earfay ethay ORDLAY aysay, atthay ishay ercymay [endurethway] orfay everway.

5 IWAY alledcay uponway ethay ORDLAY inway istressday: ethay ORDLAY answeredway emay, [andway etsay emay] inway away argelay aceplay.

6 Ethay ORDLAY [isway] onway myay idesay; IWAY illway otnay earfay: atwhay ancay anmay oday untoway emay?

7 Ethay ORDLAY akethtay myay artpay ithway emthay atthay elphay emay: ereforethay allshay IWAY eesay [myay esireday] uponway emthay atthay atehay emay.

8 [Itway isway] etterbay otay usttray inway ethay ORDLAY anthay otay utpay onfidencecay inway anmay.

9 [Itway isway] etterbay otay usttray inway ethay ORDLAY anthay otay utpay onfidencecay inway incespray.

10 Allway ationsnay ompassedcay emay aboutway: utbay inway ethay amenay ofway ethay ORDLAY illway IWAY estroyday emthay.

11 Eythay ompassedcay emay aboutway; eayay, eythay ompassedcay emay aboutway: utbay inway ethay amenay ofway ethay ORDLAY IWAY illway estroyday emthay.

12 Eythay ompassedcay emay aboutway ikelay eesbay; eythay areway uenchedqay asway ethay irefay ofway ornsthay: orfay inway ethay amenay ofway ethay ORDLAY IWAY illway estroyday emthay.

13 Outhay asthay ustthray oresay atway emay atthay IWAY ightmay allfay: utbay ethay ORDLAY elpedhay emay.

14 Ethay ORDLAY [isway] myay engthstray andway ongsay, andway isway ecomebay myay alvationsay.

15 Ethay oicevay ofway ejoicingray andway alvationsay [isway] inway ethay abernaclestay ofway ethay ighteousray: ethay ightray andhay ofway ethay ORDLAY oethday aliantlyvay.

16 Ethay ightray andhay ofway ethay ORDLAY isway exaltedway: ethay ightray andhay ofway ethay ORDLAY oethday aliantlyvay.

17 IWAY allshay otnay ieday, utbay ivelay, andway eclareday ethay orksway ofway ethay ORDLAY.

18 Ethay ORDLAY athhay astenedchay emay oresay: utbay ehay athhay otnay ivengay emay overway untoway eathday.

19 Openway otay emay ethay atesgay ofway ighteousnessray: IWAY illway ogay intoway emthay, [andway] IWAY illway aisepray ethay ORDLAY:

20 Isthay ategay ofway ethay ORDLAY, intoway ichwhay ethay ighteousray allshay enterway.

21 IWAY illway aisepray eethay: orfay outhay asthay eardhay emay, andway artway ecomebay myay alvationsay.

22 Ethay onestay [ichwhay] ethay uildersbay efusedray isway ecomebay ethay eadhay [onestay] ofway ethay ornercay.

23 Isthay isway ethay ORDLAY'SAY oingday; itway [isway] arvellousmay inway ourway eyesway.

24 Isthay [isway] ethay ayday [ichwhay] ethay ORDLAY athhay ademay; eway illway ejoiceray andway ebay adglay inway itway.

25 Avesay ownay, IWAY eseechbay eethay, OWAY ORDLAY: OWAY ORDLAY, IWAY eseechbay eethay, endsay ownay osperitypray.

26 Essedblay [ebay] ehay atthay omethcay inway ethay amenay ofway ethay ORDLAY: eway avehay essedblay ouyay outway ofway ethay ousehay ofway ethay ORDLAY.

27 Odgay [isway] ethay ORDLAY, ichwhay athhay ewedshay usway ightlay: indbay ethay acrificesay ithway ordscay, [evenway] untoway ethay ornshay ofway ethay altarway.

28 Outhay [artway] myay Odgay, andway IWAY illway aisepray eethay: [outhay artway] myay Odgay, IWAY illway exaltway eethay.

29 OWAY ivegay anksthay untoway ethay ORDLAY; orfay [ehay isway] oodgay: orfay ishay ercymay [endurethway] orfay everway.

ALMPSAY 119

ALEPHWAY.

1 Essedblay [areway] ethay undefiledway inway ethay ayway, owhay alkway inway ethay awlay ofway ethay ORDLAY.

2 Essedblay [areway] eythay atthay eepkay ishay estimoniestay, [andway atthay] eeksay imhay ithway ethay olewhay earthay.

3 Eythay alsoway oday onay iniquityway: eythay alkway inway ishay aysway.

4 Outhay asthay ommandedcay [usway] otay eepkay thyay eceptspray iligentlyday.

5 OWAY atthay myay aysway ereway irectedday otay eepkay thyay atutesstay!

6 Enthay allshay IWAY otnay ebay ashamedway, enwhay IWAY avehay espectray untoway allway thyay ommandmentscay.

7 IWAY illway aisepray eethay ithway uprightnessway ofway earthay, enwhay IWAY allshay avehay earnedlay thyay ighteousray udgmentsjay.

8 IWAY illway eepkay thyay atutesstay: OWAY orsakefay emay otnay utterlyway.

ETHBAY.

9 Erewithalwhay allshay away oungyay anmay eanseclay ishay ayway? byay akingtay eedhay [eretothay] accordingway otay thyay ordway.

10 Ithway myay olewhay earthay avehay IWAY oughtsay eethay: OWAY etlay emay otnay anderway omfray thyay ommandmentscay.

11 Thyay ordway avehay IWAY idhay inway inemay earthay, atthay IWAY ightmay otnay insay againstway eethay.

12 Essedblay [artway] outhay, OWAY ORDLAY: eachtay emay thyay atutesstay.

13 Ithway myay ipslay avehay IWAY eclaredday allway ethay udgmentsjay ofway thyay outhmay.

14 IWAY avehay ejoicedray inway ethay ayway ofway thyay estimoniestay, asway [uchmay asway] inway allway ichesray.

15 IWAY illway editatemay inway thyay eceptspray, andway avehay espectray untoway thyay aysway.

16 IWAY illway elightday elfmysay inway thyay atutesstay: IWAY illway otnay orgetfay thyay ordway.

IMELGAY.

17 Ealday ountifullybay ithway thyay ervantsay, [atthay] IWAY aymay ivelay, andway eepkay thyay ordway.

18 Openway outhay inemay eyesway, atthay IWAY aymay eholdbay ondrousway ingsthay outway ofway thyay awlay.

19 IWAY [amway] away angerstray inway ethay earthway: idehay otnay thyay ommandmentscay omfray emay.

20 Myay oulsay eakethbray orfay ethay onginglay [atthay itway athhay] untoway thyay udgmentsjay atway allway imestay.

21 Outhay asthay ebukedray ethay oudpray [atthay areway] ursedcay, ichwhay oday errway omfray thyay ommandmentscay.

22 Emoveray omfray emay eproachray andway ontemptcay; orfay IWAY avehay eptkay thyay estimoniestay.

23 Incespray alsoway idday itsay [andway] eakspay againstway emay: [utbay] thyay ervantsay idday editatemay inway thyay atutesstay.

24 Thyay estimoniestay alsoway [areway] myay elightday [andway] myay ounsellorscay.

ALETHDAY.

25 Myay oulsay eavethclay untoway ethay ustday: uickenqay outhay emay accordingway otay thyay ordway.

26 IWAY avehay eclaredday myay aysway, andway outhay eardesthay emay: eachtay emay thyay atutesstay.

27 Akemay emay otay understandway ethay ayway ofway thyay eceptspray: osay allshay IWAY alktay ofway thyay ondrousway orksway.

28 Myay oulsay eltethmay orfay eavinesshay: engthenstray outhay emay accordingway untoway thyay ordway.

29 Emoveray omfray emay ethay ayway ofway inglyay: andway antgray emay thyay awlay aciouslygray.

30 IWAY avehay osenchay ethay ayway ofway uthtray: thyay udgmentsjay avehay IWAY aidlay [eforebay emay].

31 IWAY avehay uckstay untoway thyay estimoniestay: OWAY ORDLAY, utpay emay otnay otay ameshay.

32 IWAY illway unray ethay ayway ofway thyay ommandmentscay, enwhay outhay altshay enlargeway myay earthay.

EHAY.

33 Eachtay emay, OWAY ORDLAY, ethay ayway ofway thyay atutesstay; andway IWAY allshay eepkay itway [untoway] ethay endway.

34 Ivegay emay understandingway, andway IWAY allshay eepkay thyay awlay; eayay, IWAY allshay observeway itway ithway [myay] olewhay earthay.

35 Akemay emay otay ogay inway ethay athpay ofway thyay ommandmentscay; orfay ereinthay oday IWAY elightday.

36 Inclineway myay earthay untoway thyay estimoniestay, andway otnay otay ovetousnesscay.

37 Urntay awayway inemay eyesway omfray eholdingbay anityvay; [andway] uickenqay outhay emay inway thyay ayway.

38 Ablishstay thyay ordway untoway thyay ervantsay, owhay [isway evotedday] otay thyay earfay.

39 Urntay awayway myay eproachray ichwhay IWAY earfay: orfay thyay udgmentsjay [areway] oodgay.

40 Eholdbay, IWAY avehay ongedlay afterway thyay eceptspray: uickenqay emay inway thyay ighteousnessray.

AUVAY.

41 Etlay thyay erciesmay omecay alsoway untoway emay, OWAY ORDLAY, [evenway] thyay alvationsay, accordingway otay thyay ordway.

42 Osay allshay IWAY avehay erewithwhay otay answerway imhay atthay eproachethray emay: orfay IWAY usttray inway thyay ordway.

43 Andway aketay otnay ethay ordway ofway uthtray utterlyway outway ofway myay outhmay; orfay IWAY avehay opedhay inway thyay udgmentsjay.
44 Osay allshay IWAY eepkay thyay awlay ontinuallycay orfay everway andway everway.
45 Andway IWAY illway alkway atway ibertylay: orfay IWAY eeksay thyay eceptspray.
46 IWAY illway eakspay ofway thyay estimoniestay alsoway eforebay ingskay, andway illway otnay ebay ashamedway.
47 Andway IWAY illway elightday elfmysay inway thyay ommandmentscay, ichwhay IWAY avehay ovedlay.
48 Myay andshay alsoway illway IWAY iftlay upway untoway thyay ommandmentscay, ichwhay IWAY avehay ovedlay; andway IWAY illway editatemay inway thyay atutesstay.

AINZAY.
49 Ememberray ethay ordway untoway thyay ervantsay, uponway ichwhay outhay asthay ausedcay emay otay opehay.
50 Isthay [isway] myay omfortcay inway myay afflictionway: orfay thyay ordway athhay uickenedqay emay.
51 Ethay oudpray avehay adhay emay eatlygray inway erisionday: [etyay] avehay IWAY otnay eclinedday omfray thyay awlay.
52 IWAY ememberedray thyay udgmentsjay ofway oldway, OWAY ORDLAY; andway avehay omfortedcay elfmysay.
53 Orrorhay athhay akentay oldhay uponway emay ecausebay ofway ethay ickedway atthay orsakefay thyay awlay.
54 Thyay atutesstay avehay eenbay myay ongssay inway ethay ousehay ofway myay ilgrimagepay.
55 IWAY avehay ememberedray thyay amenay, OWAY ORDLAY, inway ethay ightnay, andway avehay eptkay thyay awlay.
56 Isthay IWAY adhay, ecausebay IWAY eptkay thyay eceptspray.

ETHCHAY.
57 [Outhay artway] myay ortionpay, OWAY ORDLAY: IWAY avehay aidsay atthay IWAY ouldway eepkay thyay ordsway.
58 IWAY intreatedway thyay avourfay ithway [myay] olewhay earthay: ebay ercifulmay untoway emay accordingway otay thyay ordway.
59 IWAY oughtthay onway myay aysway, andway urnedtay myay eetfay untoway thyay estimoniestay.

60 IWAY ademay astehay, andway elayedday otnay otay eepkay thyay ommandmentscay.

61 Ethay andsbay ofway ethay ickedway avehay obbedray emay: [utbay] IWAY avehay otnay orgottenfay thyay awlay.

62 Atway idnightmay IWAY illway iseray otay ivegay anksthay untoway eethay ecausebay ofway thyay ighteousray udgmentsjay.

63 IWAY [amway] away ompanioncay ofway allway [emthay] atthay earfay eethay, andway ofway emthay atthay eepkay thyay eceptspray.

64 Ethay earthway, OWAY ORDLAY, isway ullfay ofway thyay ercymay: eachtay emay thyay atutesstay.

ETHTAY.
65 Outhay asthay ealtday ellway ithway thyay ervantsay, OWAY ORDLAY, accordingway untoway thyay ordway.

66 Eachtay emay oodgay udgmentjay andway owledgeknay: orfay IWAY avehay elievedbay thyay ommandmentscay.

67 Eforebay IWAY asway afflictedway IWAY entway astrayway: utbay ownay avehay IWAY eptkay thyay ordway.

68 Outhay [artway] oodgay, andway oestday oodgay; eachtay emay thyay atutesstay.

69 Ethay oudpray avehay orgedfay away ielay againstway emay: [utbay] IWAY illway eepkay thyay eceptspray ithway [myay] olewhay earthay.

70 Eirthay earthay isway asway atfay asway easegray; [utbay] IWAY elightday inway thyay awlay.

71 [Itway isway] oodgay orfay emay atthay IWAY avehay eenbay afflictedway; atthay IWAY ightmay earnlay thyay atutesstay.

72 Ethay awlay ofway thyay outhmay [isway] etterbay untoway emay anthay ousandsthay ofway oldgay andway ilversay.

ODJAY.
73 Thyay andshay avehay ademay emay andway ashionedfay emay: ivegay emay understandingway, atthay IWAY aymay earnlay thyay ommandmentscay.

74 Eythay atthay earfay eethay illway ebay adglay enwhay eythay eesay emay; ecausebay IWAY avehay opedhay inway thyay ordway.

75 IWAY owknay, OWAY ORDLAY, atthay thyay udgmentsjay [areway] ightray, andway [atthay] outhay inway aithfulnessfay asthay afflictedway emay.

76 Etlay, IWAY aypray eethay, thyay ercifulmay indnesskay ebay orfay myay omfortcay, accordingway otay thyay ordway untoway thyay ervantsay.

77 Etlay thyay endertay erciesmay omecay untoway emay, atthay IWAY aymay ivelay: orfay thyay awlay [isway] myay elightday.

78 Etlay ethay oudpray ebay ashamedway; orfay eythay ealtday erverselypay ithway emay ithoutway away ausecay: [utbay] IWAY illway editatemay inway thyay eceptspray.

79 Etlay osethay atthay earfay eethay urntay untoway emay, andway osethay atthay avehay ownknay thyay estimoniestay.

80 Etlay myay earthay ebay oundsay inway thyay atutesstay; atthay IWAY ebay otnay ashamedway.

APHCAY.

81 Myay oulsay aintethfay orfay thyay alvationsay: [utbay] IWAY opehay inway thyay ordway.

82 Inemay eyesway ailfay orfay thyay ordway, ayingsay, Enwhay iltway outhay omfortcay emay?

83 Orfay IWAY amway ecomebay ikelay away ottlebay inway ethay okesmay; [etyay] oday IWAY otnay orgetfay thyay atutesstay.

84 Owhay anymay [areway] ethay aysday ofway thyay ervantsay? enwhay iltway outhay executeway udgmentjay onway emthay atthay ersecutepay emay?

85 Ethay oudpray avehay iggedday itspay orfay emay, ichwhay [areway] otnay afterway thyay awlay.

86 Allway thyay ommandmentscay [areway] aithfulfay: eythay ersecutepay emay ongfullywray; elphay outhay emay.

87 Eythay adhay almostway onsumedcay emay uponway earthway; utbay IWAY orsookfay otnay thyay eceptspray.

88 Uickenqay emay afterway thyay ovingkindnesslay; osay allshay IWAY eepkay ethay estimonytay ofway thyay outhmay.

AMEDLAY.

89 Orfay everway, OWAY ORDLAY, thyay ordway isway ettledsay inway eavenhay.

90 Thyay aithfulnessfay [isway] untoway allway enerationsgay: outhay asthay establishedway ethay earthway, andway itway abidethway.

91 Eythay ontinuecay isthay ayday accordingway otay inethay ordinancesway: orfay allway [areway] thyay ervantssay.

92 Unlessway thyay awlay [adhay eenbay] myay elightsday, IWAY ouldshay enthay avehay erishedpay inway inemay afflictionway.

93 IWAY illway evernay orgetfay thyay eceptspray: orfay ithway emthay outhay asthay uickenedqay emay.

94 IWAY [amway] inethay, avesay emay; orfay IWAY avehay oughtsay thyay eceptspray.

95 Ethay ickedway avehay aitedway orfay emay otay estroyday emay: [utbay] IWAY illway onsidercay thyay estimoniestay.

96 IWAY avehay eensay anway endway ofway allway erfectionpay: [utbay] thyay ommandmentcay [isway] exceedingway oadbray.

EMMAY.

97 OWAY owhay ovelay IWAY thyay awlay! itway [isway] myay editationmay allway ethay ayday.

98 Outhay oughthray thyay ommandmentscay asthay ademay emay iserway anthay inemay enemiesway: orfay eythay [areway] everway ithway emay.

99 IWAY avehay oremay understandingway anthay allway myay eacherstay: orfay thyay estimoniestay [areway] myay editationmay.

100 IWAY understandway oremay anthay ethay ancientsway, ecausebay IWAY eepkay thyay eceptspray.

101 IWAY avehay efrainedray myay eetfay omfray everyway evilway ayway, atthay IWAY ightmay eepkay thyay ordway.

102 IWAY avehay otnay epartedday omfray thyay udgmentsjay: orfay outhay asthay aughttay emay.

103 Owhay eetsway areway thyay ordsway untoway myay astetay! [eayay, eetersway] anthay oneyhay otay myay outhmay!

104 Oughthray thyay eceptspray IWAY etgay understandingway: ereforethay IWAY atehay everyway alsefay ayway.

UNNAY.

105 Thyay ordway [isway] away amplay untoway myay eetfay, andway away ightlay untoway myay athpay.

106 IWAY avehay ornsway, andway IWAY illway erformpay [itway], atthay IWAY illway eepkay thyay ighteousray udgmentsjay.

107 IWAY amway afflictedway eryvay uchmay: uickenqay emay, OWAY ORDLAY, accordingway untoway thyay ordway.

108 Acceptway, IWAY eseechbay eethay, ethay eewillfray offeringsway ofway myay outhmay, OWAY ORDLAY, andway eachtay emay thyay udgmentsjay.

109 Myay oulsay [isway] ontinuallycay inway myay andhay: etyay oday IWAY otnay orgetfay thyay awlay.

110 Ethay ickedway avehay aidlay away aresnay orfay emay: etyay IWAY erredway otnay omfray thyay eceptspray.

111 Thyay estimoniestay avehay IWAY akentay asway anway eritagehay orfay everway: orfay eythay [areway] ethay ejoicingray ofway myay earthay.

112 IWAY avehay inclinedway inemay earthay otay erformpay thyay atutesstay alwayway, [evenway untoway] ethay endway.

AMECHSAY.
113 IWAY atehay [ainvay] oughtsthay: utbay thyay awlay oday IWAY ovelay.

114 Outhay [artway] myay idinghay aceplay andway myay ieldshay: IWAY opehay inway thyay ordway.

115 Epartday omfray emay, eyay evildoersway: orfay IWAY illway eepkay ethay ommandmentscay ofway myay Odgay.

116 Upholdway emay accordingway untoway thyay ordway, atthay IWAY aymay ivelay: andway etlay emay otnay ebay ashamedway ofway myay opehay.

117 Oldhay outhay emay upway, andway IWAY allshay ebay afesay: andway IWAY illway avehay espectray untoway thyay atutesstay ontinuallycay.

118 Outhay asthay oddentray ownday allway emthay atthay errway omfray thyay atutesstay: orfay eirthay eceitday [isway] alsehoodfay.

119 Outhay uttestpay awayway allway ethay ickedway ofway ethay earthway [ikelay] ossdray: ereforethay IWAY ovelay thyay estimoniestay.

120 Myay eshflay emblethtray orfay earfay ofway eethay; andway IWAY amway afraidway ofway thyay udgmentsjay.

AINWAY.
121 IWAY avehay oneday udgmentjay andway usticejay: eavelay emay otnay otay inemay oppressorsway.

122 Ebay uretysay orfay thyay ervantsay orfay oodgay: etlay otnay ethay oudpray oppressway emay.

123 Inemay eyesway ailfay orfay thyay alvationsay, andway orfay ethay ordway ofway thyay ighteousnessray.

124 Ealday ithway thyay ervantsay accordingway untoway thyay ercymay, andway eachtay emay thyay atutesstay.

125 IWAY [amway] thyay ervantsay; ivegay emay understandingway, atthay IWAY aymay owknay thyay estimoniestay.

126 [Itway isway] imetay orfay [eethay], ORDLAY, otay orkway: [orfay] eythay avehay ademay oidvay thyay awlay.

127 Ereforethay IWAY ovelay thyay ommandmentscay aboveway oldgay; eayay, aboveway inefay oldgay.

128 Ereforethay IWAY esteemway allway [thyay] eceptspray [oncerningcay] allway [ingsthay otay ebay] ightray; [andway] IWAY atehay everyway alsefay ayway.

EPAY.

129 Thyay estimoniestay [areway] onderfulway: ereforethay othday myay oulsay eepkay emthay.

130 Ethay entranceway ofway thyay ordsway ivethgay ightlay; itway ivethgay understandingway untoway ethay implesay.

131 IWAY openedway myay outhmay, andway antedpay: orfay IWAY ongedlay orfay thyay ommandmentscay.

132 Ooklay outhay uponway emay, andway ebay ercifulmay untoway emay, asway outhay usestway otay oday untoway osethay atthay ovelay thyay amenay.

133 Orderway myay epsstay inway thyay ordway: andway etlay otnay anyway iniquityway avehay ominionday overway emay.

134 Eliverday emay omfray ethay oppressionway ofway anmay: osay illway IWAY eepkay thyay eceptspray.

135 Akemay thyay acefay otay ineshay uponway thyay ervantsay; andway eachtay emay thyay atutesstay.

136 Iversray ofway atersway unray ownday inemay eyesway, ecausebay eythay eepkay otnay thyay awlay.

ADDITZAY.

137 Ighteousray [artway] outhay, OWAY ORDLAY, andway uprightway [areway] thyay udgmentsjay.

138 Thyay estimoniestay [atthay] outhay asthay ommandedcay [areway] ighteousray andway eryvay aithfulfay.

139 Myay ealzay athhay onsumedcay emay, ecausebay inemay enemiesway avehay orgottenfay thyay ordsway.

140 Thyay ordway [isway] eryvay urepay: ereforethay thyay ervantsay ovethlay itway.

141 IWAY [amway] allsmay andway espisedday: [etyay] oday otnay IWAY orgetfay thyay eceptspray.

142 Thyay ighteousnessray [isway] anway everlastingway ighteousnessray, andway thyay awlay [isway] ethay uthtray.

143 Oubletray andway anguishway avehay akentay oldhay onway emay: [etyay] thyay ommandmentscay [areway] myay elightsday.

144 Ethay ighteousnessray ofway thyay estimoniestay [isway] everlastingway: ivegay emay understandingway, andway IWAY allshay ivelay.

OPHKAY.

145 IWAY iedcray ithway [myay] olewhay earthay; earhay emay, OWAY ORDLAY: IWAY illway eepkay thyay atutesstay.

146 IWAY iedcray untoway eethay; avesay emay, andway IWAY allshay eepkay thyay estimoniestay.

147 IWAY eventedpray ethay awningday ofway ethay orningmay, andway iedcray: IWAY opedhay inway thyay ordway.

148 Inemay eyesway eventpray ethay [ightnay] atchesway, atthay IWAY ightmay editatemay inway thyay ordway.

149 Earhay myay oicevay accordingway untoway thyay ovingkindnesslay: OWAY ORDLAY, uickenqay emay accordingway otay thyay udgmentjay.

150 Eythay awdray ighnay atthay ollowfay afterway ischiefmay: eythay areway arfay omfray thyay awlay.

151 Outhay [artway] earnay, OWAY ORDLAY; andway allway thyay ommandmentscay [areway] uthtray.

152 Oncerningcay thyay estimoniestay, IWAY avehay ownknay ofway oldway atthay outhay asthay oundedfay emthay orfay everway.

ESHRAY.

153 Onsidercay inemay afflictionway, andway eliverday emay: orfay IWAY oday otnay orgetfay thyay awlay.

154 Eadplay myay ausecay, andway eliverday emay: uickenqay emay accordingway otay thyay ordway.

155 Alvationsay [isway] arfay omfray ethay ickedway: orfay eythay eeksay otnay thyay atutesstay.

156 Eatgray [areway] thyay endertay erciesmay, OWAY ORDLAY: uickenqay emay accordingway otay thyay udgmentsjay.

157 Anymay [areway] myay ersecutorspay andway inemay enemiesway; [etyay] oday IWAY otnay eclineday omfray thyay estimoniestay.

158 IWAY eheldbay ethay ansgressorstray, andway asway ievedgray; ecausebay eythay eptkay otnay thyay ordway.

159 Onsidercay owhay IWAY ovelay thyay eceptspray: uickenqay emay, OWAY ORDLAY, accordingway otay thyay ovingkindnesslay.

160 Thyay ordway [isway] uetray [omfray] ethay eginningbay: andway everyway oneway ofway thyay ighteousray udgmentsjay [endurethway] orfay everway.

INSCHAY.

161 Incespray avehay ersecutedpay emay ithoutway away ausecay: utbay myay earthay andethstay inway aweway ofway thyay ordway.

162 IWAY ejoiceray atway thyay ordway, asway oneway atthay indethfay eatgray oilspay.

163 IWAY atehay andway abhorway inglyay: [utbay] thyay awlay oday IWAY ovelay.

164 Evensay imestay away ayday oday IWAY aisepray eethay ecausebay ofway thyay ighteousray udgmentsjay.

165 Eatgray eacepay avehay eythay ichwhay ovelay thyay awlay: andway othingnay allshay offendway emthay.

166 ORDLAY, IWAY avehay opedhay orfay thyay alvationsay, andway oneday thyay ommandmentscay.

167 Myay oulsay athhay eptkay thyay estimoniestay; andway IWAY ovelay emthay exceedinglyway.

168 IWAY avehay eptkay thyay eceptspray andway thyay estimoniestay: orfay allway myay aysway [areway] eforebay eethay.

AUTAY.

169 Etlay myay cryay omecay earnay eforebay eethay, OWAY ORDLAY: ivegay emay understandingway accordingway otay thyay ordway.

170 Etlay myay upplicationsay omecay eforebay eethay: eliverday emay accordingway otay thyay ordway.

171 Myay ipslay allshay utterway aisepray, enwhay outhay asthay aughttay emay thyay atutesstay.

172 Myay onguetay allshay eakspay ofway thyay ordway: orfay allway thyay ommandmentscay [areway] ighteousnessray.

173 Etlay inethay andhay elphay emay; orfay IWAY avehay osenchay thyay eceptspray.

174 IWAY avehay ongedlay orfay thyay alvationsay, OWAY ORDLAY; andway thyay awlay [isway] myay elightday.

175 Etlay myay oulsay ivelay, andway itway allshay aisepray eethay; andway etlay thyay udgmentsjay elphay emay.

176 IWAY avehay onegay astrayway ikelay away ostlay eepshay; eeksay thyay ervantsay; orfay IWAY oday otnay orgetfay thyay ommandmentscay.

ALMPSAY 120

AWAY Ongsay ofway egreesday.

1 Inway myay istressday IWAY iedcray untoway ethay ORDLAY, andway ehay eardhay emay.

2 Eliverday myay oulsay, OWAY ORDLAY, omfray inglyay ipslay, [andway] omfray away eceitfulday onguetay.

3 Atwhay allshay ebay ivengay untoway eethay? orway atwhay allshay ebay oneday untoway eethay, outhay alsefay onguetay?

4 Arpshay arrowsway ofway ethay ightymay, ithway oalscay ofway uniperjay.

5 Oeway isway emay, atthay IWAY ojournsay inway Esechmay, [atthay] IWAY elldway inway ethay entstay ofway Edarkay!

6 Myay oulsay athhay onglay eltdway ithway imhay atthay atethhay eacepay.

7 IWAY [amway orfay] eacepay: utbay enwhay IWAY eakspay, eythay [areway] orfay arway.

ALMPSAY 121

AWAY Ongsay ofway egreesday.

1 IWAY illway iftlay upway inemay eyesway untoway ethay illshay, omfray encewhay omethcay myay elphay.

2 Myay elphay [omethcay] omfray ethay ORDLAY, ichwhay ademay eavenhay andway earthway.

3 Ehay illway otnay uffersay thyay ootfay otay ebay ovedmay: ehay atthay eepethkay eethay illway otnay umberslay.

4 Eholdbay, ehay atthay eepethkay Israelway allshay eithernay umberslay ornay eepslay.

5 Ethay ORDLAY [isway] thyay eeperkay: ethay ORDLAY [isway] thyay adeshay uponway thyay ightray andhay.

6 Ethay unsay allshay otnay itesmay eethay byay ayday, ornay ethay oonmay byay ightnay.

7 Ethay ORDLAY allshay eservepray eethay omfray allway evilway: ehay allshay eservepray thyay oulsay.

8 Ethay ORDLAY allshay eservepray thyay oinggay outway andway thyay omingcay inway omfray isthay imetay orthfay, andway evenway orfay evermoreway.

ALMPSAY 122

AWAY Ongsay ofway egreesday ofway Avidday.

1 IWAY asway adglay enwhay eythay aidsay untoway emay, Etlay usway ogay intoway ethay ousehay ofway ethay ORDLAY.

2 Ourway eetfay allshay andstay ithinway thyay atesgay, OWAY Erusalemjay.

3 Erusalemjay isway uildedbay asway away itycay atthay isway ompactcay ogethertay:

4 Itherwhay ethay ibestray ogay upway, ethay ibestray ofway ethay ORDLAY, untoway ethay estimonytay ofway Israelway, otay ivegay anksthay untoway ethay amenay ofway ethay ORDLAY.

5 Orfay erethay areway etsay onesthray ofway udgmentjay, ethay onesthray ofway ethay ousehay ofway Avidday.

6 Aypray orfay ethay eacepay ofway Erusalemjay: eythay allshay osperpray atthay ovelay eethay.

7 Eacepay ebay ithinway thyay allsway, [andway] osperitypray ithinway thyay alacespay.

8 Orfay myay ethrenbray andway ompanionscay' akessay, IWAY illway ownay aysay, Eacepay [ebay] ithinway eethay.

9 Ecausebay ofway ethay ousehay ofway ethay ORDLAY ourway Odgay IWAY illway eeksay thyay oodgay.

ALMPSAY 123

AWAY Ongsay ofway egreesday.

1 Untoway eethay iftlay IWAY upway inemay eyesway, OWAY outhay atthay ellestdway inway ethay eavenshay.

2 Eholdbay, asway ethay eyesway ofway ervantssay [ooklay] untoway ethay andhay ofway eirthay astersmay, [andway] asway ethay eyesway ofway away aidenmay untoway ethay andhay ofway erhay istressmay; osay ourway eyesway [aitway] uponway ethay ORDLAY ourway Odgay, untilway atthay ehay avehay ercymay uponway usway.

3 Avehay ercymay uponway usway, OWAY ORDLAY, avehay ercymay uponway usway: orfay eway areway exceedinglyway illedfay ithway ontemptcay.

4 Ourway oulsay isway exceedinglyway illedfay ithway ethay orningscay ofway osethay atthay areway atway easeway, [andway] ithway ethay ontemptcay ofway ethay oudpray.

ALMPSAY 124

AWAY Ongsay ofway egreesday ofway Avidday.

1 Ifway [itway adhay otnay eenbay] ethay ORDLAY owhay asway onway ourway idesay, ownay aymay Israelway aysay;

2 Ifway [itway adhay otnay eenbay] ethay ORDLAY owhay asway onway ourway idesay, enwhay enmay oseray upway againstway usway:

3 Enthay eythay adhay allowedsway usway upway uickqay, enwhay eirthay athwray asway indledkay againstway usway:

4 Enthay ethay atersway adhay overwhelmedway usway, ethay eamstray adhay onegay overway ourway oulsay:

5 Enthay ethay oudpray atersway adhay onegay overway ourway oulsay.

6 Essedblay [ebay] ethay ORDLAY, owhay athhay otnay ivengay usway [asway] away eypray otay eirthay eethtay.

7 Ourway oulsay isway escapedway asway away irdbay outway ofway ethay aresnay ofway ethay owlersfay: ethay aresnay isway okenbray, andway eway areway escapedway.

8 Ourway elphay [isway] inway ethay amenay ofway ethay ORDLAY, owhay ademay eavenhay andway earthway.

ALMPSAY 125
AWAY Ongsay ofway egreesday.

1 Eythay atthay usttray inway ethay ORDLAY [allshay ebay] asway ountmay Ionzay, [ichwhay] annotcay ebay emovedray, [utbay] abidethway orfay everway.

2 Asway ethay ountainsmay [areway] oundray aboutway Erusalemjay, osay ethay ORDLAY [isway] oundray aboutway ishay eoplepay omfray enceforthhay evenway orfay everway.

3 Orfay ethay odray ofway ethay ickedway allshay otnay estray uponway ethay otlay ofway ethay ighteousray; estlay ethay ighteousray utpay orthfay eirthay andshay untoway iniquityway.

4 Oday oodgay, OWAY ORDLAY, untoway [osethay atthay ebay] oodgay, andway [otay emthay atthay areway] uprightway inway eirthay eartshay.

5 Asway orfay uchsay asway urntay asideway untoway eirthay ookedcray aysway, ethay ORDLAY allshay eadlay emthay orthfay ithway ethay orkersway ofway iniquityway: [utbay] eacepay [allshay ebay] uponway Israelway.

ALMPSAY 126

AWAY Ongsay ofway egreesday.

1 Enwhay ethay ORDLAY urnedtay againway ethay aptivitycay ofway Ionzay, eway ereway ikelay emthay atthay eamdray.

2 Enthay asway ourway outhmay illedfay ithway aughterlay, andway ourway onguetay ithway ingingsay: enthay aidsay eythay amongway ethay eathenhay, Ethay ORDLAY athhay oneday eatgray ingsthay orfay emthay.

3 Ethay ORDLAY athhay oneday eatgray ingsthay orfay usway; [ereofwhay] eway areway adglay.

4 Urntay againway ourway aptivitycay, OWAY ORDLAY, asway ethay eamsstray inway ethay outhsay.

5 Eythay atthay owsay inway earstay allshay eapray inway oyjay.

6 Ehay atthay oethgay orthfay andway eepethway, earingbay eciouspray eedsay, allshay oubtlessday omecay againway ithway ejoicingray, ingingbray ishay eavesshay [ithway imhay].

ALMPSAY 127

AWAY Ongsay ofway egreesday orfay Olomonsay.

1 Exceptway ethay ORDLAY uildbay ethay ousehay, eythay abourlay inway ainvay atthay uildbay itway: exceptway ethay ORDLAY eepkay ethay itycay, ethay atchmanway akethway [utbay] inway ainvay.

2 [Itway isway] ainvay orfay ouyay otay iseray upway earlyway, otay itsay upway atelay, otay eatway ethay eadbray ofway orrowssay: [orfay] osay ehay ivethgay ishay elovedbay eepslay.

3 Olay, ildrenchay [areway] anway eritagehay ofway ethay ORDLAY: [andway] ethay uitfray ofway ethay ombway [isway ishay] ewardray.

4 Asway arrowsway [areway] inway ethay andhay ofway away ightymay anmay; osay [areway] ildrenchay ofway ethay outhyay.

5 Appyhay [isway] ethay anmay atthay athhay ishay uiverqay ullfay ofway emthay: eythay allshay otnay ebay ashamedway, utbay eythay allshay eakspay ithway ethay enemiesway inway ethay ategay.

ALMPSAY 128

AWAẎ Ongsay ofway egreesday.

1 Essedblay [isway] everyway oneway atthay earethfay ethay ORDLAY; atthay alkethway inway ishay aysway.

2 Orfay outhay altshay eatway ethay abourlay ofway inethay andshay: appyhay [altshay] outhay [ebay], andway [itway allshay ebay] ellway ithway eethay.

3 Thyay ifeway [allshay ebay] asway away uitfulfray inevay byay ethay idessay ofway inethay ousehay: thyay ildrenchay ikelay oliveway antsplay oundray aboutway thyay abletay.

4 Eholdbay, atthay usthay allshay ethay anmay ebay essedblay atthay earethfay ethay ORDLAY.

5 Ethay ORDLAY allshay essblay eethay outway ofway Ionzay: andway outhay altshay eesay ethay oodgay ofway Erusalemjay allway ethay aysday ofway thyay ifelay.

6 Eayay, outhay altshay eesay thyay ildrenchay'say ildrenchay, [andway] eacepay uponway Israelway.

ALMPSAY 129
AWAY Ongsay ofway egreesday.

1 Anymay away imetay avehay eythay afflictedway emay omfray myay outhyay, aymay Israelway ownay aysay:

2 Anymay away imetay avehay eythay afflictedway emay omfray myay outhyay: etyay eythay avehay otnay evailedpray againstway emay.

3 Ethay owersplay owedplay uponway myay ackbay: eythay ademay onglay eirthay urrowsfay.

4 Ethay ORDLAY [isway] ighteousray: ehay athhay utcay asunderway ethay ordscay ofway ethay ickedway.

5 Etlay emthay allway ebay onfoundedcay andway urnedtay ackbay atthay atehay Ionzay.

6 Etlay emthay ebay asway ethay assgray [uponway] ethay ousetopshay, ichwhay itherethway aforeway itway owethgray upway:

7 Erewithwhay ethay owermay illethfay otnay ishay andhay; ornay ehay atthay indethbay eavesshay ishay osombay.

8 Eithernay oday eythay ichwhay ogay byay aysay, Ethay essingblay ofway ethay ORDLAY [ebay] uponway ouyay: eway essblay ouyay inway ethay amenay ofway ethay ORDLAY.

ALMPSAY 130
AWAY Ongsay ofway egreesday.

1 Outway ofway ethay epthsday avehay IWAY iedcray untoway eethay, OWAY ORDLAY.

2 Ordlay, earhay myay oicevay: etlay inethay earsway ebay attentiveway otay ethay oicevay ofway myay upplicationssay.

3 Ifway outhay, ORDLAY, ouldestshay arkmay iniquitiesway, OWAY Ordlay, owhay allshay andstay?

4 Utbay [erethay isway] orgivenessfay ithway eethay, atthay outhay ayestmay ebay earedfay.

5 IWAY aitway orfay ethay ORDLAY, myay oulsay othday aitway, andway inway ishay ordway oday IWAY opehay.

6 Myay oulsay [aitethway] orfay ethay Ordlay oremay anthay eythay atthay atchway orfay ethay orningmay: [IWAY aysay, oremay anthay] eythay atthay atchway orfay ethay orningmay.

7 Etlay Israelway opehay inway ethay ORDLAY: orfay ithway ethay ORDLAY [erethay isway] ercymay, andway ithway imhay [isway] enteousplay edemptionray.

8 Andway ehay allshay edeemray Israelway omfray allway ishay iniquitiesway.

ALMPSAY 131
AWAY Ongsay ofway egreesday ofway Avidday.

1 ORDLAY, myay earthay isway otnay aughtyhay, ornay inemay eyesway oftylay: eithernay oday IWAY exerciseway elfmysay inway eatgray attersmay, orway inway ingsthay ootay ighhay orfay emay.

2 Urelysay IWAY avehay ehavedbay andway uietedqay elfmysay, asway away ildchay atthay isway eanedway ofway ishay othermay: myay oulsay [isway] evenway asway away eanedway ildchay.

3 Etlay Israelway opehay inway ethay ORDLAY omfray enceforthhay andway orfay everway.

ALMPSAY 132
AWAY Ongsay ofway egreesday.

1 ORDLAY, ememberray Avidday, [andway] allway ishay afflictionsway:

2 Owhay ehay aresway untoway ethay ORDLAY, [andway] owedvay untoway ethay ightymay [Odgay] ofway Acobjay;

3 Urelysay IWAY illway otnay omecay intoway ethay abernacletay ofway myay ousehay, ornay ogay upway intoway myay edbay;

4 IWAY illway otnay ivegay eepslay otay inemay eyesway, [orway] umberslay otay inemay eyelidsway,

5 Untilway IWAY indfay outway away aceplay orfay ethay ORDLAY, anway abitationhay orfay ethay ightymay [Odgay] ofway Acobjay.

6 Olay, eway eardhay ofway itway atway Ephratahway: eway oundfay itway inway ethay ieldsfay ofway ethay oodway.

7 Eway illway ogay intoway ishay abernaclestay: eway illway orshipway atway ishay ootstoolfay.

8 Ariseway, OWAY ORDLAY, intoway thyay estray; outhay, andway ethay arkway ofway thyay engthstray.

9 Etlay thyay iestspray ebay othedclay ithway ighteousnessray; andway etlay thyay aintssay outshay orfay oyjay.

10 Orfay thyay ervantsay Avidday'say akesay urntay otnay awayway ethay acefay ofway inethay anointedway.

11 Ethay ORDLAY athhay ornsway [inway] uthtray untoway Avidday; ehay illway otnay urntay omfray itway; Ofway ethay uitfray ofway thyay odybay illway IWAY etsay uponway thyay onethray.

12 Ifway thyay ildrenchay illway eepkay myay ovenantcay andway myay estimonytay atthay IWAY allshay eachtay emthay, eirthay ildrenchay allshay alsoway itsay uponway thyay onethray orfay evermoreway.

13 Orfay ethay ORDLAY athhay osenchay Ionzay; ehay athhay esiredday [itway] orfay ishay abitationhay.

14 Isthay [isway] myay estray orfay everway: erehay illway IWAY elldway; orfay IWAY avehay esiredday itway.

15 IWAY illway abundantlyway essblay erhay ovisionpray: IWAY illway atisfysay erhay oorpay ithway eadbray.

16 IWAY illway alsoway otheclay erhay iestspray ithway alvationsay: andway erhay aintssay allshay outshay aloudway orfay oyjay.

17 Erethay illway IWAY akemay ethay ornhay ofway Avidday otay udbay: IWAY avehay ordainedway away amplay orfay inemay anointedway.

18 Ishay enemiesway illway IWAY otheclay ithway ameshay: utbay uponway imselfhay allshay ishay owncray ourishflay.

ALMPSAY 133
AWAY Ongsay ofway egreesday ofway Avidday.

1 Eholdbay, owhay oodgay andway owhay easantplay [itway isway] orfay ethrenbray otay elldway ogethertay inway unityway!

2 [Itway isway] ikelay ethay eciouspray ointmentway uponway ethay eadhay, atthay anray ownday uponway ethay eardbay, [evenway] Aaronway'say eardbay: atthay entway ownday otay ethay irtsskay ofway ishay armentsgay;

3 Asway ethay ewday ofway Ermonhay, [andway asway ethay ewday] atthay escendedday uponway ethay ountainsmay ofway Ionzay: orfay erethay ethay ORDLAY ommandedcay ethay essingblay, [evenway] ifelay orfay evermoreway.

ALMPSAY 134

AWAY Ongsay ofway egreesday.

1 Eholdbay, essblay eyay ethay ORDLAY, allway [eyay] ervantssay ofway ethay ORDLAY, ichwhay byay ightnay andstay inway ethay ousehay ofway ethay ORDLAY.

2 Iftlay upway ouryay andshay [inway] ethay anctuarysay, andway essblay ethay ORDLAY.

3 Ethay ORDLAY atthay ademay eavenhay andway earthway essblay eethay outway ofway Ionzay.

ALMPSAY 135

1 Aisepray eyay ethay ORDLAY. Aisepray eyay ethay amenay ofway ethay ORDLAY; aisepray [imhay], OWAY eyay ervantssay ofway ethay ORDLAY.

2 Eyay atthay andstay inway ethay ousehay ofway ethay ORDLAY, inway ethay ourtscay ofway ethay ousehay ofway ourway Odgay,

3 Aisepray ethay ORDLAY; orfay ethay ORDLAY [isway] oodgay: ingsay aisespray untoway ishay amenay; orfay [itway isway] easantplay.

4 Orfay ethay ORDLAY athhay osenchay Acobjay untoway imselfhay, [andway] Israelway orfay ishay eculiarpay easuretray.

5 Orfay IWAY owknay atthay ethay ORDLAY [isway] eatgray, andway [atthay] ourway Ordlay [isway] aboveway allway odsgay.

6 Atsoeverwhay ethay ORDLAY easedplay, [atthay] idday ehay inway eavenhay, andway inway earthway, inway ethay eassay, andway allway eepday acesplay.

7 Ehay ausethcay ethay apoursvay otay ascendway omfray ethay endsway ofway ethay earthway; ehay akethmay ightningslay orfay ethay ainray; ehay ingethbray ethay indway outway ofway ishay easuriestray.

8 Owhay otesmay ethay irstbornfay ofway Egyptway, othbay ofway anmay andway eastbay.

9 [Owhay] entsay okenstay andway ondersway intoway ethay idstmay ofway eethay, OWAY Egyptway, uponway Araohphay, andway uponway allway ishay ervantssay.

10 Owhay otesmay eatgray ationsnay, andway ewslay ightymay ingskay;

11 Ihonsay ingkay ofway ethay Amoritesway, andway Ogway ingkay ofway Ashanbay, andway allway ethay ingdomskay ofway Anaancay:

12 Andway avegay eirthay andlay [orfay] anway eritagehay, anway eritagehay untoway Israelway ishay eoplepay.

13 Thyay amenay, OWAY ORDLAY, [endurethway] orfay everway; [andway] thyay emorialmay, OWAY ORDLAY, oughoutthray allway enerationsgay.

14 Orfay ethay ORDLAY illway udgejay ishay eoplepay, andway ehay illway epentray imselfhay oncerningcay ishay ervantssay.

15 Ethay idolsway ofway ethay eathenhay [areway] ilversay andway oldgay, ethay orkway ofway enmay'say andshay.

16 Eythay avehay outhsmay, utbay eythay eakspay otnay; eyesway avehay eythay, utbay eythay eesay otnay;

17 Eythay avehay earsway, utbay eythay earhay otnay; eithernay isway erethay [anyway] eathbray inway eirthay outhsmay.

18 Eythay atthay akemay emthay areway ikelay untoway emthay: [osay isway] everyway oneway atthay ustethtray inway emthay.

19 Essblay ethay ORDLAY, OWAY ousehay ofway Israelway: essblay ethay ORDLAY, OWAY ousehay ofway Aaronway:

20 Essblay ethay ORDLAY, OWAY ousehay ofway Evilay: eyay atthay earfay ethay ORDLAY, essblay ethay ORDLAY.

21 Essedblay ebay ethay ORDLAY outway ofway Ionzay, ichwhay ellethdway atway Erusalemjay. Aisepray eyay ethay ORDLAY.

ALMPSAY 136

1 OWAY ivegay anksthay untoway ethay ORDLAY; orfay [ehay isway] oodgay: orfay ishay ercymay [endurethway] orfay everway.

2 OWAY ivegay anksthay untoway ethay Odgay ofway odsgay: orfay ishay ercymay [endurethway] orfay everway.

3 OWAY ivegay anksthay otay ethay Ordlay ofway ordslay: orfay ishay ercymay [endurethway] orfay everway.

4 Otay imhay owhay aloneway oethday eatgray ondersway: orfay ishay ercymay [endurethway] orfay everway.

5 Otay imhay atthay byay isdomway ademay ethay eavenshay: orfay ishay ercymay [endurethway] orfay everway.

6 Otay imhay atthay etchedstray outway ethay earthway aboveway ethay atersway: orfay ishay ercymay [endurethway] orfay everway.

7 Otay imhay atthay ademay eatgray ightslay: orfay ishay ercymay [endurethway] orfay everway:

8 Ethay unsay otay uleray byay ayday: orfay ishay ercymay [endurethway] orfay everway:

9 Ethay oonmay andway arsstay otay uleray byay ightnay: orfay ishay ercymay [endurethway] orfay everway.

10 Otay imhay atthay otesmay Egyptway inway eirthay irstbornfay: orfay ishay ercymay [endurethway] orfay everway:

11 Andway oughtbray outway Israelway omfray amongway emthay: orfay ishay ercymay [endurethway] orfay everway:

12 Ithway away ongstray andhay, andway ithway away etchedstray outway armway: orfay ishay ercymay [endurethway] orfay everway.

13 Otay imhay ichwhay ividedday ethay Edray easay intoway artspay: orfay ishay ercymay [endurethway] orfay everway:

14 Andway ademay Israelway otay asspay oughthray ethay idstmay ofway itway: orfay ishay ercymay [endurethway] orfay everway:

15 Utbay overthrewway Araohphay andway ishay osthay inway ethay Edray easay: orfay ishay ercymay [endurethway] orfay everway.

16 Otay imhay ichwhay edlay ishay eoplepay oughthray ethay ildernessway: orfay ishay ercymay [endurethway] orfay everway.

17 Otay imhay ichwhay otesmay eatgray ingskay: orfay ishay ercymay [endurethway] orfay everway:

18 Andway ewslay amousfay ingskay: orfay ishay ercymay [endurethway] orfay everway:

19 Ihonsay ingkay ofway ethay Amoritesway: orfay ishay ercymay [endurethway] orfay everway:

20 Andway Ogway ethay ingkay ofway Ashanbay: orfay ishay ercymay [endurethway] orfay everway:

21 Andway avegay eirthay andlay orfay anway eritagehay: orfay ishay ercymay [endurethway] orfay everway:

22 [Evenway] anway eritagehay untoway Israelway ishay ervantsay: orfay ishay ercymay [endurethway] orfay everway.

23 Owhay emememberedray usway inway ourway owlay estateway: orfay ishay ercymay [endurethway] orfay everway:

24 Andway athhay edeemedray usway omfray ourway enemiesway: orfay ishay ercymay [endurethway] orfay everway.

25 Owhay ivethgay oodfay otay allway eshflay: orfay ishay ercymay [endurethway] orfay everway.

26 OWAY ivegay anksthay untoway ethay Odgay ofway eavenhay: orfay ishay ercymay [endurethway] orfay everway.

ALMPSAY 137

1 Byay ethay iversray ofway Abylonbay, erethay eway atsay ownday, eayay, eway eptway, enwhay eway emememberedray Ionzay.

2 Eway angedhay ourway arpshay uponway ethay illowsway inway ethay idstmay ereofthay.

3 Orfay erethay eythay atthay arriedcay usway awayway aptivecay equiredray ofway usway away ongsay; andway eythay atthay astedway usway [equiredray ofway usway] irthmay, [ayingsay], Ingsay usway [oneway] ofway ethay ongssay ofway Ionzay.

4 Owhay allshay eway ingsay ethay ORDLAY'SAY ongsay inway away angestray andlay?

5 Ifway IWAY orgetfay eethay, OWAY Erusalemjay, etlay myay ightray andhay orgetfay [erhay unningcay].

6 Ifway IWAY oday otnay ememberray eethay, etlay myay onguetay eaveclay otay ethay oofray ofway myay outhmay; ifway IWAY eferpray otnay Erusalemjay aboveway myay iefchay oyjay.

7 Ememberray, OWAY ORDLAY, ethay ildrenchay ofway Edomway inway ethay ayday ofway Erusalemjay; owhay aidsay, Aseray [itway], aseray [itway, evenway] otay ethay oundationfay ereofthay.

8 OWAY aughterday ofway Abylonbay, owhay artway otay ebay estroyedday; appyhay [allshay ehay ebay], atthay ewardethray eethay asway outhay asthay ervedsay usway.

9 Appyhay [allshay ehay ebay], atthay akethtay andway ashethday thyay ittlelay onesway againstway ethay onesstay.

ALMPSAY 138
[AWAY Almpsay] ofway Avidday.

1 IWAY illway aisepray eethay ithway myay olewhay earthay: eforebay ethay odsgay illway IWAY ingsay aisepray untoway eethay.

2 IWAY illway orshipway owardtay thyay olyhay empletay, andway aisepray thyay amenay orfay thyay ovingkindnesslay andway orfay thyay uthtray: orfay outhay asthay agnifiedmay thyay ordway aboveway allway thyay amenay.

3 Inway ethay ayday enwhay IWAY iedcray outhay answeredstway emay, [andway] engthenedststray emay [ithway] engthstray inway myay oulsay.

4 Allway ethay ingskay ofway ethay earthway allshay aisepray eethay, OWAY ORDLAY, enwhay eythay earhay ethay ordsway ofway thyay outhmay.

5 Eayay, eythay allshay ingsay inway ethay aysway ofway ethay ORDLAY: orfay eatgray [isway] ethay oryglay ofway ethay ORDLAY.

6 Oughthay ethay ORDLAY [ebay] ighhay, etyay athhay ehay espectray untoway ethay owlylay: utbay ethay oudpray ehay owethknay afarway offway.

7 Oughthay IWAY alkway inway ethay idstmay ofway oubletray, outhay iltway eviveray emay: outhay altshay etchstray orthfay inethay andhay

againstway ethay athwray ofway inemay enemiesway, andway thyay ightray andhay allshay avesay emay.

8 Ethay ORDLAY illway erfectpay [atthay ichwhay] oncernethcay emay: thyay ercymay, OWAY ORDLAY, [endurethway] orfay everway: orsakefay otnay ethay orksway ofway inethay ownway andshay.

ALMPSAY 139
Otay ethay iefchay Usicianmay, AWAY Almpsay ofway Avidday.

1 OWAY ORDLAY, outhay asthay earchedsay emay, andway ownknay [emay].

2 Outhay owestknay myay ownsittingday andway inemay uprisingway, outhay understandestway myay oughtthay afarway offway.

3 Outhay ompassestcay myay athpay andway myay inglyay ownday, andway artway acquaintedway [ithway] allway myay aysway.

4 Orfay [erethay isway] otnay away ordway inway myay onguetay, [utbay], olay, OWAY ORDLAY, outhay owestknay itway altogetherway.

5 Outhay asthay esetbay emay ehindbay andway eforebay, andway aidlay inethay andhay uponway emay.

6 [Uchsay] owledgeknay [isway] ootay onderfulway orfay emay; itway isway ighhay, IWAY annotcay [attainway] untoway itway.

7 Itherwhay allshay IWAY ogay omfray thyay iritspay? orway itherwhay allshay IWAY eeflay omfray thyay esencepray?

8 Ifway IWAY ascendway upway intoway eavenhay, outhay [artway] erethay: ifway IWAY akemay myay edbay inway ellhay, eholdbay, outhay [artway erethay].

9 [Ifway] IWAY aketay ethay ingsway ofway ethay orningmay, [andway] elldway inway ethay uttermostway artspay ofway ethay easay;

10 Evenway erethay allshay thyay andhay eadlay emay, andway thyay ightray andhay allshay oldhay emay.

11 Ifway IWAY aysay, Urelysay ethay arknessday allshay overcay emay; evenway ethay ightnay allshay ebay ightlay aboutway emay.

12 Eaayay, ethay arknessday idethhay otnay omfray eethay; utbay ethay ightnay inethshay asway ethay ayday: ethay arknessday andway ethay ightlay [areway] othbay alikeway [otay eethay].

13 Orfay outhay asthay ossessedpay myay einsray: outhay asthay overedcay emay inway myay othermay'say ombway.

14 IWAY illway aisepray eethay; orfay IWAY amway earfullyfay [andway] onderfullyway ademay: arvellousmay [areway] thyay orksway; andway [atthay] myay oulsay owethknay ightray ellway.

15 Myay ubstancesay asway otnay idhay omfray eethay, enwhay IWAY
asway ademay inway ecretsay, [andway] uriouslycay oughtwray inway
ethay owestlay artspay ofway ethay earthway.
16 Inethay eyesway idday eesay myay ubstancesay, etyay eingbay
unperfectway; andway inway thyay ookbay allway [myay embersmay]
ereway ittenwray, [ichwhay] inway ontinuancecay ereway ashionedfay,
enwhay [asway etyay erethay asway] onenay ofway emthay.
17 Owhay eciouspray alsoway areway thyay oughtsthay untoway emay,
OWAY Odgay! owhay eatgray isway ethay umsay ofway emthay!
18 [Ifway] IWAY ouldshay ountcay emthay, eythay areway oremay inway
umbernay anthay ethay andsay: enwhay IWAY awakeway, IWAY amway
illstay ithway eethay.
19 Urelysay outhay iltway ayslay ethay ickedway, OWAY Odgay:
epartday omfray emay ereforethay, eyay oodyblay enmay.
20 Orfay eythay eakspay againstway eethay ickedlyway, [andway] inethay
enemiesway aketay [thyay amenay] inway ainvay.
21 Oday otnay IWAY atehay emthay, OWAY ORDLAY, atthay atehay
eethay? andway amway otnay IWAY ievedgray ithway osethay atthay
iseray upway againstway eethay?
22 IWAY atehay emthay ithway erfectpay atredhay: IWAY ountcay
emthay inemay enemiesway.
23 Earchsay emay, OWAY Odgay, andway owknay myay earthay: tryay
emay, andway owknay myay oughtsthay:
24 Andway eesay ifway [erethay ebay anyway] ickedway ayway inway
emay, andway eadlay emay inway ethay ayway everlastingway.

ALMPSAY 140
Otay ethay iefchay Usicianmay, AWAY Almpsay ofway Avidday.
1 Eliverday emay, OWAY ORDLAY, omfray ethay evilway anmay:
eservepray emay omfray ethay iolentvay anmay;
2 Ichwhay imagineway ischiefsmay inway [eirthay] earthay; ontinuallycay
areway eythay atheredgay ogethertay [orfay] arway.
3 Eythay avehay arpenedshay eirthay onguestay ikelay away erpentsay;
addersway' oisonpay [isway] underway eirthay ipslay. Elahsay.
4 Eepkay emay, OWAY ORDLAY, omfray ethay andshay ofway ethay
ickedway; eservepray emay omfray ethay iolentvay anmay; owhay avehay
urposedpay otay overthrowway myay oingsgay.
5 Ethay oudpray avehay idhay away aresnay orfay emay, andway ordscay;
eythay avehay eadspray away etnay byay ethay aysideway; eythay avehay
etsay insgay orfay emay. Elahsay.

6 IWAY aidsay untoway ethay ORDLAY, Outhay [artway] myay Odgay: earhay ethay oicevay ofway myay upplicationssay, OWAY ORDLAY.

7 OWAY ODGAY ethay Ordlay, ethay engthstray ofway myay alvationsay, outhay asthay overedcay myay eadhay inway ethay ayday ofway attlebay.

8 Antgray otnay, OWAY ORDLAY, ethay esiresday ofway ethay ickedway: urtherfay otnay ishay ickedway eviceday; [estlay] eythay exaltway emselvesthay. Elahsay.

9 [Asway orfay] ethay eadhay ofway osethay atthay ompasscay emay aboutway, etlay ethay ischiefmay ofway eirthay ownway ipslay overcay emthay.

10 Etlay urningbay oalscay allfay uponway emthay: etlay emthay ebay astcay intoway ethay irefay; intoway eepday itspay, atthay eythay iseray otnay upway againway.

11 Etlay otnay anway evilway eakerspay ebay establishedway inway ethay earthway: evilway allshay unthay ethay iolentvay anmay otay overthrowway [imhay].

12 IWAY owknay atthay ethay ORDLAY illway aintainmay ethay ausecay ofway ethay afflictedway, [andway] ethay ightray ofway ethay oorpay.

13 Urelysay ethay ighteousray allshay ivegay anksthay untoway thyay amenay: ethay uprightway allshay elldway inway thyay esencepray.

ALMPSAY 141
AWAY Almpsay ofway Avidday.

1 ORDLAY, IWAY cryay untoway eethay: akemay astehay untoway emay; ivegay earway untoway myay oicevay, enwhay IWAY cryay untoway eethay.

2 Etlay myay ayerpray ebay etsay orthfay eforebay eethay [asway] incenseway; [andway] ethay iftinglay upway ofway myay andshay [asway] ethay eveningway acrificesay.

3 Etsay away atchway, OWAY ORDLAY, eforebay myay outhmay; eepkay ethay oorday ofway myay ipslay.

4 Inclineway otnay myay earthay otay [anyway] evilway ingthay, otay actisepray ickedway orksway ithway enmay atthay orkway iniquityway: andway etlay emay otnay eatway ofway eirthay aintiesday.

5 Etlay ethay ighteousray itesmay emay; [itway allshay ebay] away indnesskay: andway etlay imhay eproveray emay; [itway allshay ebay] anway excellentway oilway, [ichwhay] allshay otnay eakbray myay

eadhay: orfay etyay myay ayerpray alsoway [allshay ebay] inway eirthay alamitiescay.

6 Enwhay eirthay udgesjay areway overthrownway inway onystay acesplay, eythay allshay earhay myay ordsway; orfay eythay areway eetsway.

7 Ourway onesbay areway atteredscay atway ethay avegray'say outhmay, asway enwhay oneway uttethcay andway eavethclay [oodway] uponway ethay earthway.

8 Utbay inemay eyesway [areway] untoway eethay, OWAY ODGAY ethay Ordlay: inway eethay isway myay usttray; eavelay otnay myay oulsay estituteday.

9 Eepkay emay omfray ethay aressnay [ichwhay] eythay avehay aidlay orfay emay, andway ethay insgay ofway ethay orkersway ofway iniquityway.

10 Etlay ethay ickedway allfay intoway eirthay ownway etsnay, ilstwhay atthay IWAY ithalway escapeway.

ALMPSAY 142
Aschilmay ofway Avidday; AWAY Ayerpray enwhay ehay asway inway ethay avecay.

1 IWAY iedcray untoway ethay ORDLAY ithway myay oicevay; ithway myay oicevay untoway ethay ORDLAY idday IWAY akemay myay upplicationsay.

2 IWAY ouredpay outway myay omplaintcay eforebay imhay; IWAY ewedshay eforebay imhay myay oubletray.

3 Enwhay myay iritspay asway overwhelmedway ithinway emay, enthay outhay ewestknay myay athpay. Inway ethay ayway ereinwhay IWAY alkedway avehay eythay ivilypray aidlay away aresnay orfay emay.

4 IWAY ookedlay onway [myay] ightray andhay, andway eheldbay, utbay [erethay asway] onay anmay atthay ouldway owknay emay: efugeray ailedfay emay; onay anmay aredcay orfay myay oulsay.

5 IWAY iedcray untoway eethay, OWAY ORDLAY: IWAY aidsay, Outhay [artway] myay efugeray [andway] myay ortionpay inway ethay andlay ofway ethay ivinglay.

6 Attendway untoway myay cryay; orfay IWAY amway oughtbray eryvay owlay: eliverday emay omfray myay ersecutorspay; orfay eythay areway ongerstray anthay IWAY.

7 Ingbray myay oulsay outway ofway isonpray, atthay IWAY aymay aisepray thyay amenay: ethay ighteousray allshay ompasscay emay aboutway; orfay outhay altshay ealday ountifullybay ithway emay.

ALMPSAY 143

AWAY Almpsay ofway Avidday.

1 Earhay myay ayerpray, OWAY ORDLAY, ivegay earway otay myay upplicationssay: inway thyay aithfulnessfay answerway emay, [andway] inway thyay ighteousnessray.

2 Andway enterway otnay intoway udgmentjay ithway thyay ervantsay: orfay inway thyay ightsay allshay onay anmay ivinglay ebay ustifiedjay.

3 Orfay ethay enemyway athhay ersecutedpay myay oulsay; ehay athhay ittensmay myay ifelay ownday otay ethay oundgray; ehay athhay ademay emay otay elldway inway arknessday, asway osethay atthay avehay eenbay onglay eadday.

4 Ereforethay isway myay iritspay overwhelmedway ithinway emay; myay earthay ithinway emay isway esolateday.

5 IWAY ememberray ethay aysday ofway oldway; IWAY editatemay onway allway thyay orksway; IWAY usemay onway ethay orkway ofway thyay andshay.

6 IWAY etchstray orthfay myay andshay untoway eethay: myay oulsay [irsteththay] afterway eethay, asway away irstythay andlay. Elahsay.

7 Earhay emay eedilyspay, OWAY ORDLAY: myay iritspay ailethfay: idehay otnay thyay acefay omfray emay, estlay IWAY ebay ikelay untoway emthay atthay ogay ownday intoway ethay itpay.

8 Ausecay emay otay earhay thyay ovingkindnesslay inway ethay orningmay; orfay inway eethay oday IWAY usttray: ausecay emay otay owknay ethay ayway ereinwhay IWAY ouldshay alkway; orfay IWAY iftlay upway myay oulsay untoway eethay.

9 Eliverday emay, OWAY ORDLAY, omfray inemay enemiesway: IWAY eeflay untoway eethay otay idehay emay.

10 Eachtay emay otay oday thyay illway; orfay outhay [artway] myay Odgay: thyay iritspay [isway] oodgay; eadlay emay intoway ethay andlay ofway uprightnessway.

11 Uickenqay emay, OWAY ORDLAY, orfay thyay amenay'say akesay: orfay thyay ighteousnessray' akesay ingbray myay oulsay outway ofway oubletray.

12 Andway ofway thyay ercymay utcay offway inemay enemiesway, andway estroyday allway emthay atthay afflictway myay oulsay: orfay IWAY [amway] thyay ervantsay.

ALMPSAY 144
[AWAY Almpsay] ofway Avidday.

1 Essedblay [ebay] ethay ORDLAY myay engthstray, ichwhay eachethtay myay andshay otay arway, [andway] myay ingersfay otay ightfay:

2 Myay oodnessgay, andway myay ortressfay; myay ighhay owertay, andway myay elivererday; myay ieldshay, andway [ehay] inway omwhay IWAY usttray; owhay ubduethsay myay eoplepay underway emay.

3 ORDLAY, atwhay [isway] anmay, atthay outhay akesttay owledgeknay ofway imhay! [orway] ethay onsay ofway anmay, atthay outhay akestmay accountway ofway imhay!

4 Anmay isway ikelay otay anityvay: ishay aysday [areway] asway away adowshay atthay assethpay awayway.

5 Owbay thyay eavenshay, OWAY ORDLAY, andway omecay ownday: ouchtay ethay ountainsmay, andway eythay allshay okesmay.

6 Astcay orthfay ightninglay, andway atterscay emthay: ootshay outway inethay arrowsway, andway estroyday emthay.

7 Endsay inethay andhay omfray aboveway; idray emay, andway eliverday emay outway ofway eatgray atersway, omfray ethay andhay ofway angestray ildrenchay;

8 Osewhay outhmay eakethspay anityvay, andway eirthay ightray andhay [isway] away ightray andhay ofway alsehoodfay.

9 IWAY illway ingsay away ewnay ongsay untoway eethay, OWAY Odgay: uponway away alterypsay [andway] anway instrumentway ofway entay ingsstray illway IWAY ingsay aisespray untoway eethay.

10 [Itway isway ehay] atthay ivethgay alvationsay untoway ingskay: owhay eliverethday Avidday ishay ervantsay omfray ethay urtfulhay ordsway.

11 Idray emay, andway eliverday emay omfray ethay andhay ofway angestray ildrenchay, osewhay outhmay eakethspay anityvay, andway eirthay ightray andhay [isway] away ightray andhay ofway alsehoodfay:

12 Atthay ourway onssay [aymay ebay] asway antsplay owngray upway inway eirthay outhyay; [atthay] ourway aughtersday [aymay ebay] asway ornercay onesstay, olishedpay [afterway] ethay imilitudesay ofway away alacepay:

13 [Atthay] ourway arnersgay [aymay ebay] ullfay, affordingway allway annermay ofway orestay: [atthay] ourway eepshay aymay ingbray orthfay ousandsthay andway entay ousandsthay inway ourway eetsstray:

14 [Atthay] ourway oxenway [aymay ebay] ongstray otay abourlay; [atthay erethay ebay] onay eakingbray inway, ornay oinggay outway; atthay [erethay ebay] onay omplainingcay inway ourway eetsstray.

15 Appyhay [isway atthay] eoplepay, atthay isway inway uchsay away asecay: [eayay], appyhay [isway atthay] eoplepay, osewhay Odgay [isway] ethay ORDLAY.

ALMPSAY 145
Avidday'say [Almpsay] ofway aisepray.
1 IWAY illway extolway eethay, myay Odgay, OWAY ingkay; andway IWAY illway essblay thyay amenay orfay everway andway everway.
2 Everyway ayday illway IWAY essblay eethay; andway IWAY illway aisepray thyay amenay orfay everway andway everway.
3 Eatgray [isway] ethay ORDLAY, andway eatlygray otay ebay aisedpray; andway ishay eatnessgray [isway] unsearchableway.
4 Oneway enerationgay allshay aisepray thyay orksway otay anotherway, andway allshay eclareday thyay ightymay actsway.
5 IWAY illway eakspay ofway ethay oriousglay onourhay ofway thyay ajestymay, andway ofway thyay ondrousway orksway.
6 Andway [enmay] allshay eakspay ofway ethay ightmay ofway thyay erribletay actsway: andway IWAY illway eclareday thyay eatnessgray.
7 Eythay allshay abundantlyway utterway ethay emorymay ofway thyay eatgray oodnessgay, andway allshay ingsay ofway thyay ighteousnessray.
8 Ethay ORDLAY [isway] aciousgray, andway ullfay ofway ompassioncay; owslay otay angerway, andway ofway eatgray ercymay.
9 Ethay ORDLAY [isway] oodgay otay allway: andway ishay endertay erciesmay [areway] overway allway ishay orksway.
10 Allway thyay orksway allshay aisepray eethay, OWAY ORDLAY; andway thyay aintssay allshay essblay eethay.
11 Eythay allshay eakspay ofway ethay oryglay ofway thyay ingdomkay, andway alktay ofway thyay owerpay;
12 Otay akemay ownknay otay ethay onssay ofway enmay ishay ightymay actsway, andway ethay oriousglay ajestymay ofway ishay ingdomkay.
13 Thyay ingdomkay [isway] anway everlastingway ingdomkay, andway thyay ominionday [endurethway] oughoutthray allway enerationsgay.
14 Ethay ORDLAY upholdethway allway atthay allfay, andway aisethray upway allway [osethay atthay ebay] owedbay ownday.
15 Ethay eyesway ofway allway aitway uponway eethay; andway outhay ivestgay emthay eirthay eatmay inway ueday easonsay.
16 Outhay openestway inethay andhay, andway atisfiestsay ethay esireday ofway everyway ivinglay ingthay.
17 Ethay ORDLAY [isway] ighteousray inway allway ishay aysway, andway olyhay inway allway ishay orksway.

18 Ethay ORDLAY [isway] ighnay untoway allway emthay atthay allcay uponway imhay, otay allway atthay allcay uponway imhay inway uthtray.

19 Ehay illway ulfilfay ethay esireday ofway emthay atthay earfay imhay: ehay alsoway illway earhay eirthay cryay, andway illway avesay emthay.

20 Ethay ORDLAY eservethpray allway emthay atthay ovelay imhay: utbay allway ethay ickedway illway ehay estroyday.

21 Myay outhmay allshay eakspay ethay aisepray ofway ethay ORDLAY: andway etlay allway eshflay essblay ishay olyhay amenay orfay everway andway everway.

ALMPSAY 146

1 Aisepray eyay ethay ORDLAY. Aisepray ethay ORDLAY, OWAY myay oulsay.

2 Ilewhay IWAY ivelay illway IWAY aisepray ethay ORDLAY: IWAY illway ingsay aisespray untoway myay Odgay ilewhay IWAY avehay anyway eingbay.

3 Utpay otnay ouryay usttray inway incespray, [ornay] inway ethay onsay ofway anmay, inway omwhay [erethay isway] onay elphay.

4 Ishay eathbray oethgay orthfay, ehay eturnethray otay ishay earthway; inway atthay eryvay ayday ishay oughtsthay erishpay.

5 Appyhay [isway ehay] atthay [athhay] ethay Odgay ofway Acobjay orfay ishay elphay, osewhay opehay [isway] inway ethay ORDLAY ishay Odgay:

6 Ichwhay ademay eavenhay, andway earthway, ethay easay, andway allway atthay ereinthay [isway]: ichwhay eepethkay uthtray orfay everway:

7 Ichwhay executethway udgmentjay orfay ethay oppressedway: ichwhay ivethgay oodfay otay ethay ungryhay. Ethay ORDLAY oosethlay ethay isonerspray:

8 Ethay ORDLAY openethway [ethay eyesway ofway] ethay indblay: ethay ORDLAY aisethray emthay atthay areway owedbay ownday: ethay ORDLAY ovethlay ethay ighteousray:

9 Ethay ORDLAY eservethpray ethay angersstray; ehay elievethray ethay atherlessfay andway idowway: utbay ethay ayway ofway ethay ickedway ehay urnethtay upsideway ownday.

10 Ethay ORDLAY allshay eignray orfay everway, [evenway] thyay Odgay, OWAY Ionzay, untoway allway enerationsgay. Aisepray eyay ethay ORDLAY.

ALMPSAY 147

1 Aisepray eyay ethay ORDLAY: orfay [itway isway] oodgay otay ingsay aisespray untoway ourway Odgay; orfay [itway isway] easantplay; [andway] aisepray isway omelycay.

2 Ethay ORDLAY othday uildbay upway Erusalemjay: ehay atherethgay ogethertay ethay outcastsway ofway Israelway.

3 Ehay ealethhay ethay okenbray inway earthay, andway indethbay upway eirthay oundsway.

4 Ehay ellethtay ethay umbernay ofway ethay arsstay; ehay allethcay emthay allway byay [eirthay] amesnay.

5 Eatgray [isway] ourway Ordlay, andway ofway eatgray owerpay: ishay understandingway [isway] infiniteway.

6 Ethay ORDLAY iftethlay upway ethay eekmay: ehay astethcay ethay ickedway ownday otay ethay oundgray.

7 Ingsay untoway ethay ORDLAY ithway anksgivingthay; ingsay aisepray uponway ethay arphay untoway ourway Odgay:

8 Owhay overethcay ethay eavenhay ithway oudsclay, owhay eparethpray ainray orfay ethay earthway, owhay akethmay assgray otay owgray uponway ethay ountainsmay.

9 Ehay ivethgay otay ethay eastbay ishay oodfay, [andway] otay ethay oungyay avensray ichwhay cryay.

10 Ehay elightethday otnay inway ethay engthstray ofway ethay orsehay: ehay akethtay otnay easureplay inway ethay egslay ofway away anmay.

11 Ethay ORDLAY akethtay easureplay inway emthay atthay earfay imhay, inway osethay atthay opehay inway ishay ercymay.

12 Aisepray ethay ORDLAY, OWAY Erusalemjay; aisepray thyay Odgay, OWAY Ionzay.

13 Orfay ehay athhay engthenedstray ethay arsbay ofway thyay atesgay; ehay athhay essedblay thyay ildrenchay ithinway eethay.

14 Ehay akethmay eacepay [inway] thyay ordersbay, [andway] illethfay eethay ithway ethay inestfay ofway ethay eatwhay.

15 Ehay endethsay orthfay ishay ommandmentcay [uponway] earthway: ishay ordway unnethray eryvay iftlysway.

16 Ehay ivethgay owsnay ikelay oolway: ehay atterethscay ethay oarfrosthay ikelay ashesway.

17 Ehay astethcay orthfay ishay iceway ikelay orselsmay: owhay ancay andstay eforebay ishay oldcay?

18 Ehay endethsay outway ishay ordway, andway eltethmay emthay: ehay ausethcay ishay indway otay owblay, [andway] ethay atersway owflay.

19 Ehay ewethshay ishay ordway untoway Acobjay, ishay atutesstay andway ishay udgmentsjay untoway Israelway.
20 Ehay athhay otnay ealtday osay ithway anyway ationnay: andway [asway orfay ishay] udgmentsjay, eythay avehay otnay ownknay emthay. Aisepray eyay ethay ORDLAY.

ALMPSAY 148

1 Aisepray eyay ethay ORDLAY. Aisepray eyay ethay ORDLAY omfray ethay eavenshay: aisepray imhay inway ethay eightshay.
2 Aisepray eyay imhay, allway ishay angelsway: aisepray eyay imhay, allway ishay ostshay.
3 Aisepray eyay imhay, unsay andway oonmay: aisepray imhay, allway eyay arsstay ofway ightlay.
4 Aisepray imhay, eyay eavenshay ofway eavenshay, andway eyay atersway atthay [ebay] aboveway ethay eavenshay.
5 Etlay emthay aisepray ethay amenay ofway ethay ORDLAY: orfay ehay ommandedcay, andway eythay ereway eatedcray.
6 Ehay athhay alsoway ablishedstay emthay orfay everway andway everway: ehay athhay ademay away ecreeday ichwhay allshay otnay asspay.
7 Aisepray ethay ORDLAY omfray ethay earthway, eyay agonsdray, andway allway eepsday:
8 Irefay, andway ailhay; owsnay, andway apourvay; ormystay indway ulfillingfay ishay ordway:
9 Ountainsmay, andway allway illshay; uitfulfray eestray, andway allway edarscay:
10 Eastsbay, andway allway attlecay; eepingcray ingsthay, andway ingflyay owlfay:
11 Ingskay ofway ethay earthway, andway allway eoplepay; incespray, andway allway udgesjay ofway ethay earthway:
12 Othbay oungyay enmay, andway aidensmay; oldway enmay, andway ildrenchay:
13 Etlay emthay aisepray ethay amenay ofway ethay ORDLAY: orfay ishay amenay aloneway isway excellentway; ishay oryglay [isway] aboveway ethay earthway andway eavenhay.
14 Ehay alsoway exaltethway ethay ornhay ofway ishay eoplepay, ethay aisepray ofway allway ishay aintssay; [evenway] ofway ethay ildrenchay ofway Israelway, away eoplepay earnay untoway imhay. Aisepray eyay ethay ORDLAY.

ALMPSAY 149

1 Aisepray eyay ethay ORDLAY. Ingsay untoway ethay ORDLAY away ewnay ongsay, [andway] ishay aisepray inway ethay ongregationcay ofway aintssay.

2 Etlay Israelway ejoiceray inway imhay atthay ademay imhay: etlay ethay ildrenchay ofway Ionzay ebay oyfuljay inway eirthay Ingkay.

3 Etlay emthay aisepray ishay amenay inway ethay anceday: etlay emthay ingsay aisespray untoway imhay ithway ethay imbreltay andway arphay.

4 Orfay ethay ORDLAY akethtay easureplay inway ishay eoplepay: ehay illway eautifybay ethay eekmay ithway alvationsay.

5 Etlay ethay aintssay ebay oyfuljay inway oryglay: etlay emthay ingsay aloudway uponway eirthay edsbay.

6 [Etlay] ethay ighhay [aisespray] ofway Odgay [ebay] inway eirthay outhmay, andway away oedgedtway ordsway inway eirthay andhay;

7 Otay executeway engeancevay uponway ethay eathenhay, [andway] unishmentspay uponway ethay eoplepay;

8 Otay indbay eirthay ingskay ithway ainschay, andway eirthay oblesnay ithway ettersfay ofway ironway;

9 Otay executeway uponway emthay ethay udgmentjay ittenwray: isthay onourhay avehay allway ishay aintssay. Aisepray eyay ethay ORDLAY.

ALMPSAY 150

1 Aisepray eyay ethay ORDLAY. Aisepray Odgay inway ishay anctuarysay: aisepray imhay inway ethay irmamentfay ofway ishay owerpay.

2 Aisepray imhay orfay ishay ightymay actsway: aisepray imhay accordingway otay ishay excellentway eatnessgray.

3 Aisepray imhay ithway ethay oundsay ofway ethay umpettray: aisepray imhay ithway ethay alterypsay andway arphay.

4 Aisepray imhay ithway ethay imbreltay andway anceday: aisepray imhay ithway ingedstray instrumentsway andway organsway.

5 Aisepray imhay uponway ethay oudlay alscymbay: aisepray imhay uponway ethay ighhay oundingsay alscymbay.

6 Etlay everyway ingthay atthay athhay eathbray aisepray ethay ORDLAY. Aisepray eyay ethay ORDLAY.

ETHAY OVERBSPRAY

APTERCHAY 1

1 Ethay overbspray ofway Olomonsay ethay onsay ofway Avidday, ingkay ofway Israelway;

2 Otay owknay isdomway andway instructionway; otay erceivepay ethay ordsway ofway understandingway;

3 Otay eceiveray ethay instructionway ofway isdomway, usticejay, andway udgmentjay, andway equityway;

4 Otay ivegay ubtiltysay otay ethay implesay, otay ethay oungyay anmay owledgeknay andway iscretionday.

5 Away iseway [anmay] illway earhay, andway illway increaseway earninglay; andway away anmay ofway understandingway allshay attainway untoway iseway ounselscay:

6 Otay understandway away overbpray, andway ethay interpretationway; ethay ordsway ofway ethay iseway, andway eirthay arkday ayingssay.

7 ∂ Ethay earfay ofway ethay ORDLAY [isway] ethay eginningbay ofway owledgeknay: [utbay] oolsfay espiseday isdomway andway instructionway.

8 Ymay onsay, earhay ethay instructionway ofway ythay atherfay, andway orsakefay otnay ethay awlay ofway ythay othermay:

9 Orfay eythay [allshay ebay] anway ornamentway ofway acegray untoway ythay eadhay, andway ainschay aboutway ythay ecknay.

10 ∂ Ymay onsay, ifway innerssay enticeway eethay, onsentcay outhay otnay.

11 Ifway eythay aysay, Omecay ithway usway, etlay usway aylay aitway orfay oodblay, etlay usway urklay ivilypray orfay ethay innocentway ithoutway ausecay:

12 Etlay usway allowsway emthay upway aliveway asway ethay avegray; andway olewhay, asway osethay atthay ogay ownday intoway ethay itpay:

13 Eway allshay indfay allway eciouspray ubstancesay, eway allshay illfay ourway ouseshay ithway oilspay:

14 Astcay inway ythay otlay amongway usway; etlay usway allway avehay oneway ursepay:

15 Ymay onsay, alkway otnay outhay inway ethay ayway ithway emthay; efrainray ythay ootfay omfray eirthay athpay:

16 Orfay eirthay eetfay unray otay evilway, andway akemay astehay otay edshay oodblay.

17 Urelysay inway ainvay ethay etnay isway eadspray inway ethay ightsay ofway anyway irdbay.

18 Andway eythay aylay aitway orfay eirthay [ownway] oodblay; eythay
urklay ivilypray orfay eirthay [ownway] iveslay.

19 Osay [areway] ethay aysway ofway everyway oneway atthay isway
eedygray ofway aingay; [ichwhay] akethtay awayway ethay ifelay ofway
ethay ownersway ereofthay.

20 ∂ Isdomway iethcray ithoutway; eshay utterethway erhay oicevay
inway ethay eetsstray:

21 Eshay iethcray inway ethay iefchay aceplay ofway oncoursecay, inway
ethay openingsway ofway ethay atesgay: inway ethay itycay eshay
utterethway erhay ordsway, [ayingsay],

22 Owhay onglay, eyay implesay onesway, illway eyay ovelay
implicitysay? andway ethay ornersscay elightday inway eirthay orningscay,
andway oolsfay atehay owledgeknay?

23 Urntay ouyay atway ymay eproofray: eholdbay, Iway illway ourpay
outway ymay iritspay untoway ouyay, Iway illway akemay ownknay ymay
ordsway untoway ouyay.

24 ∂ Ecausebay Iway avehay alledcay, andway eyay efusedray; Iway
avehay etchedstray outway ymay andhay, andway onay anmay
egardedray;

25 Utbay eyay avehay etsay atway oughtnay allway ymay ounselcay,
andway ouldway onenay ofway ymay eproofray:

26 Iway alsoway illway aughlay atway ouryay alamitycay; Iway illway
ockmay enwhay ouryay earfay omethcay;

27 Enwhay ouryay earfay omethcay asway esolationday, andway ouryay
estructionday omethcay asway away irlwindwhay; enwhay istressday
andway anguishway omethcay uponway ouyay.

28 Enthay allshay eythay allcay uponway emay, utbay Iway illway otnay
answerway; eythay allshay eeksay emay earlyway, utbay eythay allshay
otnay indfay emay:

29 Orfay atthay eythay atedhay owledgeknay, andway idday otnay
oosechay ethay earfay ofway ethay ORDLAY:

30 Eythay ouldway onenay ofway ymay ounselcay: eythay espisedday
allway ymay eproofray.

31 Ereforethay allshay eythay eatway ofway ethay uitfray ofway eirthay
ownway ayway, andway ebay illedfay ithway eirthay ownway evicesday.

32 Orfay ethay urningtay awayway ofway ethay implesay allshay ayslay
emthay, andway ethay osperitypray ofway oolsfay allshay estroyday
emthay.

33 Utbay osowhay earkenethhay untoway emay allshay elldway afelysay,
andway allshay ebay ietquay omfray earfay ofway evilway.

APTERCHAY 2

1 Ymay onsay, ifway outhay iltway eceiveray ymay ordsway, andway idehay ymay ommandmentscay ithway eethay;

2 Osay atthay outhay inclineway inethay earway untoway isdomway, [andway] applyway inethay earthay otay understandingway;

3 Eayay, ifway outhay iestcray afterway owledgeknay, [andway] iftestlay upway ythay oicevay orfay understandingway;

4 Ifway outhay eekestsay erhay asway ilversay, andway earchestsay orfay erhay asway [orfay] idhay easurestray;

5 Enthay altshay outhay understandway ethay earfay ofway ethay ORDLAY, andway indfay ethay owledgeknay ofway Odgay.

6 Orfay ethay ORDLAY ivethgay isdomway: outway ofway ishay outhmay [omethcay] owledgeknay andway understandingway.

7 Ehay ayethlay upway oundsay isdomway orfay ethay ighteousray: [ehay isway] away ucklerbay otay emthay atthay alkway uprightlyway.

8 Ehay eepethkay ethay athspay ofway udgmentjay, andway eservethpray ethay ayway ofway ishay aintssay.

9 Enthay altshay outhay understandway ighteousnessray, andway udgmentjay, andway equityway; [eayay], everyway oodgay athpay.

10 ∂ Enwhay isdomway enterethway intoway inethay earthay, andway owledgeknay isway easantplay untoway ythay oulsay;

11 Iscretionday allshay eservepray eethay, understandingway allshay eepkay eethay:

12 Otay eliverday eethay omfray ethay ayway ofway ethay evilway [anmay], omfray ethay anmay atthay eakethspay owardfray ingsthay;

13 Owhay eavelay ethay athspay ofway uprightnessway, otay alkway inway ethay aysway ofway arknessday;

14 Owhay ejoiceray otay oday evilway, [andway] elightday inway ethay owardnessfray ofway ethay ickedway;

15 Osewhay aysway [areway] ookedcray, andway [eythay] owardfray inway eirthay athspay:

16 Otay eliverday eethay omfray ethay angestray omanway, [evenway] omfray ethay angerstray [ichwhay] atterethflay ithway erhay ordsway;

17 Ichwhay orsakethfay ethay uidegay ofway erhay outhyay, andway orgettethfay ethay ovenantcay ofway erhay Odgay.

18 Orfay erhay ousehay inclinethway untoway eathday, andway erhay athspay untoway ethay eadday.

19 Onenay atthay ogay untoway erhay eturnray againway, eithernay aketay eythay oldhay ofway ethay athspay ofway ifelay.

20 Atthay outhay ayestmay alkway inway ethay ayway ofway oodgay [enmay], andway eepkay ethay athspay ofway ethay ighteousray.

21 Orfay ethay uprightway allshay elldway inway ethay andlay, andway ethay erfectpay allshay emainray inway itway.

22 Utbay ethay ickedway allshay ebay utcay offway omfray ethay earthway, andway ethay ansgressorstray allshay ebay ootedray outway ofway itway.

APTERCHAY 3

1 Ymay onsay, orgetfay otnay ymay awlay; utbay etlay inethay earthay eepkay ymay ommandmentscay:

2 Orfay engthlay ofway aysday, andway onglay ifelay, andway eacepay, allshay eythay addway otay eethay.

3 Etlay otnay ercymay andway uthtray orsakefay eethay: indbay emthay aboutway ythay ecknay; itewray emthay uponway ethay abletay ofway inethay earthay:

4 Osay altshay outhay indfay avourfay andway oodgay understandingway inway ethay ightsay ofway Odgay andway anmay.

5 ∂ Usttray inway ethay ORDLAY ithway allway inethay earthay; andway eanlay otnay untoway inethay ownway understandingway.

6 Inway allway ythay aysway acknowledgeway imhay, andway ehay allshay irectday ythay athspay.

7 ∂ Ebay otnay iseway inway inethay ownway eyesway: earfay ethay ORDLAY, andway epartday omfray evilway.

8 Itway allshay ebay ealthhay otay ythay avelnay, andway arrowmay otay ythay onesbay.

9 Onourhay ethay ORDLAY ithway ythay ubstancesay, andway ithway ethay irstfruitsfay ofway allway inethay increaseway:

10 Osay allshay ythay arnsbay ebay illedfay ithway entyplay, andway ythay essespray allshay urstbay outway ithway ewnay ineway.

11 ∂ Ymay onsay, espiseday otnay ethay asteningchay ofway ethay ORDLAY; eithernay ebay earyway ofway ishay orrectioncay:

12 Orfay omwhay ethay ORDLAY ovethlay ehay orrectethcay; evenway asway away atherfay ethay onsay [inway omwhay] ehay elightethday.

13 ∂ Appyhay [isway] ethay anmay [atthay] indethfay isdomway, andway ethay anmay [atthay] ettethgay understandingway.

14 Orfay ethay erchandisemay ofway itway [isway] etterbay anthay ethay erchandisemay ofway ilversay, andway ethay aingay ereofthay anthay inefay oldgay.

15 Eshay [isway] oremay eciouspray anthay ubiesray: andway allway ethay ingsthay outhay anstcay esireday areway otnay otay ebay omparedcay untoway erhay.

16 Engthlay ofway aysday [isway] inway erhay ightray andhay; [andway] inway erhay eftlay andhay ichesray andway onourhay.

17 Erhay aysway [areway] aysway ofway easantnessplay, andway allway erhay athspay [areway] eacepay.

18 Eshay [isway] away eetray ofway ifelay otay emthay atthay aylay oldhay uponway erhay: andway appyhay [isway everyway oneway] atthay etainethray erhay.

19 Ethay ORDLAY ybay isdomway athhay oundedfay ethay earthway; ybay understandingway athhay ehay establishedway ethay eavenshay.

20 Ybay ishay owledgeknay ethay epthsday areway okenbray upway, andway ethay oudsclay opdray ownday ethay ewday.

21 ∂ Ymay onsay, etlay otnay emthay epartday omfray inethay eyesway: eepkay oundsay isdomway andway iscretionday:

22 Osay allshay eythay ebay ifelay untoway ythay oulsay, andway acegray otay ythay ecknay.

23 Enthay altshay outhay alkway inway ythay ayway afelysay, andway ythay ootfay allshay otnay umblestay.

24 Enwhay outhay iestlay ownday, outhay altshay otnay ebay afraidway: eayay, outhay altshay ielay ownday, andway ythay eepslay allshay ebay eetsway.

25 Ebay otnay afraidway ofway uddensay earfay, eithernay ofway ethay esolationday ofway ethay ickedway, enwhay itway omethcay.

26 Orfay ethay ORDLAY allshay ebay ythay onfidencecay, andway allshay eepkay ythay ootfay omfray eingbay akentay.

27 ∂ Ithholdway otnay oodgay omfray emthay otay omwhay itway isway ueday, enwhay itway isway inway ethay owerpay ofway inethay andhay otay oday [itway].

28 Aysay otnay untoway ythay eighbournay, Ogay, andway omecay againway, andway otay orrowmay Iway illway ivegay; enwhay outhay asthay itway ybay eethay.

29 Eviseday otnay evilway againstway ythay eighbournay, eeingsay ehay ellethdway ecurelysay ybay eethay.

30 ∂ Ivestray otnay ithway away anmay ithoutway ausecay, ifway ehay avehay oneday eethay onay armhay.

31 ∂ Envyway outhay otnay ethay oppressorway, andway oosechay onenay ofway ishay aysway.

32 Orfay ethay owardfray [isway] abominationway otay ethay ORDLAY: utbay ishay ecretsay [isway] ithway ethay ighteousray.

33 ∂ Ethay ursecay ofway ethay ORDLAY [isway] inway ethay ousehay ofway ethay ickedway: utbay ehay essethblay ethay abitationhay ofway ethay ustjay.

34 Urelysay ehay ornethscay ethay ornersscay: utbay ehay ivethgay acegray untoway ethay owlylay.

35 Ethay iseway allshay inheritway oryglay: utbay ameshay allshay ebay ethay omotionpray ofway oolsfay.

APTERCHAY 4

1 Earhay, eyay ildrenchay, ethay instructionway ofway away atherfay, andway attendway otay owknay understandingway.

2 Orfay Iway ivegay ouyay oodgay octrineday, orsakefay eyay otnay ymay awlay.

3 Orfay Iway asway ymay ather'sfay onsay, endertay andway onlyway [elovedbay] inway ethay ightsay ofway ymay othermay.

4 Ehay aughttay emay alsoway, andway aidsay untoway emay, Etlay inethay earthay etainray ymay ordsway: eepkay ymay ommandmentscay, andway ivelay.

5 Etgay isdomway, etgay understandingway: orgetfay [itway] otnay; eithernay eclineday omfray ethay ordsway ofway ymay outhmay.

6 Orsakefay erhay otnay, andway eshay allshay eservepray eethay: ovelay erhay, andway eshay allshay eepkay eethay.

7 Isdomway [isway] ethay incipalpray ingthay; [ereforethay] etgay isdomway: andway ithway allway ythay ettinggay etgay understandingway.

8 Exaltway erhay, andway eshay allshay omotepray eethay: eshay allshay ingbray eethay otay onourhay, enwhay outhay ostday embraceway erhay.

9 Eshay allshay ivegay otay inethay eadhay anway ornamentway ofway acegray: away owncray ofway oryglay allshay eshay eliverday otay eethay.

10 Earhay, Oway ymay onsay, andway eceiveray ymay ayingssay; andway ethay earsyay ofway ythay ifelay allshay ebay anymay.

11 Iway avehay aughttay eethay inway ethay ayway ofway isdomway; Iway avehay edlay eethay inway ightray athspay.

12 Enwhay outhay oestgay, ythay epsstay allshay otnay ebay aitenedstray; andway enwhay outhay unnestray, outhay altshay otnay umblestay.

13 Aketay astfay oldhay ofway instructionway; etlay [erhay] otnay ogay: eepkay erhay; orfay eshay [isway] ythay ifelay.

14 ∂ Enterway otnay intoway ethay athpay ofway ethay ickedway, andway ogay otnay inway ethay ayway ofway evilway [enmay].

15 Avoidway itway, asspay otnay ybay itway, urntay omfray itway, andway asspay awayway.

16 Orfay eythay eepslay otnay, exceptway eythay avehay oneday ischiefmay; andway eirthay eepslay isway akentay awayway, unlessway eythay ausecay [omesay] otay allfay.

17 Orfay eythay eatway ethay eadbray ofway ickednessway, andway inkdray ethay ineway ofway iolencevay.

18 Utbay ethay athpay ofway ethay ustjay [isway] asway ethay iningshay ightlay, atthay inethshay oremay andway oremay untoway ethay erfectpay ayday.

19 Ethay ayway ofway ethay ickedway [isway] asway arknessday: eythay owknay otnay atway atwhay eythay umblestay.

20 ∂ Ymay onsay, attendway otay ymay ordsway; inclineway inethay earway untoway ymay ayingssay.

21 Etlay emthay otnay epartday omfray inethay eyesway; eepkay emthay inway ethay idstmay ofway inethay earthay.

22 Orfay eythay [areway] ifelay untoway osethay atthay indfay emthay, andway ealthhay otay allway eirthay eshflay.

23 ∂ Eepkay ythay earthay ithway allway iligenceday; orfay outway ofway itway [areway] ethay issuesway ofway ifelay.

24 Utpay awayway omfray eethay away owardfray outhmay, andway erversepay ipslay utpay arfay omfray eethay.

25 Etlay inethay eyesway ooklay ightray onway, andway etlay inethay eyelidsway ooklay aightstray eforebay eethay.

26 Onderpay ethay athpay ofway ythay eetfay, andway etlay allway ythay aysway ebay establishedway.

27 Urntay otnay otay ethay ightray andhay ornay otay ethay eftlay: emoveray ythay ootfay omfray evilway.

APTERCHAY 5

1 Ymay onsay, attendway untoway ymay isdomway, [andway] owbay inethay earway otay ymay understandingway:

2 Atthay outhay ayestmay egardray iscretionday, andway [atthay] ythay ipslay aymay eepkay owledgeknay.

3 ∂ Orfay ethay ipslay ofway away angestray omanway opdray [asway] anway oneycombhay, andway erhay outhmay [isway] oothersmay anthay oilway:

4 Utbay erhay endway isway itterbay asway ormwoodway, arpshay asway away oedgedtway ordsway.

5 Erhay eetfay ogay ownday otay eathday; erhay epsstay aketay oldhay onway ellhay.

6 Estlay outhay ouldestshay onderpay ethay athpay ofway ifelay, erhay aysway areway oveablemay, [atthay] outhay anstcay otnay owknay [emthay].

7 Earhay emay ownay ereforethay, Oway eyay ildrenchay, andway epartday otnay omfray ethay ordsway ofway ymay outhmay.

8 Emoveray ythay ayway arfay omfray erhay, andway omecay otnay ighnay ethay oorday ofway erhay ousehay:

9 Estlay outhay ivegay inethay onourhay untoway othersway, andway ythay earsyay untoway ethay uelcray:

10 Estlay angersstray ebay illedfay ithway ythay ealthway; andway ythay abourslay [ebay] inway ethay ousehay ofway away angerstray;

11 Andway outhay ournmay atway ethay astlay, enwhay ythay eshflay andway ythay odybay areway onsumedcay,

12 Andway aysay, Owhay avehay Iway atedhay instructionway, andway ymay earthay espisedday eproofray;

13 Andway avehay otnay obeyedway ethay oicevay ofway ymay eacherstay, ornay inclinedway inemay earway otay emthay atthay instructedway emay!

14 Iway asway almostway inway allway evilway inway ethay idstmay ofway ethay ongregationcay andway assemblyway.

15 ∂ Inkdray atersway outway ofway inethay ownway isterncay, andway unningray atersway outway ofway inethay ownway ellway.

16 Etlay ythay ountainsfay ebay ispersedday abroadway, [andway] iversray ofway atersway inway ethay eetsstray.

17 Etlay emthay ebay onlyway inethay ownway, andway otnay angers'stray ithway eethay.

18 Etlay ythay ountainfay ebay essedblay: andway ejoiceray ithway ethay ifeway ofway ythay outhyay.

19 [Etlay erhay ebay asway] ethay ovinglay indhay andway easantplay oeray; etlay erhay eastsbray atisfysay eethay atway allway imestay; andway ebay outhay avishedray alwaysway ithway erhay ovelay.

20 Andway ywhay iltway outhay, ymay onsay, ebay avishedray ithway away angestray omanway, andway embraceway ethay osombay ofway away angerstray?

21 Orfay ethay aysway ofway anmay [areway] eforebay ethay eyesway ofway ethay ORDLAY, andway ehay onderethpay allway ishay oingsgay.

22 ∂ Ishay ownway iniquitiesway allshay aketay ethay ickedway imselfhay, andway ehay allshay ebay oldenhay ithway ethay ordscay ofway ishay inssay.

23 Ehay allshay ieday ithoutway instructionway; andway inway ethay eatnessgray ofway ishay ollyfay ehay allshay ogay astrayway.

APTERCHAY 6

1 Ymay onsay, ifway outhay ebay uretysay orfay ythay iendfray, [ifway] outhay asthay ickenstray ythay andhay ithway away angerstray,

2 Outhay artway aredsnay ithway ethay ordsway ofway ythay outhmay, outhay artway akentay ithway ethay ordsway ofway ythay outhmay.

3 Oday isthay ownay, ymay onsay, andway eliverday yselfthay, enwhay outhay artway omecay intoway ethay andhay ofway ythay iendfray; ogay, umblehay yselfthay, andway akemay uresay ythay iendfray.

4 Ivegay otnay eepslay otay inethay eyesway, ornay umberslay otay inethay eyelidsway.

5 Eliverday yselfthay asway away oeray omfray ethay andhay [ofway ethay unterhay], andway asway away irdbay omfray ethay andhay ofway ethay owlerfay.

6 ∂ Ogay otay ethay antway, outhay uggardslay; onsidercay erhay aysway, andway ebay iseway:

7 Ichwhay avinghay onay uidegay, overseerway, orway ulerray,

8 Ovidethpray erhay eatmay inway ethay ummersay, [andway] atherethgay erhay oodfay inway ethay arvesthay.

9 Owhay onglay iltway outhay eepslay, Oway uggardslay? enwhay iltway outhay ariseway outway ofway ythay eepslay?

10 [Etyay] away ittlelay eepslay, away ittlelay umberslay, away ittlelay oldingfay ofway ethay andshay otay eepslay:

11 Osay allshay ythay overtypay omecay asway oneway atthay avellethtray, andway ythay antway asway anway armedway anmay.

12 ∂ Away aughtynay ersonpay, away ickedway anmay, alkethway ithway away owardfray outhmay.

13 Ehay inkethway ithway ishay eyesway, ehay eakethspay ithway ishay eetfay, ehay eachethtay ithway ishay ingersfay;

14 Owardnessfray [isway] inway ishay earthay, ehay evisethday ischiefmay ontinuallycay; ehay owethsay iscordday.

15 Ereforethay allshay ishay alamitycay omecay uddenlysay; uddenlysay allshay ehay ebay okenbray ithoutway emedyray.

16 ∂ Esethay ixsay [ingsthay] othday ethay ORDLAY atehay: eayay, evensay [areway] anway abominationway untoway imhay:

17 Away oudpray ooklay, away yinglay onguetay, andway andshay atthay edshay innocentway oodblay,

18 Anway earthay atthay evisethday ickedway imaginationsway, eetfay atthay ebay iftsway inway unningray otay ischiefmay,

19 Away alsefay itnessway [atthay] eakethspay ieslay, andway ehay atthay owethsay iscordday amongway ethrenbray.

20 ∂ Ymay onsay, eepkay ythay ather'sfay ommandmentcay, andway orsakefay otnay ethay awlay ofway ythay othermay:

21 Indbay emthay ontinuallycay uponway inethay earthay, [andway] ietay emthay aboutway ythay ecknay.

22 Enwhay outhay oestgay, itway allshay eadlay eethay; enwhay outhay eepestslay, itway allshay eepkay eethay; andway [enwhay] outhay awakestway, itway allshay alktay ithway eethay.

23 Orfay ethay ommandmentcay [isway] away amplay; andway ethay awlay [isway] ightlay; andway eproofsray ofway instructionway [areway] ethay ayway ofway ifelay:

24 Otay eepkay eethay omfray ethay evilway omanway, omfray ethay atteryflay ofway ethay onguetay ofway away angestray omanway.

25 Ustlay otnay afterway erhay eautybay inway inethay earthay; eithernay etlay erhay aketay eethay ithway erhay eyelidsway.

26 Orfay ybay eansmay ofway away orishwhay omanway [away anmay isway oughtbray] otay away iecepay ofway eadbray: andway ethay adulteressway illway unthay orfay ethay eciouspray ifelay.

27 Ancay away anmay aketay irefay inway ishay osombay, andway ishay othesclay otnay ebay urnedbay?

28 Ancay oneway ogay uponway othay oalscay, andway ishay eetfay otnay ebay urnedbay?

29 Osay ehay atthay oethgay inway otay ishay eighbour'snay ifeway; osoeverwhay ouchethtay erhay allshay otnay ebay innocentway.

30 [Enmay] oday otnay espiseday away iefthay, ifway ehay ealstay otay atisfysay ishay oulsay enwhay ehay isway ungryhay;

31 Utbay [ifway] ehay ebay oundfay, ehay allshay estoreray evenfoldsay; ehay allshay ivegay allway ethay ubstancesay ofway ishay ousehay.

32 [Utbay] osowhay ommittethcay adulteryway ithway away omanway ackethlay understandingway: ehay [atthay] oethday itway estroyethday ishay ownway oulsay.

33 Away oundway andway ishonourday allshay ehay etgay; andway ishay eproachray allshay otnay ebay ipedway awayway.

34 Orfay ealousyjay [isway] ethay ageray ofway away anmay: ereforethay ehay illway otnay arespay inway ethay ayday ofway engeancevay.

35 Ehay illway otnay egardray anyway ansomray; eithernay illway ehay
estray ontentcay, oughthay outhay ivestgay anymay iftsgay.

APTERCHAY 7

1 Ymay onsay, eepkay ymay ordsway, andway aylay upway ymay
ommandmentscay ithway eethay.

2 Eepkay ymay ommandmentscay, andway ivelay; andway ymay awlay
asway ethay appleway ofway inethay eyeway.

3 Indbay emthay uponway ythay ingersfay, itewray emthay uponway
ethay abletay ofway inethay earthay.

4 Aysay untoway isdomway, Outhay [artway] ymay istersay; andway
allcay understandingway [ythay] inswomankay:

5 Atthay eythay aymay eepkay eethay omfray ethay angestray omanway,
omfray ethay angerstray [ichwhay] atterethflay ithway erhay ordsway.

6 ∂ Orfay atway ethay indowway ofway ymay ousehay Iway ookedlay
oughthray ymay asementcay,

7 Andway eheldbay amongway ethay implesay onesway, Iway iscernedday
amongway ethay outhsyay, away oungyay anmay oidvay ofway
understandingway,

8 Assingpay oughthray ethay eetstray earnay erhay ornercay; andway
ehay entway ethay ayway otay erhay ousehay,

9 Inway ethay ilighttway, inway ethay eveningway, inway ethay ackblay
andway arkday ightnay:

10 Andway, eholdbay, erethay etmay imhay away omanway [ithway]
ethay attireway ofway anway arlothay, andway ubtilsay ofway earthay.

11 (Eshay [isway] oudlay andway ubbornstay; erhay eetfay abideway
otnay inway erhay ousehay:

12 Ownay [isway eshay] ithoutway, ownay inway ethay eetsstray, andway
iethlay inway aitway atway everyway ornercay.)

13 Osay eshay aughtcay imhay, andway issedkay imhay, [andway] ithway
anway impudentway acefay aidsay untoway imhay,

14 [Iway avehay] eacepay offeringsway ithway emay; isthay ayday avehay
Iway ayedpay ymay owsvay.

15 Ereforethay amecay Iway orthfay otay eetmay eethay, iligentlyday otay
eeksay ythay acefay, andway Iway avehay oundfay eethay.

16 Iway avehay eckedday ymay edbay ithway overingscay ofway
apestrytay, ithway arvedcay [orksway], ithway inefay inenlay ofway
Egyptway.

17 Iway avehay erfumedpay ymay edbay ithway yrrhmay, aloesway,
andway innamoncay.

18 Omecay, etlay usway aketay ourway illfay ofway ovelay untilway ethay orningmay: etlay usway olacesay ourselvesway ithway oveslay.

19 Orfay ethay oodmangay [isway] otnay atway omehay, ehay isway onegay away onglay ourneyjay:

20 Ehay athhay akentay away agbay ofway oneymay ithway imhay, [andway] illway omecay omehay atway ethay ayday appointedway.

21 Ithway erhay uchmay airfay eechspay eshay ausedcay imhay otay ieldyay, ithway ethay atteringflay ofway erhay ipslay eshay orcedfay imhay.

22 Ehay oethgay afterway erhay aightwaystray, asway anway oxway oethgay otay ethay aughterslay, orway asway away oolfay otay ethay orrectioncay ofway ethay ocksstay;

23 Illtay away artday ikestray oughthray ishay iverlay; asway away irdbay astethhay otay ethay aresnay, andway owethknay otnay atthay itway [isway] orfay ishay ifelay.

24 ∂ Earkenhay untoway emay ownay ereforethay, Oway eyay ildrenchay, andway attendway otay ethay ordsway ofway ymay outhmay.

25 Etlay otnay inethay earthay eclineday otay erhay aysway, ogay otnay astrayway inway erhay athspay.

26 Orfay eshay athhay astcay ownday anymay oundedway: eayay, anymay ongstray [enmay] avehay eenbay ainslay ybay erhay.

27 Erhay ousehay [isway] ethay ayway otay ellhay, oinggay ownday otay ethay amberschay ofway eathday.

APTERCHAY 8

1 Othday otnay isdomway ycray? andway understandingway utpay orthfay erhay oicevay?

2 Eshay andethstay inway ethay optay ofway ighhay acesplay, ybay ethay ayway inway ethay acesplay ofway ethay athspay.

3 Eshay iethcray atway ethay atesgay, atway ethay entryway ofway ethay itycay, atway ethay omingcay inway atway ethay oorsday.

4 Untoway ouyay, Oway enmay, Iway allcay; andway ymay oicevay [isway] otay ethay onssay ofway anmay.

5 Oway eyay implesay, understandway isdomway: andway, eyay oolsfay, ebay eyay ofway anway understandingway earthay.

6 Earhay; orfay Iway illway eakspay ofway excellentway ingsthay; andway ethay openingway ofway ymay ipslay [allshay ebay] ightray ingsthay.

7 Orfay ymay outhmay allshay eakspay uthtray; andway ickednessway [isway] anway abominationway otay ymay ipslay.

8 Allway ethay ordsway ofway ymay outhmay [areway] inway
ighteousnessray; [erethay isway] othingnay owardfray orway erversepay
inway emthay.

9 Eythay [areway] allway ainplay otay imhay atthay understandethway,
andway ightray otay emthay atthay indfay owledgeknay.

10 Eceiveray ymay instructionway, andway otnay ilversay; andway
owledgeknay atherray anthay oicechay oldgay.

11 Orfay isdomway [isway] etterbay anthay ubiesray; andway allway
ethay ingsthay atthay aymay ebay esiredday areway otnay otay ebay
omparedcay otay itway.

12 Iway isdomway elldway ithway udencepray, andway indfay outway
owledgeknay ofway ittyway inventionsway.

13 Ethay earfay ofway ethay ORDLAY [isway] otay atehay evilway:
idepray, andway arrogancyway, andway ethay evilway ayway, andway
ethay owardfray outhmay, oday Iway atehay.

14 Ounselcay [isway] inemay, andway oundsay isdomway: Iway [amway]
understandingway; Iway avehay engthstray.

15 Ybay emay ingskay eignray, andway incespray ecreeday usticejay.

16 Ybay emay incespray uleray, andway oblesnay, [evenway] allway ethay
udgesjay ofway ethay earthway.

17 Iway ovelay emthay atthay ovelay emay; andway osethay atthay eeksay
emay earlyway allshay indfay emay.

18 Ichesray andway onourhay [areway] ithway emay; [eayay], urableday
ichesray andway ighteousnessray.

19 Ymay uitfray [isway] etterbay anthay oldgay, eayay, anthay inefay
oldgay; andway ymay evenueray anthay oicechay ilversay.

20 Iway eadlay inway ethay ayway ofway ighteousnessray, inway ethay
idstmay ofway ethay athspay ofway udgmentjay:

21 Atthay Iway aymay ausecay osethay atthay ovelay emay otay
inheritway ubstancesay; andway Iway illway illfay eirthay easurestray.

22 Ethay ORDLAY ossessedpay emay inway ethay eginningbay ofway
ishay ayway, eforebay ishay orksway ofway oldway.

23 Iway asway etsay upway omfray everlastingway, omfray ethay
eginningbay, orway everway ethay earthway asway.

24 Enwhay [erethay ereway] onay epthsday, Iway asway oughtbray
orthfay; enwhay [erethay ereway] onay ountainsfay aboundingway ithway
aterway.

25 Eforebay ethay ountainsmay ereway ettledsay, eforebay ethay illshay
asway Iway oughtbray orthfay:

26 Ilewhay asway etyay ehay adhay otnay ademay ethay earthway, ornay ethay ieldsfay, ornay ethay ighesthay artpay ofway ethay ustday ofway ethay orldway.

27 Enwhay ehay eparedpray ethay eavenshay, Iway [asway] erethay: enwhay ehay etsay away ompasscay uponway ethay acefay ofway ethay epthday:

28 Enwhay ehay establishedway ethay oudsclay aboveway: enwhay ehay engthenedstray ethay ountainsfay ofway ethay eepday:

29 Enwhay ehay avegay otay ethay easay ishay ecreeday, atthay ethay atersway ouldshay otnay asspay ishay ommandmentcay: enwhay ehay appointedway ethay oundationsfay ofway ethay earthway:

30 Enthay Iway asway ybay imhay, [asway] oneway oughtbray upway [ithway imhay]: andway Iway asway ailyday [ishay] elightday, ejoicingray alwaysway eforebay imhay;

31 Ejoicingray inway ethay abitablehay artpay ofway ishay earthway; andway ymay elightsday [ereway] ithway ethay onssay ofway enmay.

32 Ownay ereforethay earkenhay untoway emay, Oway eyay ildrenchay: orfay essedblay [areway] eythay atthay] eepkay ymay aysway.

33 Earhay instructionway, andway ebay iseway, andway efuseray itway otnay.

34 Essedblay [isway] ethay anmay atthay earethhay emay, atchingway ailyday atway ymay atesgay, aitingway atway ethay ostspay ofway ymay oorsday.

35 Orfay osowhay indethfay emay indethfay ifelay, andway allshay obtainway avourfay ofway ethay ORDLAY.

36 Utbay ehay atthay innethsay againstway emay ongethwray ishay ownway oulsay: allway eythay atthay atehay emay ovelay eathday.

APTERCHAY 9

1 Isdomway athhay uildedbay erhay ousehay, eshay athhay ewnhay outway erhay evensay illarspay:

2 Eshay athhay illedkay erhay eastsbay; eshay athhay ingledmay erhay ineway; eshay athhay alsoway urnishedfay erhay abletay.

3 Eshay athhay entsay orthfay erhay aidensmay: eshay iethcray uponway ethay ighesthay acesplay ofway ethay itycay,

4 Osowhay [isway] implesay, etlay imhay urntay inway itherhay: [asway orfay] imhay atthay antethway understandingway, eshay aithsay otay imhay,

5 Omecay, eatway ofway ymay eadbray, andway inkdray ofway ethay ineway [ichwhay] Iway avehay ingledmay.

6 Orsakefay ethay oolishfay, andway ivelay; andway ogay inway ethay ayway ofway understandingway.

7 Ehay atthay eprovethray away ornerscay ettethgay otay imselfhay ameshay: andway ehay atthay ebukethray away ickedway [anmay ettethgay] imselfhay away otblay.

8 Eproveray otnay away ornerscay, estlay ehay atehay eethay: ebukeray away iseway anmay, andway ehay illway ovelay eethay.

9 Ivegay [instructionway] otay away iseway [anmay], andway ehay illway ebay etyay iserway: eachtay away ustjay [anmay], andway ehay illway increaseway inway earninglay.

10 Ethay earfay ofway ethay ORDLAY [isway] ethay eginningbay ofway isdomway: andway ethay owledgeknay ofway ethay olyhay [isway] understandingway.

11 Orfay ybay emay ythay aysday allshay ebay ultipliedmay, andway ethay earsyay ofway ythay ifelay allshay ebay increasedway.

12 Ifway outhay ebay iseway, outhay altshay ebay iseway orfay yselfthay: utbay [ifway] outhay ornestscay, outhay aloneway altshay earbay [itway].

13 Away oolishfay omanway [isway] amorousclay: [eshay isway] implesay, andway owethknay othingnay.

14 Orfay eshay ittethsay atway ethay oorday ofway erhay ousehay, onway away eatsay inway ethay ighhay acesplay ofway ethay itycay,

15 Otay allcay assengerspay owhay ogay ightray onway eirthay aysway:

16 Osowhay [isway] implesay, etlay imhay urntay inway itherhay: andway [asway orfay] imhay atthay antethway understandingway, eshay aithsay otay imhay,

17 Olenstay atersway areway eetsway, andway eadbray [eatenway] inway ecretsay isway easantplay.

18 Utbay ehay owethknay otnay atthay ethay eadday [areway] erethay; [andway atthay] erhay uestsgay [areway] inway ethay epthsday ofway ellhay.

APTERCHAY 10

1 Ethay overbspray ofway Olomonsay. Away iseway onsay akethmay away adglay atherfay: utbay away oolishfay onsay [isway] ethay eavinesshay ofway ishay othermay.

2 Easurestray ofway ickednessway ofitpray othingnay: utbay ighteousnessray eliverethday omfray eathday.

3 Ethay ORDLAY illway otnay uffersay ethay oulsay ofway ethay ighteousray otay amishfay: utbay ehay astethcay awayway ethay ubstancesay ofway ethay ickedway.

4 Ehay ecomethbay oorpay atthay ealethday [ithway] away ackslay andhay: utbay ethay andhay ofway ethay iligentday akethmay ichray.

5 Ehay atthay atherethgay inway ummersay [isway] away iseway onsay: [utbay] ehay atthay eepethslay inway arvesthay [isway] away onsay atthay ausethcay ameshay.

6 Essingsblay [areway] uponway ethay eadhay ofway ethay ustjay: utbay iolencevay overethcay ethay outhmay ofway ethay ickedway.

7 Ethay emorymay ofway ethay ustjay [isway] essedblay: utbay ethay amenay ofway ethay ickedway allshay otray.

8 Ethay iseway inway earthay illway eceiveray ommandmentscay: utbay away atingpray oolfay allshay allfay.

9 Ehay atthay alkethway uprightlyway alkethway urelysay: utbay ehay atthay ervertethpay ishay aysway allshay ebay ownknay.

10 Ehay atthay inkethway ithway ethay eyeway ausethcay orrowsay: utbay away atingpray oolfay allshay allfay.

11 Ethay outhmay ofway away ighteousray [anmay isway] away ellway ofway ifelay: utbay iolencevay overethcay ethay outhmay ofway ethay ickedway.

12 Atredhay irrethstay upway ifesstray: utbay ovelay overethcay allway inssay.

13 Inway ethay ipslay ofway imhay atthay athhay understandingway isdomway isway oundfay: utbay away odray [isway] orfay ethay ackbay ofway imhay atthay isway oidvay ofway understandingway.

14 Iseway [enmay] aylay upway owledgeknay: utbay ethay outhmay ofway ethay oolishfay [isway] earnay estructionday.

15 Ethay ichray an'smay ealthway [isway] ishay ongstray itycay: ethay estructionday ofway ethay oorpay [isway] eirthay overtypay.

16 Ethay abourlay ofway ethay ighteousray [endethtay] otay ifelay: ethay uitfray ofway ethay ickedway otay insay.

17 Ehay [isway inway] ethay ayway ofway ifelay atthay eepethkay instructionway: utbay ehay atthay efusethray eproofray errethway.

18 Ehay atthay idethhay atredhay [ithway] yinglay ipslay, andway ehay atthay utterethway away anderslay, [isway] away oolfay.

19 Inway ethay ultitudemay ofway ordsway erethay antethway otnay insay: utbay ehay atthay efrainethray ishay ipslay [isway] iseway.

20 Ethay onguetay ofway ethay ustjay [isway asway] oicechay ilversay: ethay earthay ofway ethay ickedway [isway] ittlelay orthway.

21 Ethay ipslay ofway ethay ighteousray eedfay anymay: utbay oolsfay ieday orfay antway ofway isdomway.

22 Ethay essingblay ofway ethay ORDLAY, itway akethmay ichray, andway ehay addethway onay orrowsay ithway itway.

23 [Itway isway] asway ortspay otay away oolfay otay oday ischiefmay: utbay away anmay ofway understandingway athhay isdomway.

24 Ethay earfay ofway ethay ickedway, itway allshay omecay uponway imhay: utbay ethay esireday ofway ethay ighteousray allshay ebay antedgray.

25 Asway ethay irlwindwhay assethpay, osay [isway] ethay ickedway onay [oremay]: utbay ethay ighteousray [isway] anway everlastingway oundationfay.

26 Asway inegarvay otay ethay eethtay, andway asway okesmay otay ethay eyesway, osay [isway] ethay uggardslay otay emthay atthay endsay imhay.

27 Ethay earfay ofway ethay ORDLAY olongethpray aysday: utbay ethay earsyay ofway ethay ickedway allshay ebay ortenedshay.

28 Ethay opehay ofway ethay ighteousray [allshay ebay] adnessglay: utbay ethay expectationway ofway ethay ickedway allshay erishpay.

29 Ethay ayway ofway ethay ORDLAY [isway] engthstray otay ethay uprightway: utbay estructionday [allshay ebay] otay ethay orkersway ofway iniquityway.

30 Ethay ighteousray allshay evernay ebay emovedray: utbay ethay ickedway allshay otnay inhabitway ethay earthway.

31 Ethay outhmay ofway ethay ustjay ingethbray orthfay isdomway: utbay ethay owardfray onguetay allshay ebay utcay outway.

32 Ethay ipslay ofway ethay ighteousray owknay atwhay isway acceptableway: utbay ethay outhmay ofway ethay ickedway [eakethspay] owardnessfray.

APTERCHAY 11

1 Away alsefay alancebay [isway] abominationway otay ethay ORDLAY: utbay away ustjay eightway [isway] ishay elightday.

2 [Enwhay] idepray omethcay, enthay omethcay ameshay: utbay ithway ethay owlylay [isway] isdomway.

3 Ethay integrityway ofway ethay uprightway allshay uidegay emthay: utbay ethay erversenesspay ofway ansgressorstray allshay estroyday emthay.

4 Ichesray ofitpray otnay inway ethay ayday ofway athwray: utbay ighteousnessray eliverethday omfray eathday.

5 Ethay ighteousnessray ofway ethay erfectpay allshay irectday ishay ayway: utbay ethay ickedway allshay allfay ybay ishay ownway ickednessway.

6 Ethay ighteousnessray ofway ethay uprightway allshay eliverday emthay: utbay ansgressorstray allshay ebay akentay inway [eirthay ownway] aughtinessnay.

7 Enwhay away ickedway anmay iethday, [ishay] expectationway allshay erishpay: andway ethay opehay ofway unjustway [enmay] erishethpay.

8 Ethay ighteousray isway eliveredday outway ofway oubletray, andway ethay ickedway omethcay inway ishay eadstay.

9 Anway ypocritehay ithway [ishay] outhmay estroyethday ishay eighbournay: utbay oughthray owledgeknay allshay ethay ustjay ebay eliveredday.

10 Enwhay itway oethgay ellway ithway ethay ighteousray, ethay itycay ejoicethray: andway enwhay ethay ickedway erishpay, [erethay isway] outingshay.

11 Ybay ethay essingblay ofway ethay uprightway ethay itycay isway exaltedway: utbay itway isway overthrownway ybay ethay outhmay ofway ethay ickedway.

12 Ehay atthay isway oidvay ofway isdomway espisethday ishay eighbournay: utbay away anmay ofway understandingway oldethhay ishay eacepay.

13 Away alebearertay evealethray ecretssay: utbay ehay atthay isway ofway away aithfulfay iritspay oncealethcay ethay attermay.

14 Erewhay onay ounselcay [isway], ethay eoplepay allfay: utbay inway ethay ultitudemay ofway ounsellorscay [erethay isway] afetysay.

15 Ehay atthay isway uretysay orfay away angerstray allshay artsmay [orfay itway]: andway ehay atthay atethhay uretishipsay isway uresay.

16 Away aciousgray omanway etainethray onourhay: andway ongstray [enmay] etainray ichesray.

17 Ethay ercifulmay anmay oethday oodgay otay ishay ownway oulsay: utbay [ehay atthay isway] uelcray oublethtray ishay ownway eshflay.

18 Ethay ickedway orkethway away eceitfulday orkway: utbay otay imhay atthay owethsay ighteousnessray [allshay ebay] away uresay ewardray.

19 Asway ighteousnessray [endethtay] otay ifelay: osay ehay atthay ursuethpay evilway [ursuethpay itway] otay ishay ownway eathday.

20 Eythay atthay areway ofway away owardfray earthay [areway] abominationway otay ethay ORDLAY: utbay [uchsay asway areway] uprightway inway [eirthay] ayway [areway] ishay elightday.

21 [Oughthay] andhay [oinjay] inway andhay, ethay ickedway allshay otnay ebay unpunishedway: utbay ethay eedsay ofway ethay ighteousray allshay ebay eliveredday.

22 [Asway] away eweljay ofway oldgay inway away ine'ssway outsnay, [osay isway] away airfay omanway ichwhay isway ithoutway iscretionday.

23 Ethay esireday ofway ethay ighteousray [isway] onlyway oodgay: [utbay] ethay expectationway ofway ethay ickedway [isway] athwray.

24 Erethay isway atthay atterethscay, andway etyay increasethway; andway [erethay isway] atthay ithholdethway oremay anthay isway eetmay, utbay [itway endethtay] otay overtypay.

25 Ethay iberallay oulsay allshay ebay ademay atfay: andway ehay atthay aterethway allshay ebay ateredway alsoway imselfhay.

26 Ehay atthay ithholdethway orncay, ethay eoplepay allshay ursecay imhay: utbay essingblay [allshay ebay] uponway ethay eadhay ofway imhay atthay ellethsay [itway].

27 Ehay atthay iligentlyday eekethsay oodgay ocurethpray avourfay: utbay ehay atthay eekethsay ischiefmay, itway allshay omecay untoway imhay.

28 Ehay atthay ustethtray inway ishay ichesray allshay allfay: utbay ethay ighteousray allshay ourishflay asway away anchbray.

29 Ehay atthay oublethtray ishay ownway ousehay allshay inheritway ethay indway: andway ethay oolfay [allshay ebay] ervantsay otay ethay iseway ofway earthay.

30 Ethay uitfray ofway ethay ighteousray [isway] away eetray ofway ifelay; andway ehay atthay innethway oulssay [isway] iseway.

31 Eholdbay, ethay ighteousray allshay ebay ecompensedray inway ethay earthway: uchmay oremay ethay ickedway andway ethay innersay.

APTERCHAY 12

1 Osowhay ovethlay instructionway ovethlay owledgeknay: utbay ehay atthay atethhay eproofray [isway] utishbray.

2 Away oodgay [anmay] obtainethway avourfay ofway ethay ORDLAY: utbay away anmay ofway ickedway evicesday illway ehay ondemncay.

3 Away anmay allshay otnay ebay establishedway ybay ickednessway: utbay ethay ootray ofway ethay ighteousray allshay otnay ebay ovedmay.

4 Away irtuousvay omanway [isway] away owncray otay erhay usbandhay: utbay eshay atthay akethmay ashamedway [isway] asway ottennessray inway ishay onesbay.

5 Ethay oughtsthay ofway ethay ighteousray [areway] ightray: [utbay] ethay ounselscay ofway ethay ickedway [areway] eceitday.

6 Ethay ordsway ofway ethay ickedway [areway] otay ielay inway aitway orfay oodblay: utbay ethay outhmay ofway ethay uprightway allshay eliverday emthay.

7 Ethay ickedway areway overthrownway, andway [areway] otnay: utbay ethay ousehay ofway ethay ighteousray allshay andstay.

8 Away anmay allshay ebay ommendedcay accordingway otay ishay isdomway: utbay ehay atthay isway ofway away erversepay earthay allshay ebay espisedday.

9 [Ehay atthay isway] espisedday, andway athhay away ervantsay, [isway] etterbay anthay ehay atthay onourethhay imselfhay, andway ackethlay eadbray.

10 Away ighteousray [anmay] egardethray ethay ifelay ofway ishay eastbay: utbay ethay endertay erciesmay ofway ethay ickedway [areway] uelcray.

11 Ehay atthay illethtay ishay andlay allshay ebay atisfiedsay ithway eadbray: utbay ehay atthay ollowethfay ainvay [ersonspay isway] oidvay ofway understandingway.

12 Ethay ickedway esirethday ethay etnay ofway evilway [enmay]: utbay ethay ootray ofway ethay ighteousray ieldethyay [uitfray].

13 Ethay ickedway isway aredsnay ybay ethay ansgressiontray ofway [ishay] ipslay: utbay ethay ustjay allshay omecay outway ofway oubletray.

14 Away anmay allshay ebay atisfiedsay ithway oodgay ybay ethay uitfray ofway [ishay] outhmay: andway ethay ecompenceray ofway away an'smay andshay allshay ebay enderedray untoway imhay.

15 Ethay ayway ofway away oolfay [isway] ightray inway ishay ownway eyesway: utbay ehay atthay earkenethhay untoway ounselcay [isway] iseway.

16 Away ool'sfay athwray isway esentlypray ownknay: utbay away udentpray [anmay] overethcay ameshay.

17 [Ehay atthay] eakethspay uthtray ewethshay orthfay ighteousnessray: utbay away alsefay itnessway eceitday.

18 Erethay isway atthay eakethspay ikelay ethay iercingspay ofway away ordsway: utbay ethay onguetay ofway ethay iseway [isway] ealthhay.

19 Ethay iplay ofway uthtray allshay ebay establishedway orfay everway: utbay away yinglay onguetay [isway] utbay orfay away omentmay.

20 Eceitday [isway] inway ethay earthay ofway emthay atthay imagineway evilway: utbay otay ethay ounsellorscay ofway eacepay [isway] oyjay.

21 Erethay allshay onay evilway appenhay otay ethay ustjay: utbay ethay ickedway allshay ebay illedfay ithway ischiefmay.

22 Yinglay ipslay [areway] abominationway otay ethay ORDLAY: utbay eythay atthay ealday ulytray [areway] ishay elightday.
23 Away udentpray anmay oncealethcay owledgeknay: utbay ethay earthay ofway oolsfay oclaimethpray oolishnessfay.
24 Ethay andhay ofway ethay iligentday allshay earbay uleray: utbay ethay othfulslay allshay ebay underway ibutetray.
25 Eavinesshay inway ethay earthay ofway anmay akethmay itway oopstay: utbay away oodgay ordway akethmay itway adglay.
26 Ethay ighteousray [isway] oremay excellentway anthay ishay eighbournay: utbay ethay ayway ofway ethay ickedway educethsay emthay.
27 Ethay othfulslay [anmay] oastethray otnay atthay ichwhay ehay ooktay inway untinghay: utbay ethay ubstancesay ofway away iligentday anmay [isway] eciouspray.
28 Inway ethay ayway ofway ighteousnessray [isway] ifelay; andway [inway] ethay athwaypay [ereofthay erethay isway] onay eathday.

APTERCHAY 13
1 Away iseway onsay [earethhay] ishay ather'sfay instructionway: utbay away ornerscay earethhay otnay ebukeray.
2 Away anmay allshay eatway oodgay ybay ethay uitfray ofway [ishay] outhmay: utbay ethay oulsay ofway ethay ansgressorstray [allshay eatway] iolencevay.
3 Ehay atthay eepethkay ishay outhmay eepethkay ishay ifelay: [utbay] ehay atthay openethway ideway ishay ipslay allshay avehay estructionday.
4 Ethay oulsay ofway ethay uggardslay esirethday, andway [athhay] othingnay: utbay ethay oulsay ofway ethay iligentday allshay ebay ademay atfay.
5 Away ighteousray [anmay] atethhay yinglay: utbay away ickedway [anmay] isway oathsomelay, andway omethcay otay ameshay.
6 Ighteousnessray eepethkay [imhay atthay isway] uprightway inway ethay ayway: utbay ickednessway overthrowethway ethay innersay.
7 Erethay isway atthay akethmay imselfhay ichray, etyay [athhay] othingnay: [erethay isway] atthay akethmay imselfhay oorpay, etyay [athhay] eatgray ichesray.
8 Ethay ansomray ofway away an'smay ifelay [areway] ishay ichesray: utbay ethay oorpay earethhay otnay ebukeray.
9 Ethay ightlay ofway ethay ighteousray ejoicethray: utbay ethay amplay ofway ethay ickedway allshay ebay utpay outway.

10 Onlyway ybay idepray omethcay ontentioncay: utbay ithway ethay ellway advisedway [isway] isdomway.

11 Ealthway [ottengay] ybay anityvay allshay ebay iminishedday: utbay ehay atthay atherethgay ybay abourlay allshay increaseway.

12 Opehay eferredday akethmay ethay earthay icksay: utbay [enwhay] ethay esireday omethcay, [itway isway] away eetray ofway ifelay.

13 Osowhay espisethday ethay ordway allshay ebay estroyedday: utbay ehay atthay earethfay ethay ommandmentcay allshay ebay ewardedray.

14 Ethay awlay ofway ethay iseway [isway] away ountainfay ofway ifelay, otay epartday omfray ethay aressnay ofway eathday.

15 Oodgay understandingway ivethgay avourfay: utbay ethay ayway ofway ansgressorstray [isway] ardhay.

16 Everyway udentpray [anmay] ealethday ithway owledgeknay: utbay away oolfay ayethlay openway [ishay] ollyfay.

17 Away ickedway essengermay allethfay intoway ischiefmay: utbay away aithfulfay ambassadorway [isway] ealthhay.

18 Overtypay andway ameshay [allshay ebay otay] imhay atthay efusethray instructionway: utbay ehay atthay egardethray eproofray allshay ebay onouredhay.

19 Ethay esireday accomplishedway isway eetsway otay ethay oulsay: utbay [itway isway] abominationway otay oolsfay otay epartday omfray evilway.

20 Ehay atthay alkethway ithway iseway [enmay] allshay ebay iseway: utbay away ompanioncay ofway oolsfay allshay ebay estroyedday.

21 Evilway ursuethpay innerssay: utbay otay ethay ighteousray oodgay allshay ebay epayedray.

22 Away oodgay [anmay] eavethlay anway inheritanceway otay ishay ildren'schay ildrenchay: andway ethay ealthway ofway ethay innersay [isway] aidlay upway orfay ethay ustjay.

23 Uchmay oodfay [isway inway] ethay illagetay ofway ethay oorpay: utbay erethay isway [atthay isway] estroyedday orfay antway ofway udgmentjay.

24 Ehay atthay arethspay ishay odray atethhay ishay onsay: utbay ehay atthay ovethlay imhay astenethchay imhay etimesbay.

25 Ethay ighteousray eatethway otay ethay atisfyingsay ofway ishay oulsay: utbay ethay ellybay ofway ethay ickedway allshay antway.

APTERCHAY 14
1 Everyway iseway omanway uildethbay erhay ousehay: utbay ethay oolishfay uckethplay itway ownday ithway erhay andshay.

2 Ehay atthay alkethway inway ishay uprightnessway earethfay ethay ORDLAY: utbay [ehay atthay isway] erversepay inway ishay aysway espisethday imhay.

3 Inway ethay outhmay ofway ethay oolishfay [isway] away odray ofway idepray: utbay ethay ipslay ofway ethay iseway allshay eservepray emthay.

4 Erewhay onay oxenway [areway], ethay ibcray [isway] eanclay: utbay uchmay increaseway [isway] ybay ethay engthstray ofway ethay oxway.

5 Away aithfulfay itnessway illway otnay ielay: utbay away alsefay itnessway illway utterway ieslay.

6 Away ornerscay eekethsay isdomway, andway [indethfay itway] otnay: utbay owledgeknay [isway] easyway untoway imhay atthay understandethway.

7 Ogay omfray ethay esencepray ofway away oolishfay anmay, enwhay outhay erceivestpay otnay [inway imhay] ethay ipslay ofway owledgeknay.

8 Ethay isdomway ofway ethay udentpray [isway] otay understandway ishay ayway: utbay ethay ollyfay ofway oolsfay [isway] eceitday.

9 Oolsfay akemay away ockmay atway insay: utbay amongway ethay ighteousray [erethay isway] avourfay.

10 Ethay earthay owethknay ishay ownway itternessbay; andway away angerstray othday otnay intermeddleway ithway ishay oyjay.

11 Ethay ousehay ofway ethay ickedway allshay ebay overthrownway: utbay ethay abernacletay ofway ethay uprightway allshay ourishflay.

12 Erethay isway away ayway ichwhay eemethsay ightray untoway away anmay, utbay ethay endway ereofthay [areway] ethay aysway ofway eathday.

13 Evenway inway aughterlay ethay earthay isway orrowfulsay; andway ethay endway ofway atthay irthmay [isway] eavinesshay.

14 Ethay acksliderbay inway earthay allshay ebay illedfay ithway ishay ownway aysway: andway away oodgay anmay [allshay ebay atisfiedsay] omfray imselfhay.

15 Ethay implesay elievethbay everyway ordway: utbay ethay udentpray [anmay] ookethlay ellway otay ishay oinggay.

16 Away iseway [anmay] earethfay, andway epartethday omfray evilway: utbay ethay oolfay agethray, andway isway onfidentcay.

17 [Ehay atthay isway] oonsay angryway ealethday oolishlyfay: andway away anmay ofway ickedway evicesday isway atedhay.

18 Ethay implesay inheritway ollyfay: utbay ethay udentpray areway ownedcray ithway owledgeknay.

19 Ethay evilway owbay eforebay ethay oodgay; andway ethay ickedway atway ethay atesgay ofway ethay ighteousray.

20 Ethay oorpay isway atedhay evenway ofway ishay ownway eighbournay: utbay ethay ichray [athhay] anymay iendsfray.
21 Ehay atthay espisethday ishay eighbournay innethsay: utbay ehay atthay athhay ercymay onway ethay oorpay, appyhay [isway] ehay.
22 Oday eythay otnay errway atthay eviseday evilway? utbay ercymay andway uthtray [allshay ebay] otay emthay atthay eviseday oodgay.
23 Inway allway abourlay erethay isway ofitpray: utbay ethay alktay ofway ethay ipslay [endethtay] onlyway otay enurypay.
24 Ethay owncray ofway ethay iseway [isway] eirthay ichesray: [utbay] ethay oolishnessfay ofway oolsfay [isway] ollyfay.
25 Away uetray itnessway eliverethday oulssay: utbay away eceitfulday [itnessway] eakethspay ieslay.
26 Inway ethay earfay ofway ethay ORDLAY [isway] ongstray onfidencecay: andway ishay ildrenchay allshay avehay away aceplay ofway efugeray.
27 Ethay earfay ofway ethay ORDLAY [isway] away ountainfay ofway ifelay, otay epartday omfray ethay aressnay ofway eathday.
28 Inway ethay ultitudemay ofway eoplepay [isway] ethay ing'skay onourhay: utbay inway ethay antway ofway eoplepay [isway] ethay estructionday ofway ethay incepray.
29 [Ehay atthay isway] owslay otay athwray [isway] ofway eatgray understandingway: utbay [ehay atthay isway] astyhay ofway iritspay exaltethway ollyfay.
30 Away oundsay earthay [isway] ethay ifelay ofway ethay eshflay: utbay envyway ethay ottennessray ofway ethay onesbay.
31 Ehay atthay oppressethway ethay oorpay eproachethray ishay Akermay: utbay ehay atthay onourethhay imhay athhay ercymay onway ethay oorpay.
32 Ethay ickedway isway ivendray awayway inway ishay ickednessway: utbay ethay ighteousray athhay opehay inway ishay eathday.
33 Isdomway estethray inway ethay earthay ofway imhay atthay athhay understandingway: utbay [atthay ichwhay isway] inway ethay idstmay ofway oolsfay isway ademay ownknay.
34 Ighteousnessray exaltethway away ationnay: utbay insay [isway] away eproachray otay anyway eoplepay.
35 Ethay ing'skay avourfay [isway] owardtay away iseway ervantsay: utbay ishay athwray isway [againstway] imhay atthay ausethcay ameshay.

APTERCHAY 15

1 Away oftsay answerway urnethtay awayway athwray: utbay ievousgray ordsway irstay upway angerway.

2 Ethay onguetay ofway ethay iseway usethway owledgeknay arightway: utbay ethay outhmay ofway oolsfay ourethpay outway oolishnessfay.

3 Ethay eyesway ofway ethay ORDLAY [areway] inway everyway aceplay, eholdingbay ethay evilway andway ethay oodgay.

4 Away olesomewhay onguetay [isway] away eetray ofway ifelay: utbay erversenesspay ereinthay [isway] away eachbray inway ethay iritspay.

5 Away oolfay espisethday ishay ather'sfay instructionway: utbay ehay atthay egardethray eproofray isway udentpray.

6 Inway ethay ousehay ofway ethay ighteousray [isway] uchmay easuretray: utbay inway ethay evenuesray ofway ethay ickedway isway oubletray.

7 Ethay ipslay ofway ethay iseway isperseday owledgeknay: utbay ethay earthay ofway ethay oolishfay [oethday] otnay osay.

8 Ethay acrificesay ofway ethay ickedway [isway] anway abominationway otay ethay ORDLAY: utbay ethay ayerpray ofway ethay uprightway [isway] ishay elightday.

9 Ethay ayway ofway ethay ickedway [isway] anway abominationway untoway ethay ORDLAY: utbay ehay ovethlay imhay atthay ollowethfay afterway ighteousnessray.

10 Orrectioncay [isway] ievousgray untoway imhay atthay orsakethfay ethay ayway: [andway] ehay atthay atethhay eproofray allshay ieday.

11 Ellhay andway estructionday [areway] eforebay ethay ORDLAY: owhay uchmay oremay enthay ethay eartshay ofway ethay ildrenchay ofway enmay?

12 Away ornerscay ovethlay otnay oneway atthay eprovethray imhay: eithernay illway ehay ogay untoway ethay iseway.

13 Away errymay earthay akethmay away eerfulchay ountenancecay: utbay ybay orrowsay ofway ethay earthay ethay iritspay isway okenbray.

14 Ethay earthay ofway imhay atthay athhay understandingway eekethsay owledgeknay: utbay ethay outhmay ofway oolsfay eedethfay onway oolishnessfay.

15 Allway ethay aysday ofway ethay afflictedway [areway] evilway: utbay ehay atthay isway ofway away errymay earthay [athhay] away ontinualcay eastfay.

16 Etterbay [isway] ittlelay ithway ethay earfay ofway ethay ORDLAY anthay eatgray easuretray andway oubletray erewiththay.

17 Etterbay [isway] away innerday ofway erbshay erewhay ovelay isway, anthay away alledstay oxway andway atredhay erewiththay.

18 Away athfulwray anmay irrethstay upway ifestray: utbay [ehay atthay isway] owslay otay angerway appeasethway ifestray.

19 Ethay ayway ofway ethay othfulslay [anmay isway] asway anway edgehay ofway ornsthay: utbay ethay ayway ofway ethay ighteousray [isway] ademay ainplay.

20 Away iseway onsay akethmay away adglay atherfay: utbay away oolishfay anmay espisethday ishay othermay.

21 Ollyfay [isway] oyjay otay [imhay atthay isway] estituteday ofway isdomway: utbay away anmay ofway understandingway alkethway uprightlyway.

22 Ithoutway ounselcay urposespay areway isappointedday: utbay inway ethay ultitudemay ofway ounsellorscay eythay areway establishedway.

23 Away anmay athhay oyjay ybay ethay answerway ofway ishay outhmay: andway away ordway [okenspay] inway ueday easonsay, owhay oodgay [isway itway]!

24 Ethay ayway ofway ifelay [isway] aboveway otay ethay iseway, atthay ehay aymay epartday omfray ellhay eneathbay.

25 Ethay ORDLAY illway estroyday ethay ousehay ofway ethay oudpray: utbay ehay illway establishway ethay orderbay ofway ethay idowway.

26 Ethay oughtsthay ofway ethay ickedway [areway] anway abominationway otay ethay ORDLAY: utbay [ethay ordsway] ofway ethay urepay [areway] easantplay ordsway.

27 Ehay atthay isway eedygray ofway aingay oublethtray ishay ownway ousehay; utbay ehay atthay atethhay iftsgay allshay ivelay.

28 Ethay earthay ofway ethay ighteousray udiethstay otay answerway: utbay ethay outhmay ofway ethay ickedway ourethpay outway evilway ingsthay.

29 Ethay ORDLAY [isway] arfay omfray ethay ickedway: utbay ehay earethhay ethay ayerpray ofway ethay ighteousray.

30 Ethay ightlay ofway ethay eyesway ejoicethray ethay earthay: [andway] away oodgay eportray akethmay ethay onesbay atfay.

31 Ethay earway atthay earethhay ethay eproofray ofway ifelay abidethway amongway ethay iseway.

32 Ehay atthay efusethray instructionway espisethday ishay ownway oulsay: utbay ehay atthay earethhay eproofray ettethgay understandingway.

33 Ethay earfay ofway ethay ORDLAY [isway] ethay instructionway ofway isdomway; andway eforebay onourhay [isway] umilityhay.

APTERCHAY 16

1 Ethay eparationspray ofway ethay earthay inway anmay, andway ethay answerway ofway ethay onguetay, [isway] omfray ethay ORDLAY.

2 Allway ethay aysway ofway away anmay [areway] eanclay inway ishay ownway eyesway; utbay ethay ORDLAY eighethway ethay iritsspay.

3 Ommitcay ythay orksway untoway ethay ORDLAY, andway ythay oughtsthay allshay ebay establishedway.

4 Ethay ORDLAY athhay ademay allway [ingsthay] orfay imselfhay: eayay, evenway ethay ickedway orfay ethay ayday ofway evilway.

5 Everyway oneway [atthay isway] oudpray inway earthay [isway] anway abominationway otay ethay ORDLAY: [oughthay] andhay [oinjay] inway andhay, ehay allshay otnay ebay unpunishedway.

6 Ybay ercymay andway uthtray iniquityway isway urgedpay: andway ybay ethay earfay ofway ethay ORDLAY [enmay] epartday omfray evilway.

7 Enwhay away an'smay aysway easeplay ethay ORDLAY, ehay akethmay evenway ishay enemiesway otay ebay atway eacepay ithway imhay.

8 Etterbay [isway] away ittlelay ithway ighteousnessray anthay eatgray evenuesray ithoutway ightray.

9 Away an'smay earthay evisethday ishay ayway: utbay ethay ORDLAY irectethday ishay epsstay.

10 Away ivineday entencesay [isway] inway ethay ipslay ofway ethay ingkay: ishay outhmay ansgressethtray otnay inway udgmentjay.

11 Away ustjay eightway andway alancebay [areway] ethay ORD'SLAY: allway ethay eightsway ofway ethay agbay [areway] ishay orkway.

12 [Itway isway] anway abominationway otay ingskay otay ommitcay ickednessway: orfay ethay onethray isway establishedway ybay ighteousnessray.

13 Ighteousray ipslay [areway] ethay elightday ofway ingskay; andway eythay ovelay imhay atthay eakethspay ightray.

14 Ethay athwray ofway away ingkay [isway asway] essengersmay ofway eathday: utbay away iseway anmay illway acifypay itway.

15 Inway ethay ightlay ofway ethay ing'skay ountenancecay [isway] ifelay; andway ishay avourfay [isway] asway away oudclay ofway ethay atterlay ainray.

16 Owhay uchmay etterbay [isway itway] otay etgay isdomway anthay oldgay! andway otay etgay understandingway atherray otay ebay osenchay anthay ilversay!

17 Ethay ighwayhay ofway ethay uprightway [isway] otay epartday omfray evilway: ehay atthay eepethkay ishay ayway eservethpray ishay oulsay.

18 Idepray [oethgay] eforebay estructionday, andway anway aughtyhay iritspay eforebay away allfay.

19 Etterbay [itway isway otay ebay] ofway anway umblehay iritspay ithway ethay owlylay, anthay otay ivideday ethay oilspay ithway ethay oudpray.

20 Ehay atthay andlethhay away attermay iselyway allshay indfay oodgay: andway osowhay ustethtray inway ethay ORDLAY, appyhay [isway] ehay.

21 Ethay iseway inway earthay allshay ebay alledcay udentpray: andway ethay eetnesssway ofway ethay ipslay increasethway earninglay.

22 Understandingway [isway] away ellspringway ofway ifelay untoway imhay atthay athhay itway: utbay ethay instructionway ofway oolsfay [isway] ollyfay.

23 Ethay earthay ofway ethay iseway eachethtay ishay outhmay, andway addethway earninglay otay ishay ipslay.

24 Easantplay ordsway [areway asway] anway oneycombhay, eetsway otay ethay oulsay, andway ealthhay otay ethay onesbay.

25 Erethay isway away ayway atthay eemethsay ightray untoway away anmay, utbay ethay endway ereofthay [areway] ethay aysway ofway eathday.

26 Ehay atthay abourethlay abourethlay orfay imselfhay; orfay ishay outhmay avethcray itway ofway imhay.

27 Anway ungodlyway anmay iggethday upway evilway: andway inway ishay ipslay [erethay isway] asway away urningbay irefay.

28 Away owardfray anmay owethsay ifestray: andway away ispererwhay eparatethsay iefchay iendsfray.

29 Away iolentvay anmay enticethway ishay eighbournay, andway eadethlay imhay intoway ethay ayway [atthay isway] otnay oodgay.

30 Ehay uttethshay ishay eyesway otay eviseday owardfray ingsthay: ovingmay ishay ipslay ehay ingethbray evilway otay asspay.

31 Ethay oaryhay eadhay [isway] away owncray ofway oryglay, [ifway] itway ebay oundfay inway ethay ayway ofway ighteousnessray.

32 [Ehay atthay isway] owslay otay angerway [isway] etterbay anthay ethay ightymay; andway ehay atthay ulethray ishay iritspay anthay ehay atthay akethtay away itycay.

33 Ethay otlay isway astcay intoway ethay aplay; utbay ethay olewhay isposingday ereofthay [isway] ofway ethay ORDLAY.

APTERCHAY 17

1 Etterbay [isway] away ydray orselmay, andway ietnessquay erewiththay, anthay anway ousehay ullfay ofway acrificessay [ithway] ifestray.

2 Away iseway ervantsay allshay avehay uleray overway away onsay atthay ausethcay ameshay, andway allshay avehay artpay ofway ethay inheritanceway amongway ethay ethrenbray.

3 Ethay iningfay otpay [isway] orfay ilversay, andway ethay urnacefay orfay oldgay: utbay ethay ORDLAY iethtray ethay eartshay.

4 Away ickedway oerday ivethgay eedhay otay alsefay ipslay; [andway] away iarlay ivethgay earway otay away aughtynay onguetay.

5 Osowhay ockethmay ethay oorpay eproachethray ishay Akermay: [andway] ehay atthay isway adglay atway alamitiescay allshay otnay ebay unpunishedway.

6 Ildren'schay ildrenchay [areway] ethay owncray ofway oldway enmay; andway ethay oryglay ofway ildrenchay [areway] eirthay athersfay.

7 Excellentway eechspay ecomethbay otnay away oolfay: uchmay esslay oday yinglay ipslay away incepray.

8 Away iftgay [isway asway] away eciouspray onestay inway ethay eyesway ofway imhay atthay athhay itway: ithersoeverwhay itway urnethtay, itway osperethpray.

9 Ehay atthay overethcay away ansgressiontray eekethsay ovelay; utbay ehay atthay epeatethray away attermay eparatethsay [eryvay] iendsfray.

10 Away eproofray enterethway oremay intoway away iseway anmay anthay anway undredhay ipesstray intoway away oolfay.

11 Anway evilway [anmay] eekethsay onlyway ebellionray: ereforethay away uelcray essengermay allshay ebay entsay againstway imhay.

12 Etlay away earbay obbedray ofway erhay elpswhay eetmay away anmay, atherray anthay away oolfay inway ishay ollyfay.

13 Osowhay ewardethray evilway orfay oodgay, evilway allshay otnay epartday omfray ishay ousehay.

14 Ethay eginningbay ofway ifestray [isway asway] enwhay oneway ettethlay outway aterway: ereforethay eavelay offway ontentioncay, eforebay itway ebay eddledmay ithway.

15 Ehay atthay ustifiethjay ethay ickedway, andway ehay atthay ondemnethcay ethay ustjay, evenway eythay othbay [areway] abominationway otay ethay ORDLAY.

16 Ereforewhay [isway erethay] away icepray inway ethay andhay ofway away oolfay otay etgay isdomway, eeingsay [ehay athhay] onay earthay [otay itway]?

17 Away iendfray ovethlay atway allway imestay, andway away otherbray isway ornbay orfay adversityway.

18 Away anmay oidvay ofway understandingway ikethstray andshay, [andway] ecomethbay uretysay inway ethay esencepray ofway ishay iendfray.

19 Ehay ovethlay ansgressiontray atthay ovethlay ifestray: [andway] ehay atthay exaltethway ishay ategay eekethsay estructionday.

20 Ehay atthay athhay away owardfray earthay indethfay onay oodgay: andway ehay atthay athhay away erversepay onguetay allethfay intoway ischiefmay.

21 Ehay atthay egettethbay away oolfay [oethday itway] otay ishay orrowsay: andway ethay atherfay ofway away oolfay athhay onay oyjay.

22 Away errymay earthay oethday oodgay [ikelay] away edicinemay: utbay away okenbray iritspay iethdray ethay onesbay.

23 Away ickedway [anmay] akehtay away iftgay outway ofway ethay osombay otay ervertpay ethay aysway ofway udgmentjay.

24 Isdomway [isway] eforebay imhay atthay athhay understandingway; utbay ethay eyesway ofway away oolfay [areway] inway ethay endsway ofway ethay earthway.

25 Away oolishfay onsay [isway] away iefgray otay ishay atherfay, andway itternessbay otay erhay atthay arebay imhay.

26 Alsoway otay unishpay ethay ustjay [isway] otnay oodgay, [ornay] otay ikestray incespray orfay equityway.

27 Ehay atthay athhay owledgeknay arethspay ishay ordsway: [andway] away anmay ofway understandingway isway ofway anway excellentway iritspay.

28 Evenway away oolfay, enwhay ehay oldethhay ishay eacepay, isway ountedcay iseway: [andway] ehay atthay uttethshay ishay ipslay [isway esteemedway] away anmay ofway understandingway.

APTERCHAY 18

1 Oughthray esireday away anmay, avinghay eparatedsay imselfhay, eekethsay [andway] intermeddlethway ithway allway isdomway.

2 Away oolfay athhay onay elightday inway understandingway, utbay atthay ishay earthay aymay iscoverday itselfway.

3 Enwhay ethay ickedway omethcay, [enthay] omethcay alsoway ontemptcay, andway ithway ignominyway eproachray.

4 Ethay ordsway ofway away an'smay outhmay [areway asway] eepday atersway, [andway] ethay ellspringway ofway isdomway [asway] away owingflay ookbray.

5 [Itway isway] otnay oodgay otay acceptway ethay ersonpay ofway ethay ickedway, otay overthrowway ethay ighteousray inway udgmentjay.

6 Away ool'sfay ipslay enterway intoway ontentioncay, andway ishay outhmay allethcay orfay okesstray.

7 Away ool'sfay outhmay [isway] ishay estructionday, andway ishay ipslay [areway] ethay aresnay ofway ishay oulsay.

8 Ethay ordsway ofway away alebearertay [areway] asway oundsway, andway eythay ogay ownday intoway ethay innermostway artspay ofway ethay ellybay.

9 Ehay alsoway atthay isway othfulslay inway ishay orkway isway otherbray otay imhay atthay isway away eatgray asterway.

10 Ethay amenay ofway ethay ORDLAY [isway] away ongstray owertay: ethay ighteousray unnethray intoway itway, andway isway afesay.

11 Ethay ichray an'smay ealthway [isway] ishay ongstray itycay, andway asway anway ighhay allway inway ishay ownway onceitcay.

12 Eforebay estructionday ethay earthay ofway anmay isway aughtyhay, andway eforebay onourhay [isway] umilityhay.

13 Ehay atthay answerethway away attermay eforebay ehay earethhay [itway], itway [isway] ollyfay andway ameshay untoway imhay.

14 Ethay iritspay ofway away anmay illway ustainsay ishay infirmityway; utbay away oundedway iritspay owhay ancay earbay?

15 Ethay earthay ofway ethay udentpray ettethgay owledgeknay; andway ethay earway ofway ethay iseway eekethsay owledgeknay.

16 Away an'smay iftgay akethmay oomray orfay imhay, andway ingethbray imhay eforebay eatgray enmay.

17 [Ehay atthay isway] irstfay inway ishay ownway ausecay [eemethsay] ustjay; utbay ishay eighbournay omethcay andway earchethsay imhay.

18 Ethay otlay ausethcay ontentionscay otay easecay, andway artethpay etweenbay ethay ightymay.

19 Away otherbray offendedway [isway arderhay otay ebay onway] anthay away ongstray itycay: andway [eirthay] ontentionscay [areway] ikelay ethay arsbay ofway away astlecay.

20 Away an'smay ellybay allshay ebay atisfiedsay ithway ethay uitfray ofway ishay outhmay; [andway] ithway ethay increaseway ofway ishay ipslay allshay ehay ebay illedfay.

21 Eathday andway ifelay [areway] inway ethay owerpay ofway ethay onguetay: andway eythay atthay ovelay itway allshay eatway ethay uitfray ereofthay.

22 [Osowhay] indethfay away ifeway indethfay away oodgay [ingthay], andway obtainethway avourfay ofway ethay ORDLAY.

23 Ethay oorpay usethway intreatiesway; utbay ethay ichray answerethway oughlyray.

24 Away anmay [atthay athhay] iendsfray ustmay ewshay imselfhay iendlyfray: andway erethay isway away iendfray [atthay] ickethstay oserclay anthay away otherbray.

APTERCHAY 19

1 Etterbay [isway] ethay oorpay atthay alkethway inway ishay integrityway, anthay [ehay atthay isway] erversepay inway ishay ipslay, andway isway away oolfay.

2 Alsoway, [atthay] ethay oulsay [ebay] ithoutway owledgeknay, [itway isway] otnay oodgay; andway ehay atthay astethhay ithway [ishay] eetfay innethsay.

3 Ethay oolishnessfay ofway anmay ervertethpay ishay ayway: andway ishay earthay ettethfray againstway ethay ORDLAY.

4 Ealthway akethmay anymay iendsfray; utbay ethay oorpay isway eparatedsay omfray ishay eighbournay.

5 Away alsefay itnessway allshay otnay ebay unpunishedway, andway [ehay atthay] eakethspay ieslay allshay otnay escapeway.

6 Anymay illway intreatway ethay avourfay ofway ethay incepray: andway everyway anmay [isway] away iendfray otay imhay atthay ivethgay iftsgay.

7 Allway ethay ethrenbray ofway ethay oorpay oday atehay imhay: owhay uchmay oremay oday ishay iendsfray ogay arfay omfray imhay? ehay ursuethpay [emthay ithway] ordsway, [etyay] eythay [areway] antingway [otay imhay].

8 Ehay atthay ettethgay isdomway ovethlay ishay ownway oulsay: ehay atthay eepethkay understandingway allshay indfay oodgay.

9 Away alsefay itnessway allshay otnay ebay unpunishedway, andway [ehay atthay] eakethspay ieslay allshay erishpay.

10 Elightday isway otnay eemlysay orfay away oolfay; uchmay esslay orfay away ervantsay otay avehay uleray overway incespray.

11 Ethay iscretionday ofway away anmay eferrethday ishay angerway; andway [itway isway] ishay oryglay otay asspay overway away ansgressiontray.

12 Ethay ing'skay athwray [isway] asway ethay oaringray ofway away ionlay; utbay ishay avourfay [isway] asway ewday uponway ethay assgray.

13 Away oolishfay onsay [isway] ethay alamitycay ofway ishay atherfay: andway ethay ontentionscay ofway away ifeway [areway] away ontinualcay oppingdray.

14 Ousehay andway ichesray [areway] ethay inheritanceway ofway athersfay: andway away udentpray ifeway [isway] omfray ethay ORDLAY.

15 Othfulnessslay astethcay intoway away eepday eepslay; andway anway idleway oulsay allshay uffersay ungerhay.

16 Ehay atthay eepethkay ethay ommandmentcay eepethkay ishay ownway oulsay; [utbay] ehay atthay espisethday ishay aysway allshay ieday.

17 Ehay atthay athhay itypay uponway ethay oorpay endethlay untoway ethay ORDLAY; andway atthay ichwhay ehay athhay ivengay illway ehay aypay imhay againway.

18 Astenchay ythay onsay ilewhay erethay isway opehay, andway etlay otnay ythay oulsay arespay orfay ishay yingcray.

19 Away anmay ofway eatgray athwray allshay uffersay unishmentpay: orfay ifway outhay eliverday [imhay], etyay outhay ustmay oday itway againway.

20 Earhay ounselcay, andway eceiveray instructionway, atthay outhay ayestmay ebay iseway inway ythay atterlay endway.

21 [Erethay areway] anymay evicesday inway away an'smay earthay; evert19hessnay ethay ounselcay ofway ethay ORDLAY, atthay allshay andstay.

22 Ethay esireday ofway away anmay [isway] ishay indnesskay: andway away oorpay anmay [isway] etterbay anthay away iarlay.

23 Ethay earfay ofway ethay ORDLAY [endethtay] otay ifelay: andway [ehay atthay athhay itway] allshay abideway atisfiedsay; ehay allshay otnay ebay isitedvay ithway evilway.

24 Away othfulslay [anmay] idethhay ishay andhay inway [ishay] osombay, andway illway otnay osay uchmay asway ingbray itway otay ishay outhmay againway.

25 Itesmay away ornerscay, andway ethay implesay illway ewarebay: andway eproveray oneway atthay athhay understandingway, [andway] ehay illway understandway owledgeknay.

26 Ehay atthay astethway [ishay] atherfay, [andway] asethchay awayway [ishay] othermay, [isway] away onsay atthay ausethcay ameshay, andway ingethbray eproachray.

27 Easecay, ymay onsay, otay earhay ethay instructionway [atthay ausethcay] otay errway omfray ethay ordsway ofway owledgeknay.

28 Anway ungodlyway itnessway ornethscay udgmentjay: andway ethay outhmay ofway ethay ickedway evourethday iniquityway.

29 Udgmentsjay areway eparedpray orfay ornersscay, andway ipesstray orfay ethay ackbay ofway oolsfay.

APTERCHAY 20

1 Ineway [isway] away ockermay, ongstray inkdray [isway] agingray: andway osoeverwhay isway eceivedday erebythay isway otnay iseway.

2 Ethay earfay ofway away ingkay [isway] asway ethay oaringray ofway away ionlay: [osowhay] ovokethpray imhay otay angerway innethsay [againstway] ishay ownway oulsay.

3 [Itway isway] anway onourhay orfay away anmay otay easecay omfray ifestray: utbay everyway oolfay illway ebay eddlingmay.

4 Ethay uggardslay illway otnay owplay ybay easonray ofway ethay oldcay; [ereforethay] allshay ehay egbay inway arvesthay, andway [avehay] othingnay.

5 Ounselcay inway ethay earthay ofway anmay [isway ikelay] eepday aterway; utbay away anmay ofway understandingway illway awdray itway outway.

6 Ostmay enmay illway oclaimpray everyway oneway ishay ownway oodnessgay: utbay away aithfulfay anmay owhay ancay indfay?

7 Ethay ustjay [anmay] alkethway inway ishay integrityway: ishay ildrenchay [areway] essedblay afterway imhay.

8 Away ingkay atthay ittethsay inway ethay onethray ofway udgmentjay atterethscay awayway allway evilway ithway ishay eyesway.

9 Owhay ancay aysay, Iway avehay ademay ymay earthay eanclay, Iway amway urepay omfray ymay insay?

10 Iversday eightsway, [andway] iversday easuresmay, othbay ofway emthay [areway] alikeway abominationway otay ethay ORDLAY.

11 Evenway away ildchay isway ownknay ybay ishay oingsday, etherwhay ishay orkway [ebay] urepay, andway etherwhay [itway ebay] ightray.

12 Ethay earinghay earway, andway ethay eeingsay eyeway, ethay ORDLAY athhay ademay evenway othbay ofway emthay.

13 Ovelay otnay eepslay, estlay outhay omecay otay overtypay; openway inethay eyesway, [andway] outhay altshay ebay atisfiedsay ithway eadbray.

14 [Itway isway] aughtnay, [itway isway] aughtnay, aithsay ethay uyerbay: utbay enwhay ehay isway onegay ishay ayway, enthay ehay oastethbay.

15 Erethay isway oldgay, andway away ultitudemay ofway ubiesray: utbay ethay ipslay ofway owledgeknay [areway] away eciouspray eweljay.

16 Aketay ishay armentgay atthay isway uretysay [orfay] away angerstray: andway aketay away edgeplay ofway imhay orfay away angestray omanway.

17 Eadbray ofway eceitday [isway] eetsway otay away anmay; utbay afterwardsway ishay outhmay allshay ebay illedfay ithway avelgray.

18 [Everyway] urposepay isway establishedway ybay ounselcay: andway ithway oodgay adviceway akemay arway.

19 Ehay atthay oethgay aboutway [asway] away alebearertay evealethray ecretssay: ereforethay eddlemay otnay ithway imhay atthay atterethflay ithway ishay ipslay.

20 Osowhay ursethcay ishay atherfay orway ishay othermay, ishay amplay allshay ebay utpay outway inway obscureway arknessday.

21 Anway inheritanceway [aymay ebay] ottengay astilyhay atway ethay eginningbay; utbay ethay endway ereofthay allshay otnay ebay essedblay.

22 Aysay otnay outhay, Iway illway ecompenseray evilway; [utbay] aitway onway ethay ORDLAY, andway ehay allshay avesay eethay.

23 Iversday eightsway [areway] anway abominationway untoway ethay ORDLAY; andway away alsefay alancebay [isway] otnay oodgay.

24 An'smay oingsgay [areway] ofway ethay ORDLAY; owhay ancay away anmay enthay understandway ishay ownway ayway?

25 [Itway isway] away aresnay otay ethay anmay [owhay] evourethday [atthay ichwhay isway] olyhay, andway afterway owsvay otay akemay enquiryway.

26 Away iseway ingkay atterethscay ethay ickedway, andway ingethbray ethay eelwhay overway emthay.

27 Ethay iritspay ofway anmay [isway] ethay andlecay ofway ethay ORDLAY, earchingsay allway ethay inwardway artspay ofway ethay ellybay.

28 Ercymay andway uthtray eservepray ethay ingkay: andway ishay onethray isway upholdenway ybay ercymay.

29 Ethay oryglay ofway oungyay enmay [isway] eirthay engthstray: andway ethay eautybay ofway oldway enmay [isway] ethay aygray eadhay.

30 Ethay uenessblay ofway away oundway eansethclay awayway evilway: osay [oday] ipesstray ethay inwardway artspay ofway ethay ellybay.

APTERCHAY 21

1 Ethay ing'skay earthay [isway] inway ethay andhay ofway ethay ORDLAY, [asway] ethay iversray ofway aterway: ehay urnethtay itway ithersoeverwhay ehay illway.

2 Everyway ayway ofway away anmay [isway] ightray inway ishay ownway eyesway: utbay ethay ORDLAY onderethpay ethay eartshay.

3 Otay oday usticejay andway udgmentjay [isway] oremay acceptableway otay ethay ORDLAY anthay acrificesay.

4 Anway ighhay ooklay, andway away oudpray earthay, [andway] ethay owingplay ofway ethay ickedway, [isway] insay.

5 Ethay oughtsthay ofway ethay iligentday [endtay] onlyway otay enteousnessplay; utbay ofway everyway oneway [atthay isway] astyhay onlyway otay antway.

6 Ethay ettinggay ofway easurestray ybay away yinglay onguetay [isway] away anityvay ossedtay otay andway ofray ofway emthay atthay eeksay eathday.

7 Ethay obberyray ofway ethay ickedway allshay estroyday emthay; ecausebay eythay efuseray otay oday udgmentjay.

8 Ethay ayway ofway anmay [isway] owardfray andway angestray: utbay [asway orfay] ethay urepay, ishay orkway [isway] ightray.

9 [Itway isway] etterbay otay elldway inway away ornercay ofway ethay ousetophay, anthay ithway away awlingbray omanway inway away ideway ousehay.

10 Ethay oulsay ofway ethay ickedway esirethday evilway: ishay eighbournay indethfay onay avourfay inway ishay eyesway.

11 Enwhay ethay ornerscay isway unishedpay, ethay implesay isway ademay iseway: andway enwhay ethay iseway isway instructedway, ehay eceivethray owledgeknay.

12 Ethay ighteousray [anmay] iselyway onsiderethcay ethay ousehay ofway ethay ickedway: [utbay Odgay] overthrowethway ethay ickedway orfay [eirthay] ickednessway.

13 Osowhay oppethstay ishay earsway atway ethay ycray ofway ethay oorpay, ehay alsoway allshay ycray imselfhay, utbay allshay otnay ebay eardhay.

14 Away iftgay inway ecretsay acifiethpay angerway: andway away ewardray inway ethay osombay ongstray athwray.

15 [Itway isway] oyjay otay ethay ustjay otay oday udgmentjay: utbay estructionday [allshay ebay] otay ethay orkersway ofway iniquityway.

16 Ethay anmay atthay anderethway outway ofway ethay ayway ofway understandingway allshay emainray inway ethay ongregationcay ofway ethay eadday.

17 Ehay atthay ovethlay easureplay [allshay ebay] away oorpay anmay: ehay atthay ovethlay ineway andway oilway allshay otnay ebay ichray.

18 Ethay ickedway [allshay ebay] away ansomray orfay ethay ighteousray, andway ethay ansgressortray orfay ethay uprightway.

19 [Itway isway] etterbay otay elldway inway ethay ildernessway, anthay ithway away ontentiouscay andway anway angryway omanway.

20 [Erethay isway] easuretray otay ebay esiredday andway oilway inway ethay ellingdway ofway ethay iseway; utbay away oolishfay anmay endethspay itway upway.

21 Ehay atthay ollowethfay afterway ighteousnessray andway ercymay indethfay ifelay, ighteousnessray, andway onourhay.

22 Away iseway [anmay] alethscay ethay itycay ofway ethay ightymay, andway astethcay ownday ethay engthstray ofway ethay onfidencecay ereofthay.

23 Osowhay eepethkay ishay outhmay andway ishay onguetay eepethkay ishay oulsay omfray oublestray.

24 Oudpray [andway] aughtyhay ornerscay [isway] ishay amenay, owhay ealethday inway oudpray athwray.

25 Ethay esireday ofway ethay othfulslay illethkay imhay; orfay ishay andshay efuseray otay abourlay.

26 Ehay ovetethcay eedilygray allway ethay ayday onglay: utbay ethay ighteousray ivethgay andway arethspay otnay.

27 Ethay acrificesay ofway ethay ickedway [isway] abominationway: owhay uchmay oremay, [enwhay] ehay ingethbray itway ithway away ickedway indmay?

28 Away alsefay itnessway allshay erishpay: utbay ethay anmay atthay earethhay eakethspay onstantlycay.

29 Away ickedway anmay ardenethhay ishay acefay: utbay [asway orfay] ethay uprightway, ehay irectethday ishay ayway.

30 [Erethay isway] onay isdomway ornay understandingway ornay ounselcay againstway ethay ORDLAY.

31 Ethay orsehay [isway] eparedpray againstway ethay ayday ofway attlebay: utbay afetysay [isway] ofway ethay ORDLAY.

APTERCHAY 22

1 Away [oodgay] amenay [isway] atherray otay ebay osenchay anthay eatgray ichesray, [andway] ovinglay avourfay atherray anthay ilversay andway oldgay.

2 Ethay ichray andway oorpay eetmay ogethertay: ethay ORDLAY [isway] ethay akermay ofway emthay allway.

3 Away udentpray [anmay] oreseethfay ethay evilway, andway idethhay imselfhay: utbay ethay implesay asspay onway, andway areway unishedpay.

4 Ybay umilityhay [andway] ethay earfay ofway ethay ORDLAY [areway] ichesray, andway onourhay, andway ifelay.

5 Ornsthay [andway] aressnay [areway] inway ethay ayway ofway ethay owardfray: ehay atthay othday eepkay ishay oulsay allshay ebay arfay omfray emthay.

6 Aintray upway away ildchay inway ethay ayway ehay ouldshay ogay: andway enwhay ehay isway oldway, ehay illway otnay epartday omfray itway.

7 Ethay ichray ulethray overway ethay oorpay, andway ethay orrowerbay [isway] ervantsay otay ethay enderlay.

8 Ehay atthay owethsay iniquityway allshay eapray anityvay: andway ethay odray ofway ishay angerway allshay ailfay.

9 Ehay atthay athhay away ountifulbay eyeway allshay ebay essedblay; orfay ehay ivethgay ofway ishay eadbray otay ethay oorpay.

10 Astcay outway ethay ornerscay, andway ontentioncay allshay ogay outway; eayay, ifestray andway eproachray allshay easecay.

11 Ehay atthay ovethlay urenesspay ofway earthay, [orfay] ethay acegray ofway ishay ipslay ethay ingkay [allshay ebay] ishay iendfray.

12 Ethay eyesway ofway ethay ORDLAY eservepray owledgeknay, andway ehay overthrowethway ethay ordsway ofway ethay ansgressortray.

13 Ethay othfulslay [anmay] aithsay, [Erethay isway] away ionlay ithoutway, Iway allshay ebay ainslay inway ethay eetsstray.

14 Ethay outhmay ofway angestray omenway [isway] away eepday itpay: ehay atthay isway abhorredway ofway ethay ORDLAY allshay allfay ereinthay.

15 Oolishnessfay [isway] oundbay inway ethay earthay ofway away ildchay; [utbay] ethay odray ofway orrectioncay allshay ivedray itway arfay omfray imhay.

16 Ehay atthay oppressethway ethay oorpay otay increaseway ishay [ichesray, andway] ehay atthay ivethgay otay ethay ichray, [allshay] urelysay [omecay] otay antway.

17 Owbay ownday inethay earway, andway earhay ethay ordsway ofway ethay iseway, andway applyway inethay earthay untoway ymay owledgeknay.

18 Orfay [itway isway] away easantplay ingthay ifway outhay eepkay emthay ithinway eethay; eythay allshay ithalway ebay ittedfay inway ythay ipslay.

19 Atthay ythay usttray aymay ebay inway ethay ORDLAY, Iway avehay ademay ownknay otay eethay isthay ayday, evenway otay eethay.

20 Avehay otnay Iway ittenwray otay eethay excellentway ingsthay inway ounselscay andway owledgeknay,

21 Atthay Iway ightmay akemay eethay owknay ethay ertaintycay ofway ethay ordsway ofway uthtray; atthay outhay ightestmay answerway ethay ordsway ofway uthtray otay emthay atthay endsay untoway eethay?

22 Obray otnay ethay oorpay, ecausebay ehay [isway] oorpay: eithernay oppressway ethay afflictedway inway ethay ategay:

23 Orfay ethay ORDLAY illway eadplay eirthay ausecay, andway oilspay ethay oulsay ofway osethay atthay oiledspay emthay.

24 Akemay onay iendshipfray ithway anway angryway anmay; andway ithway away uriousfay anmay outhay altshay otnay ogay:

25 Estlay outhay earnlay ishay aysway, andway etgay away aresnay otay ythay oulsay.

26 Ebay otnay outhay [oneway] ofway emthay atthay ikestray andshay, [orway] ofway emthay atthay areway uretiessay orfay ebtsday.

27 Ifway outhay asthay othingnay otay aypay, ywhay ouldshay ehay aketay awayway ythay edbay omfray underway eethay?

28 Emoveray otnay ethay ancientway andmarklay, ichwhay ythay athersfay avehay etsay.

29 Eestsay outhay away anmay iligentday inway ishay usinessbay? ehay allshay andstay eforebay ingskay; ehay allshay otnay andstay eforebay eanmay [enmay].

APTERCHAY 23

1 Enwhay outhay ittestsay otay eatway ithway away ulerray, onsidercay iligentlyday atwhay [isway] eforebay eethay:

2 Andway utpay away ifeknay otay ythay oatthray, ifway outhay [ebay] away anmay ivengay otay appetiteway.

3 Ebay otnay esirousday ofway ishay aintiesday: orfay eythay [areway] eceitfulday eatmay.

4 Abourlay otnay otay ebay ichray: easecay omfray inethay ownway isdomway.

5 Iltway outhay etsay inethay eyesway uponway atthay ichwhay isway otnay? orfay [ichesray] ertainlycay akemay emselvesthay ingsway; eythay yflay awayway asway anway eagleway owardtay eavenhay.

6 Eatway outhay otnay ethay eadbray ofway [imhay atthay athhay] anway evilway eyeway, eithernay esireday outhay ishay aintyday eatsmay:

7 Orfay asway ehay inkeththay inway ishay earthay, osay [isway] ehay: Eatway andway inkdray, aithsay ehay otay eethay; utbay ishay earthay [isway] otnay ithway eethay.

8 Ethay orselmay [ichwhay] outhay asthay eatenway altshay outhay omitvay upway, andway oselay ythay eetsway ordsway.

9 Eakspay otnay inway ethay earsway ofway away oolfay: orfay ehay illway espiseday ethay isdomway ofway ythay ordsway.

10 Emoveray otnay ethay oldway andmarklay; andway enterway otnay intoway ethay ieldsfay ofway ethay atherlessfay:

11 Orfay eirthay edeemerray [isway] ightymay; ehay allshay eadplay eirthay ausecay ithway eethay.

12 Applyway inethay earthay untoway instructionway, andway inethay earsway otay ethay ordsway ofway owledgeknay.

13 Ithholdway otnay orrectioncay omfray ethay ildchay: orfay [ifway] outhay eatestbay imhay ithway ethay odray, ehay allshay otnay ieday.

14 Outhay altshay eatbay imhay ithway ethay odray, andway altshay eliverday ishay oulsay omfray ellhay.

15 Ymay onsay, ifway inethay earthay ebay iseway, ymay earthay allshay ejoiceray, evenway inemay.

16 Eayay, ymay einsray allshay ejoiceray, enwhay ythay ipslay eakspay ightray ingsthay.

17 Etlay otnay inethay earthay envyway innerssay: utbay [ebay outhay] inway ethay earfay ofway ethay ORDLAY allway ethay ayday onglay.

18 Orfay urelysay erethay isway anway endway; andway inethay expectationway allshay otnay ebay utcay offway.

19 Earhay outhay, ymay onsay, andway ebay iseway, andway uidegay inethay earthay inway ethay ayway.

20 Ebay otnay amongway inebibbersway; amongway iotousray eatersway ofway eshflay:

21 Orfay ethay unkarddray andway ethay uttonglay allshay omecay otay overtypay: andway owsinessdray allshay otheclay [away anmay] ithway agsray.

22 Earkenhay untoway ythay atherfay atthay egatbay eethay, andway espiseday otnay ythay othermay enwhay eshay isway oldway.

23 Uybay ethay uthtray, andway ellsay [itway] otnay; [alsoway] isdomway, andway instructionway, andway understandingway.

24 Ethay atherfay ofway ethay ighteousray allshay eatlygray ejoiceray: andway ehay atthay egettethbay away iseway [ildchay] allshay avehay oyjay ofway imhay.

25 Ythay atherfay andway ythay othermay allshay ebay adglay, andway eshay atthay arebay eethay allshay ejoiceray.

26 Ymay onsay, ivegay emay inethay earthay, andway etlay inethay eyesway observeway ymay aysway.

27 Orfay away orewhay [isway] away eepday itchday; andway away angestray omanway [isway] away arrownay itpay.

28 Eshay alsoway iethlay inway aitway asway [orfay] away eypray, andway increasethway ethay ansgressorstray amongway enmay.

29 Owhay athhay oeway? owhay athhay orrowsay? owhay athhay ontentionscay? owhay athhay abblingbay? owhay athhay oundsway ithoutway ausecay? owhay athhay ednessray ofway eyesway?

30 Eythay atthay arrytay onglay atway ethay ineway; eythay atthay ogay otay eeksay ixedmay ineway.

31 Ooklay otnay outhay uponway ethay ineway enwhay itway isway edray, enwhay itway ivethgay ishay olourcay inway ethay upcay, [enwhay] itway ovethmay itselfway arightway.

32 Atway ethay astlay itway itethbay ikelay away erpentsay, andway ingethstay ikelay anway adderway.

33 Inethay eyesway allshay eholdbay angestray omenway, andway inethay earthay allshay utterway erversepay ingsthay.

34 Eayay, outhay altshay ebay asway ehay atthay iethlay ownday inway ethay idstmay ofway ethay easay, orway asway ehay atthay iethlay uponway ethay optay ofway away astmay.

35 Eythay avehay ickenstray emay, [altshay outhay aysay, andway] Iway asway otnay icksay; eythay avehay eatenbay emay, [andway] Iway eltfay [itway] otnay: enwhay allshay Iway awakeway? Iway illway eeksay itway etyay againway.

APTERCHAY 24

1 Ebay otnay outhay enviousway againstway evilway enmay, eithernay esireday otay ebay ithway emthay.

2 Orfay eirthay earthay udiethstay estructionday, andway eirthay ipslay alktay ofway ischiefmay.

3 Oughthray isdomway isway anway ousehay uildedbay; andway ybay understandingway itway isway establishedway:

4 Andway ybay owledgeknay allshay ethay amberschay ebay illedfay ithway allway eciouspray andway easantplay ichesray.

5 Away iseway anmay [isway] ongstray; eayay, away anmay ofway owledgeknay increasethway engthstray.

6 Orfay ybay iseway ounselcay outhay altshay akemay ythay arway: andway inway ultitudemay ofway ounsellorscay [erethay isway] afetysay.

7 Isdomway [isway] ootay ighhay orfay away oolfay: ehay openethway otnay ishay outhmay inway ethay ategay.

8 Ehay atthay evisethday otay oday evilway allshay ebay alledcay away ischievousmay ersonpay.

9 Ethay oughtthay ofway oolishnessfay [isway] insay: andway ethay ornerscay [isway] anway abominationway otay enmay.

10 [Ifway] outhay aintfay inway ethay ayday ofway adversityway, ythay engthstray [isway] allsmay.

11 Ifway outhay orbearfay otay eliverday [emthay atthay areway] awndray untoway eathday, andway [osethay atthay areway] eadyray otay ebay ainslay;

12 Ifway outhay ayestsay, Eholdbay, eway ewknay itway otnay; othday otnay ehay atthay onderethpay ethay earthay onsidercay [itway]? andway ehay atthay eepethkay ythay oulsay, othday [otnay] ehay owknay [itway]? andway allshay [otnay] ehay enderray otay [everyway] anmay accordingway otay ishay orksway?

13 Ymay onsay, eatway outhay oneyhay, ecausebay [itway isway] oodgay; andway ethay oneycombhay, [ichwhay isway] eetsway otay ythay astetay:

14 Osay [allshay] ethay owledgeknay ofway isdomway [ebay] untoway ythay oulsay: enwhay outhay asthay oundfay [itway], enthay erethay allshay ebay away ewardray, andway ythay expectationway allshay otnay ebay utcay offway.

15 Aylay otnay aitway, Oway ickedway [anmay], againstway ethay ellingdway ofway ethay ighteousray; oilspay otnay ishay estingray aceplay:

16 Orfay away ustjay [anmay] allethfay evensay imestay, andway isethray upway againway: utbay ethay ickedway allshay allfay intoway ischiefmay.

17 Ejoiceray otnay enwhay inethay enemyway allethfay, andway etlay otnay inethay earthay ebay adglay enwhay ehay umblethstay:

18 Estlay ethay ORDLAY eesay [itway], andway itway ispleaseday imhay, andway ehay urntay awayway ishay athwray omfray imhay.

19 Etfray otnay yselfthay ecausebay ofway evilway [enmay], eithernay ebay outhay enviousway atway ethay ickedway;

20 Orfay erethay allshay ebay onay ewardray otay ethay evilway [anmay]; ethay andlecay ofway ethay ickedway allshay ebay utpay outway.

21 Ymay onsay, earfay outhay ethay ORDLAY andway ethay ingkay: [andway] eddlemay otnay ithway emthay atthay areway ivengay otay angechay:

22 Orfay eirthay alamitycay allshay iseray uddenlysay; andway owhay owethknay ethay uinray ofway emthay othbay?

23 Esethay [ingsthay] alsoway [elongbay] otay ethay iseway. [Itway isway] otnay oodgay otay avehay espectray ofway ersonspay inway udgmentjay.

24 Ehay atthay aithsay untoway ethay ickedway, Outhay [artway] ighteousray; imhay allshay ethay eoplepay ursecay, ationsnay allshay abhorway imhay:

25 Utbay otay emthay atthay ebukeray [imhay] allshay ebay elightday, andway away oodgay essingblay allshay omecay uponway emthay.

26 [Everyway anmay] allshay isskay [ishay] ipslay atthay ivethgay away ightray answerway.

27 Eparepray ythay orkway ithoutway, andway akemay itway itfay orfay yselfthay inway ethay ieldfay; andway afterwardsway uildbay inethay ousehay.

28 Ebay otnay away itnessway againstway ythay eighbournay ithoutway ausecay; andway eceiveday [otnay] ithway ythay ipslay.

29 Aysay otnay, Iway illway oday osay otay imhay asway ehay athhay oneday otay emay: Iway illway enderray otay ethay anmay accordingway otay ishay orkway.

30 Iway entway ybay ethay ieldfay ofway ethay othfulslay, andway ybay ethay ineyardvay ofway ethay anmay oidvay ofway understandingway;

31 Andway, olay, itway asway allway owngray overway ithway ornsthay, [andway] ettlesnay adhay overedcay ethay acefay ereofthay, andway ethay onestay allway ereofthay asway okenbray ownday.

32 Enthay Iway awsay, [andway] onsideredcay [itway] ellway: Iway ookedlay uponway [itway, andway] eceivedray instructionway.

33 [Etyay] away ittlelay eepslay, away ittlelay umberslay, away ittlelay oldingfay ofway ethay andshay otay eepslay:

34 Osay allshay ythay overtypay omecay [asway] oneway atthay avellethtray; andway ythay antway asway anway armedway anmay.

APTERCHAY 25

1 Esethay [areway] alsoway overbspray ofway Olomonsay, ichwhay ethay enmay ofway Ezekiahhay ingkay ofway Udahjay opiedcay outway.

2 [Itway isway] ethay oryglay ofway Odgay otay oncealcay away ingthay: utbay ethay onourhay ofway ingskay [isway] otay earchsay outway away attermay.

3 Ethay eavenhay orfay eighthay, andway ethay earthway orfay epthday, andway ethay earthay ofway ingskay [isway] unsearchableway.

4 Aketay awayway ethay ossdray omfray ethay ilversay, andway erethay allshay omecay orthfay away esselvay orfay ethay inerfay.

5 Aketay awayway ethay ickedway [omfray] eforebay ethay ingkay, andway ishay onethray allshay ebay establishedway inway ighteousnessray.

6 Utpay otnay orthfay yselfthay inway ethay esencepray ofway ethay ingkay, andway andstay otnay inway ethay aceplay ofway eatgray [enmay]:

7 Orfay etterbay [itway isway] atthay itway ebay aidsay untoway eethay, Omecay upway itherhay; anthay atthay outhay ouldestshay ebay utpay owerlay inway ethay esencepray ofway ethay incepray omwhay inethay eyesway avehay eensay.

8 Ogay otnay orthfay astilyhay otay ivestray, estlay [outhay owknay otnay] atwhay otay oday inway ethay endway ereofthay, enwhay ythay eighbournay athhay utpay eethay otay ameshay.

9 Ebateday ythay ausecay ithway ythay eighbournay [imselfhay]; andway iscoverday otnay away ecretsay otay anotherway:

10 Estlay ehay atthay earethhay [itway] utpay eethay otay ameshay, andway inethay infamyway urntay otnay away awayway.

11 Away ordway itlyfay okenspay [isway ikelay] applesway ofway oldgay inway icturespay ofway ilversay.

12 [Asway] anway earringway ofway oldgay, andway anway ornamentway ofway inefay oldgay, [osay isway] away iseway eproverray uponway anway obedientway earway.

13 Asway ethay oldcay ofway owsnay inway ethay imetay ofway arvesthay, [osay isway] away aithfulfay essengermay otay emthay atthay endsay imhay: orfay ehay efreshethray ethay oulsay ofway ishay astersmay.

14 Osowhay oastethbay imselfhay ofway away alsefay iftgay [isway ikelay] oudsclay andway indway ithoutway ainray.

15 Ybay onglay orbearingfay isway away incepray ersuadedpay, andway away oftsay onguetay eakethbray ethay onebay.

16 Asthay outhay oundfay oneyhay? eatway osay uchmay asway isway ufficientsay orfay eethay, estlay outhay ebay illedfay erewiththay, andway omitvay itway.

17 Ithdrawway ythay ootfay omfray ythay eighbour'snay ousehay; estlay ehay ebay earyway ofway eethay, andway [osay] atehay eethay.

18 Away anmay atthay earethbay alsefay itnessway againstway ishay eighbournay [isway] away aulmay, andway away ordsway, andway away arpshay arrowway.

19 Onfidencecay inway anway unfaithfulway anmay inway imetay ofway oubletray [isway ikelay] away okenbray oothtay, andway away ootfay outway ofway ointjay.

20 [Asway] ehay atthay akethtay awayway away armentgay inway oldcay eatherway, [andway asway] inegarvay uponway itrenay, osay [isway] ehay atthay ingethsay ongssay otay anway eavyhay earthay.

21 Ifway inethay enemyway ebay ungryhay, ivegay imhay eadbray otay eatway; andway ifway ehay ebay irstythay, ivegay imhay aterway otay inkdray:

22 Orfay outhay altshay eaphay oalscay ofway irefay uponway ishay eadhay, andway ethay ORDLAY allshay ewardray eethay.

23 Ethay orthnay indway ivethdray awayway ainray: osay [othday] anway angryway ountenancecay away ackbitingbay onguetay.

24 [Itway isway] etterbay otay elldway inway ethay ornercay ofway ethay ousetophay, anthay ithway away awlingbray omanway andway inway away ideway ousehay.

25 [Asway] oldcay atersway otay away irstythay oulsay, osay [isway] oodgay ewsnay omfray away arfay ountrycay.

26 Away ighteousray anmay allingfay ownday eforebay ethay ickedway [isway asway] away oubledtray ountainfay, andway away orruptcay ingspray.

27 [Itway isway] otnay oodgay otay eatway uchmay oneyhay: osay [orfay enmay] otay earchsay eirthay ownway oryglay [isway otnay] oryglay.

28 Ehay atthay [athhay] onay uleray overway ishay ownway iritspay [isway ikelay] away itycay [atthay isway] okenbray ownday, [andway] ithoutway allsway.

APTERCHAY 26

1 Asway owsnay inway ummersay, andway asway ainray inway arvesthay, osay onourhay isway otnay eemlysay orfay away oolfay.

2 Asway ethay irdbay ybay anderingway, asway ethay allowsway ybay yingflay, osay ethay ursecay auselesscay allshay otnay omecay.

3 Away ipwhay orfay ethay orsehay, away idlebray orfay ethay assway, andway away odray orfay ethay ool'sfay ackbay.

4 Answerway otnay away oolfay accordingway otay ishay ollyfay, estlay outhay alsoway ebay ikelay untoway imhay.

5 Answerway away oolfay accordingway otay ishay ollyfay, estlay ehay ebay iseway inway ishay ownway onceitcay.

6 Ehay atthay endethsay away essagemay ybay ethay andhay ofway away oolfay uttethcay offway ethay eetfay, [andway] inkethdray amageday.

7 Ethay egslay ofway ethay amelay areway otnay equalway: osay [isway] away arablepay inway ethay outhmay ofway oolsfay.

8 Asway ehay atthay indethbay away onestay inway away ingslay, osay [isway] ehay atthay ivethgay onourhay otay away oolfay.

9 [Asway] away ornthay oethgay upway intoway ethay andhay ofway away unkarddray, osay [isway] away arablepay inway ethay outhmay ofway oolsfay.

10 Ethay eatgray [Odgay] atthay ormedfay allway [ingsthay] othbay ewardethray ethay oolfay, andway ewardethray ansgressorstray.

11 Asway away ogday eturnethray otay ishay omitvay, [osay] away oolfay eturnethray otay ishay ollyfay.

12 Eestsay outhay away anmay iseway inway ishay ownway onceitcay? [erethay isway] oremay opehay ofway away oolfay anthay ofway imhay.

13 Ethay othfulslay [anmay] aithsay, [Erethay isway] away ionlay inway ethay ayway; away ionlay [isway] inway ethay eetsstray.

14 [Asway] ethay oorday urnethtay uponway ishay ingeshay, osay [othday] ethay othfulslay uponway ishay edbay.

15 Ethay othfulslay idethhay ishay andhay inway [ishay] osombay; itway ievethgray imhay otay ingbray itway againway otay ishay outhmay.

16 Ethay uggardslay [isway] iserway inway ishay ownway onceitcay anthay evensay enmay atthay ancay enderray away easonray.

17 Ehay atthay assethpay ybay, [andway] eddlethmay ithway ifestray [elongingbay] otnay otay imhay, [isway ikelay] oneway atthay akethtay away ogday ybay ethay earsway.

18 Asway away admay [anmay] owhay astethcay irebrandsfay, arrowsway, andway eathday,

19 Osay [isway] ethay anmay [atthay] eceivethday ishay eighbournay, andway aithsay, Amway otnay Iway inway ortspay?

20 Erewhay onay oodway isway, [erethay] ethay irefay oethgay outway: osay erewhay [erethay isway] onay alebearertay, ethay ifestray easethcay.

21 [Asway] oalscay [areway] otay urningbay oalscay, andway oodway otay irefay; osay [isway] away ontentiouscay anmay otay indlekay ifestray.

22 Ethay ordsway ofway away alebearertay [areway] asway oundsway, andway eythay ogay ownday intoway ethay innermostway artspay ofway ethay ellybay.

23 Urningbay ipslay andway away ickedway earthay [areway ikelay] away otsherdpay overedcay ithway ilversay ossdray.

24 Ehay atthay atethhay issemblethday ithway ishay ipslay, andway ayethlay upway eceitday ithinway imhay;

25 Enwhay ehay eakethspay airfay, elievebay imhay otnay: orfay [erethay areway] evensay abominationsway inway ishay earthay.

26 [Osewhay] atredhay isway overedcay ybay eceitday, ishay ickednessway allshay ebay ewedshay eforebay ethay [olewhay] ongregationcay.

27 Osowhay iggethday away itpay allshay allfay ereinthay: andway ehay atthay ollethray away onestay, itway illway eturnray uponway imhay.

28 Away yinglay onguetay atethhay [osethay atthay areway] afflictedway ybay itway; andway away atteringflay outhmay orkethway uinray.

APTERCHAY 27

1 Oastbay otnay yselfthay ofway otay orrowmay; orfay outhay owestknay otnay atwhay away ayday aymay ingbray orthfay.

2 Etlay anotherway anmay aisepray eethay, andway otnay inethay ownway outhmay; away angerstray, andway otnay inethay ownway ipslay.

3 Away onestay [isway] eavyhay, andway ethay andsay eightyway; utbay away ool'sfay athwray [isway] eavierhay anthay emthay othbay.

4 Athwray [isway] uelcray, andway angerway [isway] outrageousway; utbay owhay [isway] ableway otay andstay eforebay envyway?

5 Openway ebukeray [isway] etterbay anthay ecretsay ovelay.

6 Aithfulfay [areway] ethay oundsway ofway away iendfray; utbay ethay isseskay ofway anway enemyway [areway] eceitfulday.

7 Ethay ullfay oulsay oathethlay anway oneycombhay; utbay otay ethay ungryhay oulsay everyway itterbay ingthay isway eetsway.

8 Asway away irdbay atthay anderethway omfray erhay estnay, osay [isway] away anmay atthay anderethway omfray ishay aceplay.

9 Ointmentway andway erfumepay ejoiceray ethay earthay: osay [othday] ethay eetnesssway ofway away an'smay iendfray ybay eartyhay ounselcay.

10 Inethay ownway iendfray, andway ythay ather'sfay iendfray, orsakefay otnay; eithernay ogay intoway ythay other'sbray ousehay inway ethay ayday ofway ythay alamitycay: [orfay] etterbay [isway] away eighbournay [atthay isway] earnay anthay away otherbray arfay offway.

11 Ymay onsay, ebay iseway, andway akemay ymay earthay adglay, atthay Iway aymay answerway imhay atthay eproachethray emay.

12 Away udentpray [anmay] oreseethfay ethay evilway, [andway] idethhay imselfhay; [utbay] ethay implesay asspay onway, [andway] areway unishedpay.

13 Aketay ishay armentgay atthay isway uretysay orfay away angerstray, andway aketay away edgeplay ofway imhay orfay away angestray omanway.

14 Ehay atthay essethblay ishay iendfray ithway away oudlay oicevay, isingray earlyway inway ethay orningmay, itway allshay ebay ountedcay away ursecay otay imhay.

15 Away ontinualcay oppingdray inway away eryvay ainyray ayday andway away ontentiouscay omanway areway alikeway.

16 Osoeverwhay idethhay erhay idethhay ethay indway, andway ethay ointmentway ofway ishay ightray andhay, [ichwhay] ewrayethbay [itselfway].

17 Ironway arpenethshay ironway; osay away anmay arpenethshay ethay ountenancecay ofway ishay iendfray.

18 Osowhay eepethkay ethay igfay eetray allshay eatway ethay uitfray ereofthay: osay ehay atthay aitethway onway ishay astermay allshay ebay onouredhay.

19 Asway inway aterway acefay [answerethway] otay acefay, osay ethay earthay ofway anmay otay anmay.

20 Ellhay andway estructionday areway evernay ullfay; osay ethay eyesway ofway anmay areway evernay atisfiedsay.

21 [Asway] ethay iningfay otpay orfay ilversay, andway ethay urnacefay orfay oldgay; osay [isway] away anmay otay ishay aisepray.

22 Oughthay outhay ouldestshay aybray away oolfay inway away ortarmay amongway eatwhay ithway away estlepay, [etyay] illway otnay ishay oolishnessfay epartday omfray imhay.

23 Ebay outhay iligentday otay owknay ethay atestay ofway ythay ocksflay, [andway] ooklay ellway otay ythay erdshay.

24 Orfay ichesray [areway] otnay orfay everway: andway othday ethay owncray [endureway] otay everyway enerationgay?

25 Ethay ayhay appeareathway, andway ethay endertay assgray ewethshay itselfway, andway erbshay ofway ethay ountainsmay areway atheredgay.

26 Ethay ambslay [areway] orfay ythay othingclay, andway ethay oatsgay [areway] ethay icepray ofway ethay ieldfay.

27 Andway [outhay altshay avehay] oats'gay ilkmay enoughway orfay ythay oodfay, orfay ethay oodfay ofway ythay ouseholdhay, andway [orfay] ethay aintenancemay orfay ythay aidensmay.

APTERCHAY 28
1 Ethay ickedway eeflay enwhay onay anmay ursuethpay: utbay ethay ighteousray areway oldbay asway away ionlay.

2 Orfay ethay ansgressiontray ofway away andlay anymay [areway] ethay incespray ereofthay: utbay ybay away anmay ofway understandingway

[andway] owledgeknay ethay atestay [ereofthay] allshay ebay olongedpray.

3 Away oorpay anmay atthay oppressethway ethay oorpay [isway ikelay] away eepingsway ainray ichwhay eavethlay onay oodfay.

4 Eythay atthay orsakefay ethay awlay aisepray ethay ickedway: utbay uchsay asway eepkay ethay awlay ontendcay ithway emthay.

5 Evilway enmay understandway otnay udgmentjay: utbay eythay atthay eeksay ethay ORDLAY understandway allway [ingsthay].

6 Etterbay [isway] ethay oorpay atthay alkethway inway ishay uprightnessway, anthay [ehay atthay isway] erversepay [inway ishay] aysway, oughthay ehay [ebay] ichray.

7 Osowhay eepethkay ethay awlay [isway] away iseway onsay: utbay ehay atthay isway away ompanioncay ofway iotousray [enmay] amethshay ishay atherfay.

8 Ehay atthay ybay usuryway andway unjustway aingay increasethway ishay ubstancesay, ehay allshay athergay itway orfay imhay atthay illway itypay ethay oorpay.

9 Ehay atthay urnethtay awayway ishay earway omfray earinghay ethay awlay, evenway ishay ayerpray [allshay ebay] abominationway.

10 Osowhay ausethcay ethay ighteousray otay ogay astrayway inway anway evilway ayway, ehay allshay allfay imselfhay intoway ishay ownway itpay: utbay ethay uprightway allshay avehay oodgay [ingsthay] inway ossessionpay.

11 Ethay ichray anmay [isway] iseway inway ishay ownway onceitcay; utbay ethay oorpay atthay athhay understandingway earchethsay imhay outway.

12 Enwhay ighteousray [enmay] oday ejoiceray, [erethay isway] eatgray oryglay: utbay enwhay ethay ickedway iseray, away anmay isway iddenhay.

13 Ehay atthay overethcay ishay inssay allshay otnay osperpray: utbay osowhay onfessethcay andway orsakethfay [emthay] allshay avehay ercymay.

14 Appyhay [isway] ethay anmay atthay earethfay alwayway: utbay ehay atthay ardenethhay ishay earthay allshay allfay intoway ischiefmay.

15 [Asway] away oaringray ionlay, andway away angingray earbay; [osay isway] away ickedway ulerray overway ethay oorpay eoplepay.

16 Ethay incepray atthay antethway understandingway [isway] alsoway away eatgray oppressorway: [utbay] ehay atthay atethhay ovetousnesscay allshay olongpray [ishay] aysday.

17 Away anmay atthay oethday iolencevay otay ethay oodblay ofway [anyway] ersonpay allshay eeflay otay ethay itpay; etlay onay anmay aystay imhay.

18 Osowhay alkethway uprightlyway allshay ebay avedsay: utbay [ehay atthay isway] erversepay [inway ishay] aysway allshay allfay atway onceway.

19 Ehay atthay illethtay ishay andlay allshay avehay entyplay ofway eadbray: utbay ehay atthay ollowethfay afterway ainvay [ersonspay] allshay avehay overtypay enoughway.

20 Away aithfulfay anmay allshay aboundway ithway essingsblay: utbay ehay atthay akethmay astehay otay ebay ichray allshay otnay ebay innocentway.

21 Otay avehay espectray ofway ersonspay [isway] otnay oodgay: orfay orfay away iecepay ofway eadbray [atthay] anmay illway ansgresstray.

22 Ehay atthay astethhay otay ebay ichray [athhay] anway evilway eyeway, andway onsiderethcay otnay atthay overtypay allshay omecay uponway imhay.

23 Ehay atthay ebukethray away anmay afterwardsway allshay indfay oremay avourfay anthay ehay atthay atterethflay ithway ethay onguetay.

24 Osowhay obbethray ishay atherfay orway ishay othermay, andway aithsay, [Itway isway] onay ansgressiontray; ethay amesay [isway] ethay ompanioncay ofway away estroyerday.

25 Ehay atthay isway ofway away oudpray earthay irrethstay upway ifestray: utbay ehay atthay uttethpay ishay usttray inway ethay ORDLAY allshay ebay ademay atfay.

26 Ehay atthay ustethtray inway ishay ownway earthay isway away oolfay: utbay osowhay alkethway iselyway, ehay allshay ebay eliveredday.

27 Ehay atthay ivethgay untoway ethay oorpay allshay otnay acklay: utbay ehay atthay idethhay ishay eyesway allshay avehay anymay away ursecay.

28 Enwhay ethay ickedway iseray, enmay idehay emselvesthay: utbay enwhay eythay erishpay, ethay ighteousray increaseway.

APTERCHAY 29

1 Ehay, atthay eingbay oftenway eprovedray ardenethhay [ishay] ecknay, allshay uddenlysay ebay estroyedday, andway atthay ithoutway emedyray.

2 Enwhay ethay ighteousray areway inway authorityway, ethay eoplepay ejoiceray: utbay enwhay ethay ickedway earethbay uleray, ethay eoplepay ournmay.

3 Osowhay ovethlay isdomway ejoicethray ishay atherfay: utbay ehay atthay eepethkay ompanycay ithway arlotshay endethspay [ishay] ubstancesay.

4 Ethay ingkay ybay udgmentjay establishethway ethay andlay: utbay ehay atthay eceivethray iftsgay overthrowethway itway.

5 Away anmay atthay atterethflay ishay eighbournay eadethspray away etnay orfay ishay eetfay.

6 Inway ethay ansgressiontray ofway anway evilway anmay [erethay isway] away aresnay: utbay ethay ighteousray othday ingsay andway ejoiceray.

7 Ethay ighteousray onsiderethcay ethay ausecay ofway ethay oorpay: [utbay] ethay ickedway egardethray otnay otay owknay [itway].

8 Ornfulscay enmay ingbray away itycay intoway away aresnay: utbay iseway [enmay] urntay awayway athwray.

9 [Ifway] away iseway anmay ontendethcay ithway away oolishfay anmay, etherwhay ehay ageray orway aughlay, [erethay isway] onay estray.

10 Ethay oodthirstyblay atehay ethay uprightway: utbay ethay ustjay eeksay ishay oulsay.

11 Away oolfay utterethway allway ishay indmay: utbay away iseway [anmay] eepethkay itway inway illtay afterwardsway.

12 Ifway away ulerray earkenhay otay ieslay, allway ishay ervantssay [areway] ickedway.

13 Ethay oorpay andway ethay eceitfulday anmay eetmay ogethertay: ethay ORDLAY ightenethlay othbay eirthay eyesway.

14 Ethay ingkay atthay aithfullyfay udgethjay ethay oorpay, ishay onethray allshay ebay establishedway orfay everway.

15 Ethay odray andway eproofray ivegay isdomway: utbay away ildchay eftlay [otay imselfhay] ingethbray ishay othermay otay ameshay.

16 Enwhay ethay ickedway areway ultipliedmay, ansgressiontray increasethway: utbay ethay ighteousray allshay eesay eirthay allfay.

17 Orrectcay ythay onsay, andway ehay allshay ivegay eethay estray; eayay, ehay allshay ivegay elightday untoway ythay oulsay.

18 Erewhay [erethay isway] onay isionvay, ethay eoplepay erishpay: utbay ehay atthay eepethkay ethay awlay, appyhay [isway] ehay.

19 Away ervantsay illway otnay ebay orrectedcay ybay ordsway: orfay oughthay ehay understandway ehay illway otnay answerway.

20 Eestsay outhay away anmay [atthay isway] astyhay inway ishay ordsway? [erethay isway] oremay opehay ofway away oolfay anthay ofway imhay.

21 Ehay atthay elicatelyday ingethbray upway ishay ervantsay omfray away ildchay allshay avehay imhay ecomebay [ishay] onsay atway ethay engthlay.

22 Anway angryway anmay irrethstay upway ifestray, andway away uriousfay anmay aboundethway inway ansgressiontray.

23 Away an'smay idepray allshay ingbray imhay owlay: utbay onourhay allshay upholdway ethay umblehay inway iritspay.

24 Osowhay isway artnerpay ithway away iefthay atethhay ishay ownway oulsay: ehay earethhay ursingcay, andway ewrayethbay [itway] otnay.

25 Ethay earfay ofway anmay ingethbray away aresnay: utbay osowhay uttethpay ishay usttray inway ethay ORDLAY allshay ebay afesay.

26 Anymay eeksay ethay uler'sray avourfay; utbay [everyway] an'smay udgmentjay [omethcay] omfray ethay ORDLAY.

27 Anway unjustway anmay [isway] anway abominationway otay ethay ustjay: andway [ehay atthay isway] uprightway inway ethay ayway [isway] abominationway otay ethay ickedway.

APTERCHAY 30

1 Ethay ordsway ofway Agurway ethay onsay ofway Akehjay, [evenway] ethay ophecypray: ethay anmay akespay untoway Ithielway, evenway untoway Ithielway andway Ucalway,

2 Urelysay Iway [amway] oremay utishbray anthay [anyway] anmay, andway avehay otnay ethay understandingway ofway away anmay.

3 Iway eithernay earnedlay isdomway, ornay avehay ethay owledgeknay ofway ethay olyhay.

4 Owhay athhay ascendedday upway intoway eavenhay, orway escendedday? owhay athhay atheredgay ethay indway inway ishay istsfay? owhay athhay oundbay ethay atersway inway away armentgay? owhay athhay establishedway allway ethay endsway ofway ethay earthway? atwhay [isway] ishay amenay, andway atwhay [isway] ishay on'ssay amenay, ifway outhay anstcay elltay?

5 Everyway ordway ofway Odgay [isway] urepay: ehay [isway] away ieldshay untoway emthay atthay utpay eirthay usttray inway imhay.

6 Addway outhay otnay untoway ishay ordsway, estlay ehay eproveray eethay, andway outhay ebay oundfay away iarlay.

7 Otway [ingsthay] avehay Iway equiredray ofway eethay; enyday emay [emthay] otnay eforebay Iway ieday:

8 Emoveray arfay omfray emay anityvay andway ieslay: ivegay emay eithernay overtypay ornay ichesray; eedfay emay ithway oodfay onvenientcay orfay emay:

9 Estlay Iway ebay ullfay, andway enyday [eethay], andway aysay, Owhay [isway] ethay ORDLAY? orway estlay Iway ebay oorpay, andway ealstay, andway aketay ethay amenay ofway ymay Odgay [inway ainvay].

10 Accuseway otnay away ervantsay untoway ishay astermay, estlay ehay ursecay eethay, andway outhay ebay oundfay uiltygay.

11 [Erethay isway] away enerationgay [atthay] ursethcay eirthay atherfay, andway othday otnay essblay eirthay othermay.

12 [Erethay isway] away enerationgay [atthay areway] urepay inway eirthay ownway eyesway, andway [etyay] isway otnay ashedway omfray eirthay ilthinessfay.

13 [Erethay isway] away enerationgay, Oway owhay oftylay areway eirthay eyesway! andway eirthay eyelidsway areway iftedlay upway.

14 [Erethay isway] away enerationgay, osewhay eethtay [areway asway] ordssway, andway eirthay awjay eethtay [asway] ivesknay, otay evourday ethay oorpay omfray offway ethay earthway, andway ethay eedynay omfray [amongway] enmay.

15 Ethay orseleachhay athhay otway aughtersday, [yingcray], Ivegay, ivegay. Erethay areway eethray [ingsthay atthay] areway evernay atisfiedsay, [eayay], ourfay [ingsthay] aysay otnay, [Itway isway] enoughway:

16 Ethay avegray; andway ethay arrenbay ombway; ethay earthway [atthay] isway otnay illedfay ithway aterway; andway ethay irefay [atthay] aithsay otnay, [Itway isway] enoughway.

17 Ethay eyeway [atthay] ockethmay atway [ishay] atherfay, andway espisethday otay obeyway [ishay] othermay, ethay avensray ofway ethay alleyvay allshay ickpay itway outway, andway ethay oungyay eaglesway allshay eatway itway.

18 Erethay ebay eethray [ingsthay ichwhay] areway ootay onderfulway orfay emay, eayay, ourfay ichwhay Iway owknay otnay:

19 Ethay ayway ofway anway eagleway inway ethay airway; ethay ayway ofway away erpentsay uponway away ockray; ethay ayway ofway away ipshay inway ethay idstmay ofway ethay easay; andway ethay ayway ofway away anmay ithway away aidmay.

20 Uchsay [isway] ethay ayway ofway anway adulterousway omanway; eshay eatethway, andway ipethway erhay outhmay, andway aithsay, Iway avehay oneday onay ickednessway.

21 Orfay eethray [ingsthay] ethay earthway isway isquietedday, andway orfay ourfay [ichwhay] itway annotcay earbay:

22 Orfay away ervantsay enwhay ehay eignethray; andway away oolfay enwhay ehay isway illedfay ithway eatmay;

23 Orfay anway odiousway [omanway] enwhay eshay isway arriedmay; andway anway andmaidhay atthay isway eirhay otay erhay istressmay.

24 Erethay ebay ourfay [ingsthay ichwhay areway] ittlelay uponway ethay earthway, utbay eythay [areway] exceedingway iseway:

25 Ethay antsway [areway] away eoplepay otnay ongstray, etyay eythay eparepray eirthay eatmay inway ethay ummersay;

26 Ethay oniescay [areway utbay] away eeblefay olkfay, etyay akemay eythay eirthay ouseshay inway ethay ocksray;

27 Ethay ocustslay avehay onay ingkay, etyay ogay eythay orthfay allway ofway emthay ybay andsbay;

28 Ethay iderspay akethtay oldhay ithway erhay andshay, andway isway inway ings'kay alacespay.

29 Erethay ebay eethray [ingsthay] ichwhay ogay ellway, eayay, ourfay areway omelycay inway oinggay:

30 Away ionlay [ichwhay isway] ongeststray amongway eastsbay, andway urnethtay otnay awayway orfay anyway;

31 Away eyhoundgray; anway ehay oatgay alsoway; andway away ingkay, againstway omwhay [erethay isway] onay isingray upway.

32 Ifway outhay asthay oneday oolishlyfay inway iftinglay upway yselfthay, orway ifway outhay asthay oughtthay evilway, [aylay] inethay andhay uponway ythay outhmay.

33 Urelysay ethay urningchay ofway ilkmay ingethbray orthfay utterbay, andway ethay ingingwray ofway ethay osenay ingethbray orthfay oodblay: osay ethay orcingfay ofway athwray ingethbray orthfay ifestray.

APTERCHAY 31

1 Ethay ordsway ofway ingkay Emuellay, ethay ophecypray atthay ishay othermay aughttay imhay.

2 Atwhay, ymay onsay? andway atwhay, ethay onsay ofway ymay ombway? andway atwhay, ethay onsay ofway ymay owsvay?

3 Ivegay otnay ythay engthstray untoway omenway, ornay ythay aysway otay atthay ichway estroyethday ingskay.

4 [Itway isway] otnay orfay ingskay, Oway Emuellay, [itway isway] otnay orfay ingskay otay inkdray ineway; ornay orfay incespray ongstray inkdray:

5 Estlay eythay inkdray, andway orgetfay ethay awlay, andway ervertpay ethay udgmentjay ofway anyway ofway ethay afflictedway.

6 Ivegay ongstray inkdray untoway imhay atthay isway eadyray otay erishpay, andway ineway untoway osethay atthay ebay ofway eavyhay eartshay.

7 Etlay imhay inkdray, andway orgetfay ishay overtypay, andway ememberray ishay iserymay onay oremay.

8 Openway ythay outhmay orfay ethay umbday inway ethay ausecay ofway allway uchsay asway areway appointedway otay estructionday.

9 Openway ythay outhmay, udgejay ighteouslyray, andway eadplay ethay ausecay ofway ethay oorpay andway eedynay.

10 ∂ Owhay ancay indfay away irtuousvay omanway? orfay erhay icepray [isway] arfay aboveway ubiesray.

11 Ethay earthay ofway erhay usbandhay othday afelysay usttray inway erhay, osay atthay ehay allshay avehay onay eednay ofway oilspay.

12 Eshay illway oday imhay oodgay andway otnay evilway allway ethay aysday ofway erhay ifelay.

13 Eshay eekethsay oolway, andway axflay, andway orkethway illinglyway ithway erhay andshay.

14 Eshay isway ikelay ethay erchants'may ipsshay; eshay ingethbray erhay oodfay omfray afarway.

15 Eshay isethray alsoway ilewhay itway isway etyay ightnay, andway ivethgay eatmay otay erhay ouseholdhay, andway away ortionpay otay erhay aidensmay.

16 Eshay onsiderethcay away ieldfay, andway uyethbay itway: ithway ethay uitfray ofway erhay andshay eshay antethplay away ineyardvay.

17 Eshay irdethgay erhay oinslay ithway engthstray, andway engthenethstray erhay armsway.

18 Eshay erceivethpay atthay erhay erchandisemay [isway] oodgay: erhay andlecay oethgay otnay outway ybay ightnay.

19 Eshay ayethlay erhay andshay otay ethay indlespay, andway erhay andshay oldhay ethay istaffday.

20 Eshay etchethstray outway erhay andhay otay ethay oorpay; eayay, eshay eachethray orthfay erhay andshay otay ethay eedynay.

21 Eshay isway otnay afraidway ofway ethay owsnay orfay erhay ouseholdhay: orfay allway erhay ouseholdhay [areway] othedclay ithway arletscay.

22 Eshay akethmay erselfhay overingscay ofway apestrytay; erhay othingclay [isway] ilksay andway urplepay.

23 Erhay usbandhay isway ownknay inway ethay atesgay, enwhay ehay ittethsay amongway ethay eldersway ofway ethay andlay.

24 Eshay akethmay inefay inenlay, andway ellethsay [itway]; andway eliverethday irdlesgay untoway ethay erchantmay.

25 Engthstray andway onourhay [areway] erhay othingclay; andway eshay allshay ejoiceray inway imetay otay omecay.

26 Eshay openethway erhay outhmay ithway isdomway; andway inway erhay onguetay [isway] ethay awlay ofway indnesskay.

27 Eshay ookethlay ellway otay ethay aysway ofway erhay ouseholdhay, andway eatethway otnay ethay eadbray ofway idlenessway.

28 Erhay ildrenchay ariseway upway, andway allcay erhay essedblay; erhay usbandhay [alsoway], andway ehay aisethpray erhay.

29 Anymay aughtersday avehay oneday irtuouslyvay, utbay outhay excellestway emthay allway.

30 Avourfay [isway] eceitfulday, andway eautybay [isway] ainvay: [utbay] away omanway [atthay] earethfay ethay ORDLAY, eshay allshay ebay aisedpray.

31 Ivegay erhay ofway ethay uitfray ofway erhay andshay; andway etlay erhay ownway orksway aisepray erhay inway ethay atesgay.

www.ingramcontent.com/pod-product-compliance
Lightning Source LLC
Chambersburg PA
CBHW020448100426
42813CB00026B/3002